OXFORD STUDIES IN THEOLOGICAL ETHICS

General Editor

Oliver O'Donovan

OXFORD STUDIES IN THEOLOGICAL ETHICS

The series presents discussions on topics of central concern to Christian Ethics, as it is currently taught in universities and colleges, at the level demanded by a serious student. The volumes will not be specialized monographs nor general introductions or surveys. They aim to make a contribution worthy of notice in its own right but also focussed in such a way as to provide a suitable starting point for orientation.

The titles include studies in important contributors to the Christian tradition of moral thought; explorations of current moral and social questions; and discussions of central concepts in Christian moral and political thought. Authors treat their topics in a way that will show the relevance of the Christian tradition, but with openness to neighbouring traditions of thought which have entered into dialogue with it.

The Hastening that Waits

KARL BARTH'S ETHICS

NIGEL BIGGAR

CLARENDON PRESS · OXFORD

Oxford University Press, Walton Street, Oxford OX2 6DP

Oxford New York
Athens Auckland Bangkok Bombay
Calcutta Cape Town Dar es Salaam Delhi
Florence Hong Kong Istanbul Karachi
Kuala Lumpur Madras Madrid Melbourne
Mexico City Nairobi Paris Singapore
Taipei Tokyo Toronto
and associated companies in
Berlin Ibadan

Oxford is a trade mark of Oxford University Press

Published in the United States
by Oxford University Press Inc., New York

British Library Cataloguing in Publication Data
Data available

Library of Congress Cataloging in Publication Data
The hastening that waits : Karl Barth's ethics / Nigel Biggar.
Includes bibliographical references.
1. Barth, Karl, 1886—1968—Ethics. 2. Christian ethics—
History—20th century. I. Title. II. Series.
BF1201.B54 1993 241'.092—dc20
ISBN 0–19–826390–2

1 3 5 7 9 10 8 6 4 2

Printed in Great Britain on acid-free paper by
Bookcraft (Bath) Ltd., Midsomer Norton

PREFACE

This book is the culmination of a decade of intermittent study, in the course of which I have incurred three major debts of gratitude.

Thanks are due, first, to Professor James Gustafson, who at the Divinity School of the University of Chicago marked me with his passion for theological ethics and with his (critical) admiration for Karl Barth, and who eventually supervised the doctoral dissertation in which this book had its embryonic beginnings. Next, I owe thanks to Latimer House, Oxford, for its generous support during most of the period of writing. And finally I must thank my wife Virginia for faithfully bearing me on those occasions when the end seemed to be forever receding.

N.J.B.

Oriel College, Oxford
Advent 1991

ACKNOWLEDGEMENTS

Thanks are due to T. & T. Clark, publisher and copyright holder, for permission to quote at length from Barth's *Church Dogmatics* and *The Christian Life*.

CONTENTS

ABBREVIATIONS

CD   Karl Barth, *Church Dogmatics*, 4 vols., ed. G. W. Bromiley and T. F. Torrance (Edinburgh: T. & T. Clark, 1936–77). Cited by volume number, part number, and page: e.g. *CD* i/2: 3.

Chr. L.   Karl Barth, *Das christliche Leben*, *Kirchliche Dogmatik*, iv/4, Fragmente aus dem Nachlaß, Vorlesungen 1959–61 (Zurich: Theologischer Verlag, 1976).

CL   Karl Barth, *The Christian Life*, *Church Dogmatics*, iv/4, Lecture Fragments, trans. G. W. Bromiley (Edinburgh: T. & T. Clark, 1981).

KD   Karl Barth, *Kirchliche Dogmatik*, 4 vols. (Zollikon-Zurich: Evangelischer Verlag AG, 1942–70). Cited by volume number, part number, and page: e.g. *KD* i/2: 3.

INTRODUCTION

The English-speaking world has not been generous with the attention it has paid to the ethical thought of Karl Barth. Only one book has been published that offers an account of his ethics as a whole—Robert Willis's *The Ethics of Karl Barth*;[1] and a handful of others have been devoted to the discussion of a single aspect of it.[2] The number of volumes in which Barth's ethical thought receives sustained consideration, without being itself the focus, is not great;[3] and of the three collections of essays published to mark the centenary of Barth's birth in 1986, only one gives substantial coverage to the ethical dimension of his thought.[4]

The cause of this relative neglect lies partly in the reputation that Barth acquired during the early 'dialectical' period of his thinking, when the stress on divine judgement seemed such as entirely to devalue human activity and ethical reflection upon it, and to make uncritical obeisance the only possible human response to God's will. Naturally, many found this emphasis and its ramifications unappealing, and the fact that Barth's later work was so

[1] Robert E. Willis, *The Ethics of Karl Barth* (Leiden: E. J. Brill, 1971).

[2] The aspect referred to is the political one: John Howard Yoder, *Karl Barth and the Problem of War* (Nashville: Abingdon, 1970); Robert E. Hood, *Contemporary Political Orders and Christ: Karl Barth's Christology and Political Praxis* (Pittsburgh: Pickwick Press, 1985); George Hunsinger (ed.), *Karl Barth and Radical Politics* (Philadelphia: Westminster Press, 1976); Charles Villa-Vicencio (ed.), *On Reading Karl Barth in South Africa* (Grand Rapids: Eerdmans, 1988).

[3] Charles C. West, *Communism and the Theologians* (Philadelphia: Westminster Press, 1958); Stanley Hauerwas, *Character and the Christian Life: A Study in Theological Ethics* (San Antonio: Trinity University Press, 1975); Robin W. Lovin, *Christian Faith and Public Choices: The Social Ethics of Barth, Brunner, and Bonhoeffer* (Philadelphia: Fortress Press, 1984). James M. Gustafson recurrently engages with Barth in many of his writings, e.g. *Christ and the Moral Life* (Chicago: University of Chicago Press, 1968); *Protestant and Roman Catholic Ethics: Prospects for Rapprochement* (Chicago: University of Chicago Press, 1978); *Ethics from a Theocentric Perspective*, ii: *Ethics and Theology* (Chicago: University of Chicago Press, 1984).

[4] Ethics is not the subject of any of the six essays in S. W. Sykes (ed.), *Karl Barth: Centenary Essays* (Cambridge: Cambridge University Press, 1989); and it is the subject of only one of the fourteen essays in John Thompson (ed.), *Theology beyond Christendom: Essays on the Centenary of the Birth of Karl Barth, May 10, 1886* (Pittsburgh: Pickwick Press, 1986). Nigel Biggar (ed.), *Reckoning with Barth: Essays in Commemoration of the Centenary of Karl Barth's Birth* (Oxford: Mowbray, 1988) is the exception to the rule, allotting four of its twelve essays to ethical topics.

immense in scale and so slow in being translated into English doubtless discouraged them from delving further either at all or very carefully.[5] As a consequence, the ethical thought of the mature Barth—that is, of his *Church Dogmatics*—is often supposed to propose a number of unattractive positions that, in fact, it does not. For example, it is often supposed that the concept of apprehending what is right by hearing a command of God is the ethical version of 'revelational positivism'; that is to say, that it refers to a special religious form of moral cognition that is immune from 'public' criticism. It is also commonly believed that the Christological concentration of Barth's ethics is such that the distinct existence of creation and its moral order is entirely obscured, and that the Bible utterly displaces human experience as a source of moral knowledge. And a third misconception is that, in Barth's account, the human agent virtually dissolves into her acts, and human acts into God's.

In recent years, something of a reassessment of Barth's theology has been under way in the English-speaking world, and it is time for that reassessment to extend to his ethics. This is so, not only because certain common misperceptions need correction, but also because, since Robert Willis completed his account in 1971, two important primary sources have been published for the first time: Barth's lectures on ethics at the universities of Münster (1928–9) and Bonn (1930–1), and the 1959–60 lectures on 'The Command of God the Reconciler' that would have formed the ethical conclusion to volume iv of the *Dogmatics*, had it been completed.[6] So it is the aim of this book not only to correct certain false understandings of Barth's mature ethical thought, but also to offer a fresh reading of it in the light of these newly available sources. Furthermore, we intend to relate this reading to appropriate focuses of

---

[5] The English translation of the first part of vol. i of the *Church Dogmatics* appeared in 1936, four years after its publication in German. But it took a further twenty years for the second part to appear in English (1956), eighteen years after its German counterpart.

[6] The 1928–9 lectures were published in German in 1973 and 1976, the 1959–60 lectures also in 1976. The English translations of both appeared in 1981 under the titles *Ethics* and *The Christian Life*, respectively. Willis refers only to an outline of the 1928–9 lectures that he discovered at the end (pp. 157–68) of *Das Problem der Ethik in der dialektischen Theologie* (Uppsala: Appelbergs, 1938), by John Cullberg (*Ethics of Karl Barth*, 46–52).

contemporary discussion within the field of Christian ethics, in order to suggest points at which Barth has a positive contribution to make.

Our account will proceed as follows. In Chapter 1, we shall analyse what Barth means when he proposes that human beings know what is right by hearing a command of God, and we shall explore how the event of hearing is supposed to relate to the human activity of reflection upon moral matters—that is, to ethics. In Chapter 2, we shall present a synopsis of Barth's tripartite 'special' ethics, in which he expounds the three theological dimensions of the existential context in which the event of hearing God's command occurs. It is here that we shall draw most heavily on the 1928–9 and the 1959–60 lectures. Our aim throughout will be to give an account of the 'special' ethics of the *Church Dogmatics*. But we shall use the 1928–9 lectures, partly to help in conjecturing the outline of the third part of 'special' ethics in the *Dogmatics* (which Barth did not live to begin), and partly to draw out the significance of the *Dogmatics*' arrangement of 'special' ethics by comparing and contrasting it with an earlier version. In subsequent chapters we shall explore the three sources from which, as Barth has it, theological ethics draws: Scripture (Chapter 3); the Church, past and present (Chapter 4); and the world *extra muros ecclesiae* (Chapter 5). In the course of discussing the Church, we shall deal with Barth's understanding of the formation of moral character; and in the course of discussing the world, we shall address the question of the place of empirical science in Barth's ethics.

Before we proceed, however, there is a preliminary issue of substance that we must address: namely, the freedom of the human agent. This is preliminary because, strictly, it belongs to the field of anthropology; but we need to deal with it here because it does bear directly on the question of whether human beings can be held responsible for their moral decisions, and so of whether ethics as reflection upon the exercise of this responsibility is a worthwhile activity. Barth is commonly criticized for providing an inadequate account of human freedom. In his book on the theme of autonomy in the *Church Dogmatics*, John Macken argues that Barth denies the possibility of resistance to God's reconciling grace through his insistence that human being is constituted *in* Christ. He endorses Wilfried Härle's argument that Barth's 'ontology of grace' reduces creation to an epiphenomenon of divine reconciliation.[7] Macken's account, however, does not distinguish sufficiently between human being and *real* human being, between humanity as *esse* and as *bene esse*.[8] For, when Barth speaks of human being or freedom, more often than not he is speaking of their fulfilment; and his argument is that there can be no such fulfilment except in faithful relationship to God in Christ. The freedom to which he refers is almost invariably the freedom for life according to the orders of creation, which is realized by acknowledgement of God's gracious act of reconciliation in Christ. It is the glad freedom for spontaneous co-operation on the part of human creatures with their Creator. What Barth means is something akin to *eudaimonia*, the happiness or joy of living the kind of life for which one is specifically fitted; and this, he claims, is possible for sinful creatures only through participation in the order of God's reconciling grace.

The glad freedom of fulfilled being is to be distinguished from the formal freedom of spiritual or moral choice. Barth's affirmation of this is much less clear. At one point he is to be found arguing that there is no human 'subject' except in responsibility before God. It is clear that by 'responsibility' Barth does not mean some merely formal or neutral accountability. He is not merely saying that human subjects always stand in a relationship of some kind with God. Rather, he is asserting that human subjectivity consists in the fulfilment of responsibility before God. There is only one kind of human freedom—'the freedom of a right choice', which the free man is bound to make.[9] Barth's meaning here is best understood in terms of Stephen Clark's assault on the 'liberal' notion of the freedom to choose from a position of spiritual neutrality. Clark argues that the unity or integrity of the human self depends on its accordance with a 'pre-existing pattern' which orders 'each passion, each mood, each province of meaning'. Apart from this 'divine order' the human self decomposes into elemental anarchy.[10] Barth's point is the same: apart from subordination to God, the human

---

[7] John Macken, SJ, *The Autonomy Theme in the 'Church Dogmatics': Karl Barth and His Critics* (Cambridge: Cambridge University Press, 1990), 152–3, 157.

[8] He does allude to it on one occasion when he writes that 'Barth consistently underplays the question about man's being as such in favour of a concentration on its meaning and goal in Christ' (ibid. 59).   [9] *CD* iii/2: 196–7.

[10] S. R. L. Clark, *Civil Peace and Sacred Order: Limits and Renewals* I (Oxford: Oxford University Press, 1989), 36–7.

creature is oppressed by the 'lordless powers'.[11] One could speak of insubordination as a state of 'freedom', but only in a highly ironic sense; and, given the modern history of the meaning of the word 'freedom', which assumes that God and humanity are essentially at odds with one another, such a use would tend to mislead. It is this consideration that Barth has in mind when he writes that it is God's reconciling grace that grants human beings the status of subjects.[12]

Nevertheless, granted Barth's point here, a problem remains. For he does tend to speak as if human beings were ultimately *determined* by the sovereignty of God's reconciling grace. This he does when he places *all* human beings in the order of reconciliation. It is true that he distinguishes between *de jure* and *de facto* participation in this order.[13] But he is confident that even this distinction will be overcome, eschatologically: for 'when the lordship of Jesus Christ over all creation is manifested, and with it the reconciliation of the world to God that has taken place in him', those who are not yet liberated to cry 'Our Father' 'will not finally fail to do it'.[14] Certainly, Barth's concern here is to emphasize the triumph of God's grace in Jesus Christ and how it serves human dignity. But the unavoidable implication of the manner in which he chooses to do this is that human beings are ultimately determined by God's grace, and that their liberation is in the end an inexorable necessity. At this point Barth's understanding of the lordship of God's grace lapses into incoherence. For he makes it perfectly clear that what the gracious God seeks is the free, glad, spontaneous, voluntary co-operation of his creatures. But in arguing that this freedom for God is something that all human creatures must ultimately enjoy, Barth seems to propose a form of 'compatibilist' account; namely, that human beings are *determined* to choose *freely* what is right. This yields a notion of human freedom that is more apparent than real, and it raises questions about the graciousness of a grace that does not concede to the beloved the freedom to turn away permanently. It is true, of course, that the freedom to reject the liberating grace of God is the freedom to

---

[11] See e.g. *The Humanity of God* (Richmond, Va.: John Knox Press, 1960), 77: 'Trying to escape from being in accord with God's own freedom is not human freedom. Rather, it is a compulsion wrought by powers of darkness or by man's own helplessness.' See also *CL* s. 78. 2, 'The Lordless Powers'.
[12] *CL* 102.   [13] *CD* iv/1: 92–3.   [14] *CL* 101.

enter voluntarily into bondage. But if the ultimate spiritual and moral commitments of human beings are to retain their dignity and weight, then it is just such a paradoxical freedom that they must possess.

At this point in his account of human freedom we believe that Barth fails. But we do not believe that his failure here vitiates his subsequent exposition of the good life; for the question of what comprises such life is quite distinct from that of the power by which one enters upon it and remains in it. Barth's ethical thought remains to be judged on its own merits. So, leaving preliminaries behind, we now proceed across the threshold.

I

ETHICS AS AN AID
TO HEARING

I

When the serpent promised Adam and Eve that they would become as God, what he had in mind, according to Karl Barth, was 'the establishment of ethics'.[1] Such an assertion is hardly calculated to kindle affection in the breasts of earnest moralists, and it goes a long way toward explaining why Barth has so seldom been the subject of their rapt attention. It is so outrageously counter-intuitive that more exact minds, less given to rhetorical flourishes, may be forgiven for turning away in irritation. For is not life far too short to warrant the expenditure of effort upon making sense out of careless nonsense? However, although a reaction of instant dismissal deserves some sympathy, it is none the less not to be endorsed. For polemical rhetoric deserves to be taken as such, and a measure of patience exercised in its interpretation. Treated thus, we believe that Barth's meaning here (as so often elsewhere) will disclose itself as much more worthy of consideration than his rhetorical mode of expression might suggest. So we begin our study with an examination of Barth's thought about ethics as a distinct form of intellectual activity for the apologetic reason of securing him a hearing at the very point where he tends to lose it, as well as for reasons of expository logic.

What could Barth possibly intend when he identifies ethics as the original sin? In order to answer this question, we must first ask another: What does he mean here by 'ethics'? It is immediately clear from the context of his provocative interpretation of Genesis 3: 5 that he uses 'ethics' to refer to the subjective idealist conception of the making of moral judgements as an autarkic process; that is, as a process in which the human subject is absolutely

[1] *CD* iv/1: 448.

self-determinative.[2] Against this kind of ethics, Barth argues for a theological version of ethical realism. It is God's wisdom to know, and his freedom and power to decide, what he wills and does not will, what he creates and does not create; and therefore to judge between good and evil, order and disorder, cosmos and chaos, being and non-being. God's knowledge of good and evil is the basis of all things and the source of all life; it is 'the supreme attribute and function which basically and radically distinguishes the Creator from the creature'.[3] From this Barth infers that no human creature as such is fit to perform the office of moral judge.[4] For it to pretend to do so would be to overestimate itself as 'an Atlas bearing and holding together the great building of the universe'.[5] Instead of aspiring to equal the Creator and so to play the Lord, it is proper for the human creature to recognize and accept the divine decision, stand upon it, and, by way of repetition, witness to it. It is thus that she acts well.[6] Correlatively, in so far as she seeks to make moral judgements without reference to the prior judgement of God, in so far as her ethics are not basically an attempt to correspond to that judgement, she recapitulates the original sin of pride.[7]

The autarkic refusal to acknowledge any moral authority external to the human self is one form of original sin in its primary, ethical expression. But it is not the only one. There is also the autonomous pretension of the human subject to a kind of jurisprudential mastery over the objective moral law, which expresses itself typically in a tendency to systematize. Barth defines a system

---

[2] 'Autarky' is used here to refer to absolute self-determination, in distinction from 'autonomy' as self-determination according to the moral law. See John Macken's helpful analysis of this distinction in terms of the thought of Fichte and Kant in *The Autonomy Theme in the 'Church Dogmatics'* (Cambridge: Cambridge University Press, 1990), 1–21.

[3] *CD* iii/1: 257–8, 260; iv/1: 449. Although Barth tends to prefer the voluntarist to the rationalist horn of the Euthyphro dilemma, he exhibits some ambivalence over whether what is good is so because God wills it, or God wills what is good because it is so. On one side, he writes that 'it is the judicial wisdom of God to know, and His judicial freedom and office to decide, what He wills and does on the one hand and does not will and do on the other, and *therefore* what is good and evil'. But he also writes that 'God knows what He created because He willed to create it, because He affirms it, *because He found it* good and salutary' (*CD* iii/1: 260). Author's emphasis.

[4] *CD* iii/1: 261–2.   [5] *CD* iv/1: 450.   [6] *CD* iii/1: 260; iv/1: 449.

[7] Barth's discussion of the human pretension to play moral judge occurs in *CD* iv/1, s. 60, 'The Pride and Fall of Man'.

as 'a structure of principles and their consequences, founded on the presupposition of a basic view of things ... self-contained and complete in itself';[8] and he argues that in so far as God's will is identified in an ethical system with a particular 'basic view', with a fundamental idea or principle, it is brought under human control. This is because such a principle will invariably be general and will therefore require specification in particular cases, with the result that through interpretation and application it will in practice be surrendered to private human judgement.[9] In such a casuistic system Barth reckons that, at best, the human will is obliged by the general principle; but at worst we pour 'the dictates and pronouncements of our own self-will into the empty container of a formal moral concept ... justifying our own will in the concrete situation'.[10]

In part, Barth's objection to the assertion of human control over the good by means of systematic ethics is theological; for he believes that it denies one of God's most important properties—his freedom. Negatively, this freedom is equivalent to the divine transcendence or sovereignty, that is, an absolute freedom from extrinsic compulsion. Positively, it is the freedom of the personal subject for self-revelation; and so, in the case of the personal God, for being present in creation.[11] Further, this personal freedom involves a certain irreducible spontaneity, which means that God is capable of having his presence assume different forms, and his will different meaning and content, in different situations.[12] Systematic ethical reflection, however, by identifying God's will with a particular principle or set of principles, separates the idea of what is commanded from the person of the commanding God. Thus it both robs the divine will of personal spontaneity and

---

[8] *CD* i/2: 861–2. Barth gives this definition directly with reference to philosophy or theology, but there is no good reason why it should not be extended to ethics.

[9] *CD* ii/2: 666; *CL* 5; *CD* iv/3. 1: 448; i/2: 866.

[10] *CD* ii/2: 664–5. In *Karl Barth and the Problem of War* (Nashville: Abingdon, 1970) Yoder asserts that in this section (38. 2) of the *Church Dogmatics* Barth's 'adversary was not casuistics; the word "casuistics" does not appear there. What Barth was there concerned to reject is a concept of the ideal law which would still leave men free to decide on their own what the command of God really means' (p. 71). Casuistry may not be mentioned by name, but it is surely alluded to in Barth's criticism of the process of making moral judgements by applying general principles to particular cases. For casuistry as a deductive system, see *CD* iii/4: 10, 14.

[11] *CD* ii/1: 320.   [12] Ibid.; *CL* 4.

abstracts the moral agent from relationship with the divine person.[13] Moreover, by surrendering these principles to interpretation and application by private human judgement, systematic ethics in effect compromises God's sovereignty.

Associated with this theological criticism is a further, epistemological one. For the infringement of God's freedom by systematic ethics is correlated with the assertion of the claim that human knowledge of God and his will is direct and immediate, and something for which human beings have a natural, intrinsic capacity. The truth, as Barth sees it, is quite the contrary. Because God is a living subject and enjoys freedom to an eminent degree, human knowledge of him and of his will depends entirely upon God's free giving of himself to be known. Moreover, sinful humans do not have an intrinsic capacity even to receive what God reveals. Rather, they become capable only when God constitutes them so by empowering them to participate in true humanity. To be truly human means to be a creature and to behave accordingly; that is, to be with God, to have and acknowledge him as one's origin and goal. To have and acknowledge God as origin and goal is to be grateful for the gift of his grace: 'as thanks [the creature] returns to the grace of God in which it has its source.'[14] This returning of the creature to God means that 'it opens itself to God as God first opened it to himself'.[15] To be open to God is to have the character of 'active responsibility' toward God; that is, of 'being in the act of response to the Word of God'.[16] Therefore, to be a creature is to be in the sphere where God's Word is spoken and heard, to be summoned by it, and to obey it.[17]

Actual, sinful humankind, however, contradicts real humanity. By aspiring to either the autarkic or the autonomous forms of moral mastery, they defy their creatureliness, turning away from responsibility to the Creator and so closing their ears to the Word of God. Therefore, it is only on the ground of God's reconciliation of sinful humankind to himself in Jesus Christ that man accords with his 'destiny by creation whereby he is from God and to God'.[18] It is only in Jesus Christ that human creatures enjoy ontological freedom, the freedom proper to their creaturely status: the freedom to be grateful, to be open, to be responsible to God, to hear God's

---

[13] *CD* ii/2: 676.   [14] *CD* iii/2: 174.   [15] Ibid. 199.
[16] Ibid. 174.   [17] Ibid. 149–50; *CD* iii/1: 264.   [18] *CL* 22.

Word, and to obey it. But in Jesus Christ they enjoy something more: not only the restored freedom of creatures, but also the freedom of forgiven sinners. Because they are now reconciled as well as created by God's grace, their dependence on it is intensified to the point where they 'can never lift up hands that are any other than very weak, very dirty and always very empty'.[19]

Given their sinfulness, the only knowledge of God and his will that is in fact possible to actual human beings is knowledge in faith. This is knowledge whose subject accepts and respects what is given her with humility and gratitude, repentance and obedience, as something that is not her right and that is not to be taken for granted; and it is knowledge whose object, God, is and remains at the same time a free and living subject. Human knowledge of God, then, is not such that the knower controls or possesses its object, for it involves a recognition of the utter dependence of the knower upon the known. It involves acknowledgement of the hiddenness, the incomprehensibility, the mystery of the free and living Subject who graciously gives himself to be known out of love.

Autonomous, systematic ethics is therefore epistemologically erroneous because it thinks of moral understanding in abstraction from some of the basic conditions of human existence, theologically conceived: creatureliness, sinfulness, and the state of having been reconciled to God by God.[20] It imagines that the only problem in apprehending the good is a theoretical one; that right moral understanding is possible quite apart from the fundamental religious and moral commitments of the knower. For Barth, however, the real ethical question is fundamentally not epistemic, but affective and pragmatic. 'We know and easily recognise the good as such ... but ... we do not really accept it, far less love it.'[21] The real ethical question, which 'ethics' studiously avoids, concerns 'man's actual commitment to the good, his actual distance from it and the actual overcoming of this distance'.[22] It is a question of religious praxis. By conceiving the ethical problem in terms of knowledge rather than of love and practice, 'ethics' ignores the need for affective and pragmatic reorientation or conversion, and domesticates the good in such a way as to prevent it from

---

[19] Ibid. 24.
[20] As will be made clear in Ch. 2, there is a further such condition: the state of being redeemed by God the Holy Spirit.
[21] CL 746.   [22] Ibid. 519.

presenting any challenge too deeply disturbing. By reducing it to part of an ethical system—to a particular principle or set of principles—that is under human intellectual control, 'ethics' permits the moral agent to distance herself from the critical claim which the good makes upon the whole of her self, upon her governing loves and interests.[23] This is why Barth describes casuistry as

an undertaking in which man, even though he calls upon God's grace, would like to win clear of the occurrence, the freedom and peril of this event [of ecounter with the will of God or the good], to reach dry land as it were, and to stand there like God, knowing good and evil. In it he thinks that he can be more than a recipient, beneficiary or pure beginner. . . . He thinks he can handle the command of God like a possession or domain which he has to administer. No longer now does he decide with God's decision in mind, and even when he calls others to decision, he no longer does so as directly claimed by God, and struck by his decision, and placed, terrified and consoled, before his judgement seat. At a safe distance from the ethical battlefield . . . he manipulates for himself and for others a method of correct decisions.[24]

Aiding and abetting human self-justification: this is the cardinal sin of which autonomous, systematic, casuistic ethics is, in Barth's eyes, guilty.

The rest of Barth's critique of 'ethics' bears upon two consequences of this sin for human life. For in setting the human being at odds with his creaturely destiny, the will to self-justification bereaves him of his ontological freedom and of its characteristic expression in openness, willingness, spontaneity, gladness, joy.[25] It sets him against himself and gives him over to 'the disunity of an existence in which he does not will what he does, or do what he wills'.[26] It delivers him into the hands of frustration by encouraging him to assume the (for him) impossible role of judge over good and evil; for he finds himself driven to distraction by the responsibility he has assumed. 'He now has soon to choose and decide and judge on all sides;' and yet, 'he will never satisfy all claims, and he will not really satisfy even one'.[27] Moreover, he is crippled by the lack of any method capable of apply-

[23] CD iii/4: 13; ii/2: 610.   [24] CD iii/4: 11.
[25] CD iii/2: 281–3; 'The Gift of Freedom: Foundation of Evangelical Ethics' in Barth, The Humanity of God, (Richmond, Va.: John Knox Press, 1960), 78.
[26] CD ii/2: 727.   [27] Ibid. 586–7.

ing a universal principle 'to the plenitude of conditions and possibilities of the activity of all men'.[28] In brief, by inciting the human creature to assume the responsibility of moral judge, 'ethics' surrenders him to the ravages of an anxiety which is, ironically, morally debilitating.[29]

But the evil effects of 'ethics' are not restricted to the individual, for they also find social expression in the disruption of 'moral fellowship'.[30] First of all, 'ethics' regards the human individual as an atom, and not as one properly among his fellows; whereas 'it may well be the case—indeed it will always be so—that one man has the task of interfering in respect of the conduct of another'.[31] Second, it actually divides human beings from one another. In so far as basic general moral principles are subject to the practical control of 'individualistic' (*individueller*) interpretation and application, they bring into play 'self-will, better judgement, particular standpoints, various interests, jealousies, cleavages and parties'.[32] In that casuistry fosters in practice and on the part of each would-be moral judge a 'fanatical self-instruction',[33] it destroys 'moral fellowship', which depends upon a common subordination to the sovereign decision of God—to the transcendent good:[34]

I am already putting myself in the wrong with others, and doing them wrong, when ... I confront them as one who is right, wanting to break over them as the great crisis. For when I do this I divide myself and I break the fellowship between myself and others. I can only live at unity with myself, and we can only live in fellowship with one another, when I and we subject ourselves to the right which does not dwell in us and is not manifested by us, but which is over me and us as the right of God above, and manifested to me and us only from God.[35]

The human will to play moral judge

means the emergence and conflict, the more or less tolerable harmony and conjunction of the different judges with their different rights, the battle of

---

[28] *CD* iii/4: 9–10.   [29] *CD* ii/2: 596.

[30] Indeed, it is Barth's usual policy in the *Dogmatics* to treat the social dimension first and the individual one afterwards. See e.g. his discussion of the good effects of the divine command (*CD* ii/2: 708–32); or of the Holy Spirit's realization of the effects of God's justification, sanctification, and vocation of humankind (*CD* iv/1: 643–779; iv/2: 614–840; iv/3. 2: 681–942).

[31] *CD* iii/4: 9.   [32] *CD* ii/2: 716 (*KD* ii/2: 800).   [33] *CD* iv/2: 374.

[34] *CD* ii/2: 716.   [35] *CD* iv/1: 451.

ideas formed and the principles affirmed and the standpoints adopted and the various universal or individual systems, in which at bottom no one understands the language of others because he is too much convinced of the soundness of his own seriously to want to understand others. . . . When man sets out to exercise his own power to judge is not the essential thing which he achieves . . . the formation both microcosmically and macrocosmically of a world which is darkened and disrupted and bedevilled by its own self-righteousness?[36]

It should now be patent that, when Barth identified the original sin with the establishment of ethics, he actually had a specific form of ethics in mind. Indeed, given the extensiveness of his own disciplined reflections on moral matters, it is inconceivable that he should have denied moral legitimacy to ethics as such. What kind of ethics, then, does Barth regard as legitimate? What does it look like when it does not pretend to be autonomous by abstracting itself from theological existence, bracketing questions of fundamental religious and moral commitment, and bringing the good under the systematic control of human 'reason'?

The crucial and most distinguishing feature of the legitimate form of ethics, as Barth presents it, is that it conceives human apprehension of the good in terms of hearing a command of God. It is by means of this concept that Barth thoroughly integrates moral understanding into a theological vision of human existence. This is largely because it is made into the product of an event of personal encounter between God and the human creature. The very word 'command' indicates as much because, unlike 'law', it does not denote a natural or conventional institution but rather a momentary utterance issued directly by one person to another.[37] Thus moral understanding is made to accord with some of Barth's basic theological and anthropological convictions. One of these is the idea of God as pre-eminent person and, since 'the being of a person is being in act',[38] as the original and sovereign personal

---

[36] Ibid. 447.

[37] In the light of this very common-sensical distinction between the concepts of law and command, it is hard to understand R. E. Willis's comment that '[t]he impossibility of giving expression to the command in binding propositional form as either general or specific principles or rules underlines the oddity of Barth's use of the term. When the notion of command is joined to the category of event, it is removed from the ordinary, literal meaning, and invested with a sense that borders on metaphor' (The Ethics of Karl Barth (Leiden: E. J. Brill, 1971), 193). Surely what normally distinguishes 'command' from 'law' is precisely its nature as an occasional utterance—as an event of speech. [38] CD ii/1: 268-72.

agent who is free to reveal himself spontaneously. Another is Barth's conception of human being as essentially 'historical'; that is, as being subject in a certain state to encounter by 'something other than itself and transcending its own nature', with the result that 'it is compelled and enabled to transcend itself in response and in relation to this new factor'.[39] From these two tenets it follows that the relationship between God and the human creature is understood in terms of personal encounter, encounter between the divine I and the human Thou, between divine Father and human child.[40] It is immediate, direct, and intimate in form. Indeed, God in his Word 'is present to the world and each individual and confronts him in the smallest steps and thoughts'.[41] He gives 'immediate and direct guidance'.[42] He 'does not keep silent but says something to man, telling him what he wants from him, what he for his part is to do'.[43]

The concept of hearing a command of God not only locates human apprehension of what is right in the context of an intimately personal encounter between God and his human creatures; it also implies a personal encounter of a particular kind. The word 'command' connotes a measure of compulsion; a command obliges. And it obliges in this case precisely in so far as the human creature who is commanded is a sinner; precisely as he 'does not find the divine good in himself . . . he is not at all ready on his side to will and do this good within the limits of his creatureliness'. Therefore the good 'must necessarily come in the most radical sense [from outside]'; 'as something alien, as the command of another'; as 'an imperative to which I owe absolute obedience'.[44] Because of the

---

[39] *CD* iii/2: 158.   [40] *CD* ii/2: 667, 672.   [41] Ibid. 669.
[42] Ibid. 679.   [43] *CL* 33.

[44] *CD* ii/2: 651 (*KD* ii/2: 725). Dr Harold Knight's accuracy lapses here where he has translated *von außen* as 'from within'. Barth takes issue with Roman Catholic moral theology because, as he understands it, it does not allow obligation to be genuinely heteronomous and so to become genuinely imperative. Since it grounds obligation in being, and since man participates in being, it cannot become imperative 'except with the assistance and co-operation of man, except on the presupposition of his agreement'. However, 'on this presupposition it is quite impossible that it should confront him, his being and his existence with an absolute challenge . . . From the very outset man is assured of a right of consultation and control in God's command . . . [I]t can never become for him a command that affects him personally and binds him unconditionally. It can certainly never become a command of *God*' (ibid. 532–3). On this point Barth finds reason to commend Kant for designating the moral imperative as a special category, and thereby expressing 'the essential concern' of Christian ethics 'by pointing out that of itself the concept of what is pleasing and useful and valuable does not give us the concept of what is obligatory' (ibid. 650).

nature of human existence as theologically conceived, because the human creature is estranged from the good, it necessarily meets him as heteronomous—as a command.

But the command of God is not simply heteronomous, because it is the command of the God who decided from eternity in his sovereign freedom to be for humankind in Jesus Christ, and because of that decision has created and reconciled them and is in the process of redeeming them. The divine command is therefore commanding grace.[45] So if the divine good comes to me from outside, it does so precisely 'in order that it may claim me most radically within'. It comes as 'an alien and imperious law' in diametrical opposition to 'the foolish wishes of the old man', precisely in order to perform 'a liberation and a loosing'.[46] It opposes us in our sinful destruction of our own real, creaturely being; it opposes us 'insofar as we are against ourselves' and for the sake of our 'most proper cause'.[47] The heteronomous command is addressed to us—and against us—'for our own highest good'. What it obliges is, *pace* Kant, desirable and pleasant and true and good and beautiful for humankind, though only 'in an eminent sense'. The alien command of God intends nothing less than human salvation, if only as God understands it. This is the ground of its moral authority over human beings.[48]

Because the divine command is the command of the gracious God, it has the distinctive property of bestowing freedom upon those who hear and obey. Whereas all other commands bind man, filling him with anxious fears about the use of his liberty, this one 'will not meet him with mistrust but with trust. It will not appeal to his fear but to his courage. It will instil courage, and not fear into him.' It appeals, not to absolutely alien obligation, but to the freedom to which human beings have been elected, in which we have been created, and to which we are called: the divine command 'wills only that we make use of the given permission by the grace of God to be what we are'.[49]

The freedom that the command of God bestows takes three forms. The first is the freedom to adhere to the Creator, Reconciler, and Redeemer, and so to be faithful, penitent, grateful,

---

[45] Here, of course, we have a specific manifestation of the priority, according to Barth, of Gospel to Law, as of content to form.

[46] Ibid. 602.   [47] Ibid. 595–7; *CL* 15–16.   [48] *CD* ii/2: 650–2.

[49] Ibid. 586–8, 590, 592.

open, and responsive before God. Upon this form depends the second; for in freeing the individual for adherence to the God who is for him, the divine command relieves him of 'all the care and all the fear of being for himself' and of the inner conflict that his striving for self-justification engenders. Moreover, the individual's relief from inner conflict dissipates the concomitant urge to externalize it, and so frees him to respect his fellow creatures as companions in sin and under grace, and as common hearers of the Word of God. The third form of the freedom that the divine command bestows, then, is that for 'moral fellowship'.[50]

The concept of knowing what is right by hearing a command of God lodges moral apprehension firmly in the context of a personal relationship between a definite God and a definite human being; between a God who is gracious and therefore critical, and human beings who are creaturely, sinful, reconciled to God by God, and in the process of being redeemed. It also makes of moral apprehension something which is basically atheoretical. For the divine command is not 'a norm which we have thought out for ourselves',[51] nor 'a mere theory, or vision, or moral ideal', but 'the truth of the reality of the work and activity of God'.[52] It cannot be seen 'from the safe shelter of a general theory'.[53] It cannot be kept at a comfortable arm's length by the interposition of 'supposed natural or rational truths or any timeless truths'.[54] It cannot be domesticated by bringing it under the control of a principle or method.[55] The divine command is encountered immediately because it is irreducibly personal: in it we encounter nothing less than our living Lord. Therefore it must also be absolutely definite, 'the specially relevant individual command for the decisions which we have to make at this moment and in this situation ... a specific prescription and norm for each individual case'.[56] It must be such if, in practice, it is to be sovereign; for 'in proportion as a demand remains general, formal and abstract, leaving the question of interpretation and application to those to whom it is addressed, it is not yet a command'. The divine command is beyond any determination by human will, since 'even to the smallest details it is self-interpreting'. Only then is it 'distinguishable from the answers which we ourselves have continuously given and give and will give

[50] Ibid. 597, 727–8, 716.   [51] Ibid. 666.   [52] CD i/2: 866.
[53] CD ii/2: 548.   [54] CL 4.   [55] CD iv/3. 1: 448.   [56] CD ii/2: 662–3.

to ourselves.... Only then do we stand in a relation of responsibility ... to Another, to a transcendent Commander and Judge'.[57]

It follows from its absolute immediacy and definiteness that
God's command is 'quite definitely present to and recognisable by
every man in every situation'.[58] If it appears obscure to us, that is
because of our unwillingness 'to hear carefully what is precisely
spoken to us as those to whom God is present and near'.[59] Accordingly, the question can never be 'what the command is, but how it
stands with the man confronted by it';[60] never 'whether he [God]
speaks, but only whether we hear'.[61]

This concept of the divine command allows room for only one
legitimate kind of ethical reflection; not that which engages in
theoretical enquiry into the nature of the good, but that which
takes the form of self-examination. Through this form of reflection
I ask myself 'at every moment of [my] willing and acting' whether
my life has been and will be directed toward the *telos* of real
humanity to which I have been elected in Jesus Christ; whether
my life has been and shall be moved in correspondence with the
norm of this divine decision about me; whether my life moves
from and to the grace of God. Further, since to move from and
toward grace is therefore and at the same time to move from
and toward the claim and judgement of the divine decision, self-
examination involves enquiry about my readiness at the next

---

[57] Ibid. 665–7. On these grounds Barth argues that Kant's 'categorical imperative' 'can never be more than a formula for the idea of the imperative abstracted
from the actuality of the imperatives which encounter us—"categorical" in so far as
it defines, illuminates and describes the category of the imperative, differentiating
it from all sorts of suppositions, desires and aspirations which as such cannot
constitute an imperative because they do not correspond to the necessary definition
of an imperative. But this or any similar formula can never be an imperative in
itself and as such, or "categorical" in the current (but not originally Kantian)
meaning of the term, i.e. confronting man with an absolutely obligatory demand, in
such a way that he must and will obey this formula. The categorical imperative as
such will never be a command' (ibid. 666–7).

[58] *CD* iii/4: 15.   [59] *CD* ii/2: 670.   [60] *CD* iii/4: 12.

[61] *CD* ii/2: 670. The concepts of the divine command espoused by Emil Brunner
and Dietrich Bonhoeffer share many of the same features as Barth's. See Brunner,
The Divine Imperative (Philadelphia: Westminster Press, 1937), 111–21; Bonhoeffer,
Ethics (New York: Macmillan, 1955), 277–85. Brunner however, is more prepared
than Barth to identify the content of the command with love for God and neighbour (p. 112), and so to summarize it in terms dear to the ears of act-agapists: *Dilige
et fac quod vis* (p. 119). Further, where Barth speaks of God's freedom, Brunner
tends to speak of God's holiness or sovereignty (pp. 116–17, 119), thereby alluding
to his considerably more positive regard for 'law'.

moment to encounter the divine claim and judgement upon me. Such examination is serious only if I expose nothing less than my very self to the decision, claim, and judgement of the divine command; and if I seek knowledge only in order to make genuine response to the claim made upon me—that is, in order to act responsibly. By submitting to this 'preparatory testing', I adopt a proper attitude to the sovereign divine decision: I acknowledge my accountability for the whole sequence of my life and I acknowledge the continuousness of my responsibility. Through such acknowledgements, I am rendered obedient and made ready to hear the command of God.[62]

The fact that this is the only kind of ethical reflection expressly permitted by Barth's concept of hearing a divine command presents a problem. For although this concept has the virtue of locating moral apprehension firmly in a theological context—that is, of a God who is sovereign, personally spontaneous, and has chosen to make himself known to humankind out of grace and therefore in criticism; and of human being that is creaturely, sinful, reconciled, and being redeemed—it apparently does so only by precluding any legitimate role for moral reasoning. This seems to be clearly implied by the description of God's command as presenting itself with an absolute immediacy and definiteness, and it has not gone unnoticed. The fact that the divine command meets the human being in an event and with absolute definiteness 'amounts', writes Robert Willis, 'to nothing less than a total exclusion of the necessity of deliberation in ethics'. Willis says this on the ground that 'there can be deliberation only where there are formal rules or principles to be brought into conjunction with particular cases, so that a consideration of alternative possibilities for action is made a constant factor in the ethical situation'.[63] Later he qualifies this statement when he admits that the interpretation of what in a given context the divine command is might be considered another form of deliberation. However, because Barth has so conceived things that the Holy Spirit supplies both the command and the conditions for its being apprehended, Willis reckons that he excludes even this form.[64] When James Gustafson attributes Barth's short-circuiting of rational processes to that

---

[62] CD ii/2: 566–7, 634–6, 641–2, 645–61.
[63] Willis, *Ethics of Karl Barth*, 183.   [64] Ibid. 421.

radical occasionalism which is based on the premiss that God's freedom 'might erupt in actions that could not be anticipated by the exercise of human rational capacities',[65] and which therefore 'emphasizes the uniqueness of each moment of serious moral choice',[66] or to the interpersonalism and intuitionism of the concept of hearing the divine command,[67] he is making essentially the same point. If the good is supposed to be directly apprehended by an act of hearing or intuiting the quite spontaneous utterance of the divine Commander, what place can possibly remain for ethical reflection in the sense of rational deliberation about right action?

This apparent displacement of rational deliberation has naturally attracted widespread criticism. Gustafson, for example, describes as unwarranted Barth's 'confidence in the objectivity of a particular command of God that can be heard' and his certainty that there are no genuine moral dilemmas.[68] Likewise, Willis denies 'that the situation in which we are called to respond is, as regards our precise decision and action, entirely uncluttered and free of ambiguities, so that it is immediately self-evident, without serious moral reflexion on our part, what we are to do'.[69] He finds the cause of Barth's failure to take seriously the moral ambiguity and complexity of the human situation, including that actual variety of options for action prerequisite for any notion of responsible choice, in his permitting the victory of grace in Jesus Christ and the consequent ontological transformation of humankind and the world so to absorb historical and existential realities as to obscure the necessity and possibility of drawing relative distinctions between good and evil.[70] Reinhold Niebuhr criticizes along similar lines when he blames Barth's 'realized eschatology' for encourag-

---

[65] James M. Gustafson, *Can Ethics Be Christian?* (Chicago: University of Chicago Press, 1975), 160.

[66] James M. Gustafson, *Protestant and Roman Catholic Ethics* (Chicago: University of Chicago Press, 1978), 71.

[67] James M. Gustafson, *Ethics from a Theocentric Perspective* (Chicago: University of Chicago Press, 1984), ii. 31. Gustafson recognizes that Barth himself denied that he was an intuitionist on theological grounds, but argues that his concept of the making of moral judgements nevertheless has affinities with the concept of intuition (*Protestant and Roman Catholic Ethics*, 41). Stanley Hauerwas also argues, in *Character and the Christian Life* (San Antonio: Trinity University Press, 1975), that Barth's emphasis on the concreteness of the command 'seems to imply a form of direct intuition of the good' (p. 142 n. 44).

[68] Gustafson, *Ethics from a Theocentric Perspective*, ii. 33.

[69] Willis, *Ethics of Karl Barth*, 199.   [70] Ibid. 198–9, 334.

ing irresponsible negligence of 'all the trials and perplexities, the judgements and discriminations, the tasks and duties which Christians face in the daily round of their individual and collective life'.[71]

If we take moral ambiguity and complexity seriously, we are bound to follow Paul Lehmann (as Willis does) in contending that, when people ask about the will of God, they do not do so 'merely evasively, pretending that they do not know they are to do the will of God when they really do know, but because they are genuinely perplexed by the diversity and complexity of human motivation and of behavioural options which make up the stuff of the ethical situation'.[72] Further, if moral perplexity is genuine, then so is the need for precise and refined moral guidance.

But the development of this kind of moral guidance is something that Barth's concept of hearing a divine command apparently does not allow; for it expressly repudiates the use of principles, rules, and their systematic organization in ethics. The command of God, as Barth conceives it, cannot be identified with a single principle or set of principles, nor comprehended in a rule or body of rules. We cannot derive from it a set of generic or specific features that will enable us to distinguish a good from a bad act. It cannot be said, for example, that the content of God's command is love; that love is essentially self-sacrificial and that the hearer of the command will therefore refrain from all kinds of self-defence.[73] The divine command cannot be grasped, generalized, specified, and then applied in this way. It cannot be manhandled or manipulated, but only met and heard. Speaking of Barth's thought after his adoption of an analogical method, Robin Lovin writes that, 'no less than in the dialectical method of *The Epistle to the Romans*, the theological imperative to preserve God's freedom and initiative appears to rule out the predictability and universality that systematic thinking in ethics requires'.[74] Likewise, Willis

---

[71] Reinhold Niebuhr, 'We are Men and Not God', *Christian Century*, 65/43 (27 Oct. 1948), 1138.

[72] Paul Lehmann, *Ethics in a Christian Context* (New York: Harper & Row, 1963), 76. Quoted by Willis, *Ethics of Karl Barth*, 200.

[73] Barth does, therefore, provide Robin W. Lovin with ground for his description of the the ethic of the divine command as an act-deontology. We shall argue, however, that he also provides grounds for a very different description (*Christian Faith and Public Choices* (Philadelphia: Fortress Press, 1984), 27–8).

[74] Ibid. 40.

avers that 'Barth's opposition to an ethics involving rules or principles whose introduction and application in specific contexts is made a function of human sensitivity and discernment is just as strong and unremitting in the *Dogmatics* as it was in the *Römerbrief* and the writings after it'.[75]

But if the content of God's command cannot be expressed in terms of moral principles or rules that are always applicable to appropriate cases, if its meaning cannot be specified in terms of kinds of acts, if it has no intelligible constancy, then there can be no way of charting one's way through moral perplexity by distinguishing good and bad acts in terms of their characteristic features. If there can be no legitimate reflection upon the nature or content of the good, if there can be no legitimate deliberation about which possible action is the right one, then there can be no substantive moral advice. Further, and more particularly, if the divine command cannot engender principles and rules, then it cannot free us 'to cope with innumerable recurring situations without the labor of deliberation and the likelihood of error'.[76] Nor can it give voice to distinctions between different grades of principle and rule. Therefore, in cases of conflict between different principles or rules, it can provide no rational procedure for deciding that one should override another, and so for the practical resolution of moral tensions and ambiguities.[77] What James Gustafson says of Protestant ethics in general applies prima facie to Barth in particular:

Insofar as this theological and religious problem [of overcoming the temptation to self-justification and so the emergence of legalism] has led to the elimination of general moral principles, or of clear concepts of moral values, Protestant theology has gotten into an irrational and morally dangerous ethical position. It has frequently failed to see that general principles and rules and concepts of values are necessary in the Christian life in order to give guidance (if not a sense of moral certitude) to human action.... Few persons are saints ... few have heard an unambiguous, immediate command of God.... Given this state of experience and perhaps even of being human, it is both necessary and possible to work

[75] Willis, *Ethics of Karl Barth*, 172.

[76] Basil Mitchell, 'Ideals, Roles and Rules', in Gene Outka and Paul Ramsey (eds.), *Norm and Context in Christian Ethics* (London: SCM, 1968), 362.

[77] Philip L. Quinn, 'Divine Command Ethics: A Causal Theory', in Janine Marie Idziak (ed.), *Divine Command Morality: Historical and Contemporary Readings* (New York: Edwin Mellen Press, 1979), 320.

out procedures for practical moral reasoning which provide both substantive guidance for moral choices and acts and provide clearer reasons for them.[78]

Moreover, Barth's concept of the divine command is reckoned to provide inadequate moral guidance, not only because it provides no practical means of coming to rational terms with a conflict of moral principles or rules, but also because it neglects careful analysis of the empirical data present in a situation that demands a moral response. This neglect appears to follow directly from the nature of the divine command, for, as Willis says, if the latter is absolutely definite, 'then any possibility of giving attention to factors in a situation which are relatively "non-theological" (i.e. political, economic, sociological, psychological)... is excluded from the outset'.[79] In the same vein, Charles West complains that Barth 'rushes into political and economic judgements armed only with theological insight and a limited experience, ignoring (at least from the evidence of his published writings) the vast body of social scientific literature, some of it standard for Christian understanding in these fields, which might enlighten him as to the actual human situation he confronts'.[80] Reinhold Niebuhr also makes a similar objection when he accuses Barth of 'an amateur intrusion of absolute religious judgements into the endless relativities of the political order'.[81]

---

[78] Gustafson, *Protestant and Roman Catholic Ethics*, 44, 46. For exactly the same reasons, Brunner argues for the necessity of the third, instructive use of the Law: 'It is, of course, true that Luther says: "if we had enough of the Holy Spirit, we could make 'new Decalogues' for ourselves which would be clearer than that of Moses". Yes, indeed, we could, if...! It may, indeed, be true that there is a kind of creative ingenuity in genuine love... We are all aware of that amazing penetrating intuition which characterizes the outstanding examples of Christian love, who, with an insight only to be compared with the genius of the great diagnostician, discover the hidden distress of others, and with amazing spontaneity do what no one would have expected, because this is what love commands. But few of us possess much of this creative faculty, and most of us have very little indeed. Therefore the commandments of the Bible—and for many people the considerations of an ethic as well—are absolutely necessary' (*Divine Imperative*, 148–9).

[79] Willis, *Ethics of Karl Barth*, 200.

[80] Charles C. West, *Communism and the Theologians* (Philadelphia: Westminster Press, 1958), 286.

[81] Reinhold Niebuhr, 'The Moral and Political Judgements of Christians', *Christianity and Crisis*, 19 (6 July 1959), 101. Willis also follows West in this matter (*Ethics of Karl Barth*, 418–20). John Howard Yoder moves along the same tracks when he takes Barth to task for his lack of historical realism in his treatment of the issue of war (*Karl Barth and the Problem of War*, 106).

For many, perhaps especially for the followers of Kant, the real problem with any concept of divine command such as Barth's is that it transcends rational assessment. Here, Barth's concept is understood in terms of the theological voluntarism of William of Occam or Kierkegaard. The good is literally arbitrary, purely the product of the absolute power and freedom of the divine will. It is absolutely heteronomous, and therefore irrational. It stands quite beyond the range of any human measure of what is rational and moral. It requires unquestioning obedience. It entirely displaces human autonomy; for to speak of the divine command is to speak of the capricious ejaculation of 'some Oriental potentate'.[82]

Associated with this objection, but also with that against the exclusion of principles and rules, is the complaint that the concept of hearing the divine command does not allow the formulation of any publicly intelligible justification of moral decisions. Referring again to Protestant ethics in general, James Gustafson remarks that, 'when asked for a theological and ethical reason to justify particular decisions and actions, this theology takes recourse to extraordinarily elusive sources'; and among these 'elusive sources' he numbers 'hearing God's command'.[83]

Correlatively, if the concept of divine command rules out the need and possibility of publicly intelligible justification, it rules out at the same time the need and possibility of publicly intelligible criticism. Robin Lovin notes that the ethic of the divine command 'begins with the assumption that the meaning and purpose in God's action are forever beyond human evaluation. . . . The child of God knows in action what God's will requires, but this certainty is neither visible to his neighbour nor available for his own reflection.'[84]

'Nor available for his own reflection': this brings us to the final objection raised against Barth's concept of divine command. If the divine command precludes public accountability, it cannot help but close the door on self-criticism too. If it cannot be comprehended by the formulation of principles or rules or systems of both; if it does not require, indeed actively opposes, interpretation

[82] W. G. Maclagan quoted by Ian T. Ramsey, 'Moral Judgements and God's Commands', in Ian T. Ramsey (ed.), *Christian Ethics and Contemporary Philosophy* (London: SCM, 1966), 152.
[83] Gustafson, *Protestant and Roman Catholic Ethics*, 32.
[84] Lovin, *Christian Faith and Public Choices*, 28, 41.

of any kind, then it will suffer analysis and interrogation in no
forum whatsoever, either public or private. It gives itself only to be
heard and then obeyed. But precisely in withholding itself from
public discussion and private reflection, it would appear that, in
the end, the divine command lends itself to exploitation by the
human will to self-justification and so to the destruction of moral
fellowship. Ironically, then, Barth's divine command finds itself
accused of promoting in practice precisely the ideological kind of
ethics that it was originally designed to preclude. 'What happens',
asks Charles West, 'when [Man] is liberated from the very need for
explaining and justifying his faith, from the requirement of ethical
behaviour according to principles? A greater appreciation of all
truth wherever found? A more sensitive ethical insight? Or the
erection of a new law of his own in both these areas, an orthodoxy
bearing the name of Barth?'[85]

II

If this barrage of criticism that we have just reported were unequivocally accurate, then Barth's concept of hearing God's command would be beyond redemption. It is certainly not entirely
wide of the mark; for there is indeed in Barth's thought a strand
of theological voluntarism that inclines him to depreciate the
propriety of rational deliberation, analysis, and criticism in regard
to moral issues. Nevertheless, this voluntarist element does not
consistently dominate Barth's thinking. For in spite of his
unequivocal insistence that God's command is absolutely self-
determining, reaching us with an immediacy and definiteness that
precludes interpretation, and that the only legitimate kind of ethical reflection is a sort of spiritual self-examination, Barth himself
engaged extensively in a systematic form of ethical deliberation
about right conduct. This engagement occurs pre-eminently in the
final chapters of volumes iii (chapter 12) and iv (chapter 17) of his

[85] West, *Communism and the Theologians*, 245–6. The charge that Barth, who
campaigns so vigorously against ideologies, operates ideologically himself in
reaching political decisions was first made by Reinhold Niebuhr in his review
of Barth's *Against the Stream* in *Christianity and Society* (1954/4). West endorses
this, but reckons that the word 'ideological' is too strong (*Communism and the
Theologians*, 286–7). Willis follows Niebuhr and West in detecting 'an ideological
overtone' to Barth's political thinking (*Ethics of Karl Barth*, 420).

Church Dogmatics, and would have occurred in the final chapter of volume v, had he been spared to write it. Whereas the concluding chapter (8) of volume ii comprises 'general' ethics, in which human action is considered from the objective point of view of the command of God which liberates it and makes it good, these chapters deal in 'special' ethics. 'Special' ethics, presupposing the general sort, proceeds to consider good human action in terms of its subjective matter, namely, the recognizable effects which the liberating and sanctifying command of God creates in those who actively respond to it. Here ethics becomes concrete, particular— 'special'—in accordance with the fact that actual human activity is always 'the related sequence of events in which this particular concrete man chooses and realizes a particular concrete condition and possibility'.[86]

But in what sense may we describe Barth's special ethics as systematic? We have already noted Barth's jaundiced view of system and so of casuistry. So we suffer no surprise when he takes pains to distinguish his own special ethics from the casuistical manufacturing of moral judgements about particular cases, by the mechanical application of rules that state what kinds of action are and are not expressive of moral principles. Ethics cannot be systematic in this sense, Barth insists, because it must respect both the sovereign, personal freedom of God to dispose the concrete meaning and content of his commanding, and the creaturely, personal freedom of man to be responsible in his action; 'it has to

---

[86] *CD* iii/4: 3–6. Paul Ramsey contrasts Barth with Paul Lehmann: 'it is true that under the doctrine of God (where Lehmann says [*Ethics in a Christian Context*, 271] Barth "located" ethics, neglecting the rest), Karl Barth gives extended analysis simply of the proposition that "there is no good which is not obedience to God's command" [*CD* ii/2: 541]. This is the source and the extent of Lehmann's ethics of "freedom in obedience". However, Karl Barth's undertaking for the entirety of Christian ethics requires another statement: "there must be seen and demonstrated the fact and extent of the existence of good human action under the lordship and efficacy of the divine command" [*CD* iii/4: 6]. Lehmann does not give or seek to fulfil such a description of the task of Christian ethics. . . . In his *Dogmatics* taken as a whole . . . Barth stresses as well [as the freedom and uniqueness of the divine command and claim] what is entailed for man in God's binding Himself to the world and the world to Himself; he does not hesitate to discourse upon the doctrines of creation and the nature of man, and in this connexion to elaborate a "special ethics" entailed in all this' (*Deeds and Rules in Christian Ethics*, Scottish Journal of Theology Occasional Papers No. 11 (Edinburgh: Oliver & Boyd, 1965), 53–4, 61). As we shall see shortly, Barth's elaboration of special ethics extended beyond the doctrine of creation to the doctrines of reconciliation and redemption.

respect the directness of the dealings between the commanding God and the man who obeys or disobeys him'.[87] Otherwise it will constitute 'a violation of the divine mystery of the ethical event'.[88] On the other hand, special ethics can be more than 'an obscure ethics of the *kairos* in general'.[89] It can do more than merely give 'a direction to let oneself be governed from moment to moment and situation to situation by a kind of direct and particular inspiration and guidance, and to prepare oneself, to make and keep oneself fit and ready, for the reception of such guidance, perhaps by "quiet times" or similar exercises'. 'This', Barth asserts, 'is not what is meant.'[90] What special ethics can and must do is 'to point to that event between God and man, to its uncontrollable content'.[91] Certainly, it must constantly be on guard against trying to give more than a reference to the event of God's concrete command and man's concrete obedience or disobedience; to be more than a reminder of the authority, guidance, and judgement of the Holy Spirit; to teach more than the art of how to ask appropriately and listen openly to the answer that God alone can give; to offer more than an encouragement to go to meet this event. Nevertheless, although the event of encounter and its content cannot be made theoretically captive, a certain theoretical reference to them can and must be made.[92]

The possibility of the formation of such a reference rests, in the first place, on the fact that God, though sovereign, is also constant,

---

[87] *Chr. L.* 4. [88] *CD* iii/4: 11. [89] *CL* 5. [90] *CD* iii/4: 15.
[91] *CL* 5.

[92] *CD* iii/4: 16; *CL* 6, 34. This concurs with Yoder's summary of Barth's general concept of the nature of theological ethics: 'The theological science of Christian ethics, according to Barth, does not contribute directly to moral decision, nor does it evaluate the ultimate righteousness (before God) of decisions which have been made. It has a much more modest function. Its only task is to test, technically and "scientifically", i.e. carefully, with relation to the object of Christian faith, the reasons Christians give to account for their actions before, in the course of, or after having made their decisions' (*Karl Barth and the Problem of War*, 23). And again: 'Ethics is not the process of Christian decision, but the evaluation of the reasons presented for decision, as the Christian converses, before and after his decision, with the Christian past and with the Christian brotherhood. We cannot judge whether a Christian's act is right or wrong, but we can call upon him to account for the decision he has made by presenting for examination, and for testing by the criterion of the Word of God, his reasons for deciding as he did' (p. 48). Ethics stands to moral decision as dogmatics to proclamation: as a critical science which tests the current speech and thought of the Church in the light of the principle of its being, the norm of faith, the Word of God attested by Scripture.

being faithful both to himself and to humankind.[93] He is not capricious, for his absolute power is moved by his grace. His sovereignty is informed and directed by 'the great and active Yes of his free and gracious address to the world created by him, and to man who is at the heart of it'. The substance of his positive freedom consists in his decision from eternity and in Jesus Christ to be active on behalf of humankind.[94] Now, it is true that God demonstrates faithfulness to his own nature as grace precisely in that 'every encounter with every man at every historical moment is of sufficient importance for Him on His side to encounter man in His command in a unique way, for which there is neither precedence nor recurrence'. Nevertheless, God is equally true to himself in that, in all the infinite diversity in which he gives and reveals his command, there is 'a single and unitary command' which is the expression of his one definite, good, and gracious will from all eternity to be for humankind in Jesus Christ.[95] The fact that each singular event of encounter between the commanding God and sinful human being is a moment in a history which is ordered by this definite intention of God gives to each historically contingent divine command its *ratio* and raises it above the status of one element in a chaos of individual conflicting intimations to individual human beings in individual situations.[96]

In the second place, the possibility of the formation of a reference to the event of encounter rests on the fact that each singular act of human obedience or disobedience is both expressive and formative of a certain continuity of human being, attitude, and

---

[93] *CL* 5.   [94] *CD* ii/2: 552–3; *CL* 15–18; *CD* iii/1: 370.

[95] *CD* iii/4: 16. Paul Ramsey finds Paul Lehmann's ethics wanting this Christological information of God's freedom: 'Barth can take ethics more seriously than Lehmann precisely because his theology is more adequate. While for Barth God is free (as Lehmann seems to say most of all and hence to be concerned with the exceptional all the time). He has also made Himself known quite historically in Jesus Christ. Jesus Christ becomes the datum for the moral life of a Christian in Barth in a way that he does not for Lehmann. In Him is all we know about the humanity of God (theology) and the humanity of man (anthropology). This is also all we are given to know about the freedom of God, i.e. His freedom to bind Himself to the world and the world to himself. By contrast, God's freedom in Lehmann is simply an autonomous theological speculation drawn from this world of rapid change. While there remains the possibility in Barth of entirely novel, free acts of God, there is a shape to the gospel of God and a shape to His action that enables us to reflect upon it for our knowledge into God and for our knowledge into the shape of Christian moral action' (*Deeds and Rules*, 51).

[96] *CD* ii/2: 710, 713–15; iii/4: 16–17; ii/2: 677, 701.

action—of a particular human subject; that the being of each and every subject is determined by the creative, reconciling, and redemptive action of the God by whose command it is always addressed; and that, therefore, concrete human action proceeds under a divine ordering of history which persists in all the differentiation of individual cases. Each singular event of encounter constitutes a moment in this definite history. The vertical dimension stands in a definite horizontal connection; indeed, 'only as the vertical intersects a horizontal can it be called vertical'. Therefore, the reference which special ethics must make to the singular vertical dimension of the ethical event cannot remain a mere point, but must become linear to the extent that it has to take note of the horizontal constancy of the divine command and human action as the form common to all such events. By thus describing the character that the ethical event will 'always' (*auf alle Fälle* = 'in every case') take, and the standards by which the divine Commander will 'always' decide the goodness or evil of human action, special ethics at once forbears from anticipating the moral judgement that the divine command will pronounce in the event of encounter, and yet still provides 'instructional preparation' for it.[97]

The constant, horizontal dimension of the ethical encounter, in terms of which special ethics makes its theoretical reference, consists in the history of the covenant of grace established by God with humankind. This history takes its direction, its law, its order from the *telos* that God intends; namely, the future redemption of humankind in fulfilment of their destiny by creation, through God's reconciling election of humanity in the real human being, Jesus Christ.[98] In order to represent it, therefore, special ethics must differentiate this history into the three 'spheres' of creation, reconciliation, and redemption. But it needs to be emphasized that 'always in the ethical event God commands and man acts in all three spheres at once'.[99] In each and every such event God commands simultaneously, first, as Father, Creator, and therefore sovereign Lord of human beings as his creatures; second, as Son and Reconciler to himself of human beings as sinners; and third,

---

[97] CD iii/4: 17–18 (*KD* iii/4: 18); *CL* 5. [98] CD ii/2: 694, 766.

[99] CD iii/4: 33. As the *opera Trinitatis ad extra sunt indivisa*, so the three moments of the ethical event (and the three dimensions of Christian ethics) enjoy *perichoresis* or mutual interpenetration. See Willis, *Ethics of Karl Barth*, 116, 118, 192 n. 2.

as Holy Spirit and Redeemer of human beings to eternal life from the conflict in which they stand here and now. Correlatively, in each and every ethical event the human being confronted with the divine command is always thereby defined simultaneously as the creature and therefore the covenant partner of God; as the pardoned sinner; and as the child of God led by the Holy Spirit to live during the present time of contradiction, conflict, and suffering by hope in the presence of God's future.

The three spheres or dimensions of the relationship—and therefore of the encounter—between God and humankind are determined and relatively demarcated from one another by the fact, on the one hand, that the one will of God has different forms and his one command different elements; and, on the other hand, that the one man exists before God in different respects, and his action is composed of different elements. Within each of its forms and elements, the divine will and command embrace a plenitude of particular intentions and demands; and within each of their respects and elements human existence and action are widely differentiated. It is of the utmost importance to Barth that we take note that the divine command and the obedient or disobedient action of humankind are not coincident with the spheres in which they occur, and so cannot simply be read off them. These spheres are not laws (or orders in the sense of laws) *according to* which God commands and humankind does right or wrong; rather, they are the 'general form' *within* which God commands and humans act.[100] As the general form or 'historical outline' of the ethical event, 'which is inaccessible . . . to the casuistical grasp', these spheres do not (Barth is careful to insist) make possible a return to casuistry. Nevertheless, they do give

a definite lead in the direction of an answer which is finally asked of each of us individually in his relationship to God and his fellows . . . not the answer itself; not a definition or determination of this event . . . but a reference to it by which it is generally described in a way which is generally discernible and attested in a form which is generally valid . . . a directive, or rather a series of directives, which give guidance to the individual in the form of an approximation to the knowledge of the divine command and right human action.[101]

In the ideal case of a full knowledge of the definite general spheres and relationships in which the ethical event occurs, the question

---

[100] *CD* iii/4: 29–30 (*KD* iii/4: 31).   [101] Ibid. 30–1.

of what is commanded or forbidden 'gains a sharpness in which the question almost acquires the character of an answer'. However, since the singular concrete ethical case to which an answer must always relate ultimately transcends the predictions of ethics, and since our knowledge of these general spheres and relationships will never actually be full, the question of what is commanded and forbidden will always and necessarily retain 'a certain breadth of openness'. Because it must always respect 'the final mystery' of the event of encounter, even the most special of special ethics can offer no more than general guidance.[102]

Special ethics as Barth conceives it is not self-contained and self-sufficient. It does not pretend to autonomy. It is not a closed system. But it is, nevertheless, systematic. The history of God's covenant of grace with humankind provides its organizing principle and brings about the differentiation of special ethics into consideration of the three dimensions of the one command of God the Creator, Reconciler, and Redeemer. In each of these spheres, special ethics explicates the meaning of the constant will of God in terms of a governing concept or principle. This principle is then differentiated into species, each of which is subject to further specification.

As an example of the systematic structure of special ethics we take the first part, which focuses on the sphere of the command of God the Creator.[103] Here the principle is that of freedom, which is differentiated into freedom before God, freedom in fellowship, freedom for life, and freedom in limitation. But the process of differentiation and specification does not stop there. The third species, for example, is conceived as having two facets: the freedom to treat life—especially human life—as a loan from God, and the freedom to live life in active obedience to the Creator and Lord. The first facet is then further differentiated into the freedom to respect and the freedom to protect life; and then the meaning of these latest species is explicated in terms of the two basic kinds of the taking of human life, suicide and homicide, and of the latter's various forms—abortion, euthanasia, self-defence, capital punishment, and war.

Barth's special ethics is certainly systematic, but it does not comprise a closed system. For although it proceeds by means of the systematic specification of the moral meaning of a basic theo-

---

[102] Ibid. 31.   [103] See ch. 12 in vol. iii/4.

logical principle, it does not claim the power to identify conclusively what God is commanding in a given situation. It can indicate
the normal form of God's command, but it is always open to the
possibility that God in his sovereignty may make extraordinary
demands. It allows the possibility of 'exceptional' or 'border-line
cases' (*Grenzfälle*), which cannot be brought under its control by
determining in advance, through classification and codification,
what are the circumstances in which they invariably occur. Such
predetermination is simply beyond human ability; for

> it is not the greater or lesser cogency of human reasons which decides in
> this matter ... but exclusively the judgement of God, which in the last
> analysis we must all hear in every actual or conceivable situation after
> considering the human arguments on both sides. ... [T]he possibility of
> the exceptional case is the particular possibility of God Himself. Nor
> should we merely persuade ourselves that this is given us. It is casuistical
> frivolity to try to do so. This is something we can only be told.[104]

An example of this may be found in Barth's elaboration of that
specification of God's command which gives us the rule that we
should protect life. Here, he cautions us that life is not divine and
eternal, but natural in the sense of creaturely and finite—'temporal
life is certainly not the highest of all goods'[105]—and further, that
the inner norm of its protection lies in the will of its Creator.
From this he concludes that 'the protection of life required of us is
not unlimited nor absolute. It is simply the protection which God
wills to demand of man as the Creator of this life and the Giver
of the future eternal life.'[106] Barth admits rational systematization
in ethics provided that it opens itself to the 'final mystery' of the
event of encounter between God and the human creature, by
acknowledging the possibility of an exceptional case of divine
commanding.

But at this point there presses upon us the question of whether
Barth's concept of the exceptional case ultimately leaves ethical
reasoning any ground at all. For the voluntarist tone of some of his
discussion militates against this, as when he sets the (possibly
exceptional) judgement of God over and against 'the greater and
lesser cogency of human reasons'. Such a tone is made stronger by
his express denial that we can domesticate an exceptional case

---

[104] *CD* iii/4: 411–13.   [105] Ibid. 401.   [106] Ibid. 397–8.

by classifying it in terms of its moral features 'so that we may know that in certain circumstances we are confronted by . . . [it]'.[107] This could well be interpreted as saying that God may command something that lies *in principle* beyond the rational grasp of ethics, something that is *irreducibly* exceptional to the apprehension of God's will contained in any set of moral rules; and if this interpretation is correct, then Barth has succeeded in limiting systematic ethics only by subverting it. For if I cannot count upon my systematic ethical reflection having any bearing upon what God will command; if in the end all my efforts at moral reasoning might simply be eclipsed, then why should I bother with it in the first place? The problem is not at all that my moral reasoning should be confronted by a moral case that startles it; one that my current array of moral rules cannot readily comprehend. The problem is not that my ethical system should be provoked to adjust itself to the datum of a case with an unfamiliar feature of some moral significance. The problem is not that my special ethics should be stimulated to reform itself. Not at all. Rather, the problem is that my systematic ethical reflection should be faced with a case that is simply unintelligible; and whose effect, therefore, upon the process of moral reasoning is not to correct it, but to suspend it; not to teach it to speak differently, but to strike it dumb.[108]

However, this voluntarist account of the exceptional case of an extraordinary divine command is not the only one that Barth gives us; for he does not always talk about it as an irredeemable outlaw. Indeed, whenever he discusses a concrete instance of such a case he insists that it is not simply a contradiction of the relevant rule, but rather an unusual meaning of it. So, for example, with respect to the possibility of an extraordinary command of God to take human life, Barth denies that it implies a 'limitation' of the Sixth Commandment. Rather,

it simply refers to the fact that human life has no absolute greatness or supreme value, that it is not a kind of second god, but that its proper protection must also be guided, limited and defined by the One who commands it, i.e. by the One who is a real God, the supreme good, the Lord of life. It simply means that the required protection of life must take

---

[107] Ibid. 411.

[108] Here Barth appears to propose something akin to Joseph Fletcher's 'situation ethics', according to which the discernment here and now of 'the loving thing to do' might require the simple suspension of received moral rules.

into account its limitation in relation to that which is to be protected. It cannot try to have only one mode, or to express itself only in the assertion, preservation and defence of life. These are naturally the forms of achievement which are most obvious and which call for primary treatment. And so far as possible they will continue to be the only form in which it presents itself. But since human life is of relative greatness and limited value, its protection may also consist *ultima ratione* in its surrender and sacrifice. In certain circumstances, should the commanding God so will it, it may have to break and discontinue the defence of life in which it should present itself until this boundary is reached. This will be the case only, but then in all seriousness, when God as the Lord of life so wills it.[109]

Although Barth pursues a voluntarist line here when he argues that the divine will can make the protection of life require what is normally considered to be its opposite—that is, its surrender and sacrifice—he simultaneously affirms moral reason when he asserts that such an extraordinary divine command does not require the transgression or suspension of the rule but rather an unusual mode of keeping it. He takes the same, rational line when, with regard to the possibility that God might command us to leave our families in order to follow a prophetic vocation, he denies that such an extraordinary command requires us to violate the rule that we should honour our parents.[110] Here the extraordinary command of God is presented as constituting, not so much a case that is an exception to the rule, but rather one that stands on the outer margins of its fulfilment. It is literally a *Grenzfall*—a 'borderline' case—but one standing inside the border. So understood, God's extraordinary command may meet us as a stranger, but it is not in fact a sheer outlaw. It baffles moral reason; but it baffles it into learning. It is not, therefore, irreducibly exceptional. It startles systematic ethics with something that it has not comprehended; but it does so in order that the ethical system might yet extend or refine its grasp.

This account of the role of the extraordinary case as a stimulus to moral learning accords with the dialectical-evolutionary concept of special ethics implied in a description that Barth gives of one of its formal elements, the moral principle. Moral principles, he writes, 'may be absolute in appearance, but in fact they are altogether ambiguous and dialectical. They can and must continu-

---

[109] *CD* iii/4: 398.   [110] Ibid. 260.

ally be completed and replaced by others. As they are established, recognized and applied, they constantly provoke antitheses.'[111] Moreover, the claim that Barth was really concerned to make systematic ethics systematically open to correction, rather than to emasculate or displace it, is supported by the terms in which he explains what subordination to the Word of God does and does not involve.

It certainly does not involve a *sacrificium intellectus*, which is 'only a last desperate attempt to make the knowledge of God a work of man, to have a human possibility correspond to what is God's work alone'.[112] God's Word encounters us in the midst of our intellectual humanity, with all its limitations and distortions, with all its half-truths and errors; and we must be content to meet it there. To attempt an encounter outside of our finite and fallen intellects is to aspire to approach the Word of God on equal terms and apart from our sin and creaturely finitude.[113] Subordination to God's Word, therefore, does not require us to make ourselves *tabulae rasae*:

It is not as though we had simply to abandon and forget our ideas, thoughts and convictions. We certainly cannot do that, just as little as we can free ourselves from our own shadow. . . . Subordination does not mean the elimination and annihilation of our own resources. Subordination implies that the subordinate is there as such and remains there. It means placing oneself behind, following, complying as subordinate to superior. . . . With our whole fund of reason and experience we will let ourselves be led and taught and corrected by the Word of God and therefore by Scripture, that is, by its testimony to Jesus Christ.[114]

What applies to human reason in general presumably applies to moral reason in particular. Its operations are legitimate—indeed, they are necessary—and its conclusions are valuable. Nevertheless, it must operate with its ears open, ready to learn; and it must be ready at every turn to call into question 'every answer that we and others may have given' to the ethical question, 'What ought we to do?'; and to regard as hypothetical 'all that we think we know

---

[111] *CD* ii/2: 727.   [112] *CD* i/1: 247.

[113] Barth's point here is well put by Basil Mitchell when he advises that '[i]t is perhaps wiser not to try to escape ideology altogether but to recognise the ideology one has and submit it critically to the test of reason and experience, prepared, if necessary, to revise or even reject it' ('Ideals, Roles and Rules', 365).

[114] *CD* i/2: 718, 721.

concerning the rightness and goodness of our past and recent decisions, all the rules and axioms, however good, all the inner and outer laws and necessities under which we have hitherto placed ourselves and perhaps do so again'.[115]

Clearly, Barth is proposing an ethical system that is open to correction and so to development. But if such a system is to learn anything from an encounter with an extraordinary case, then it must eventually be able to make sense of it. This it does by identifying the moral features of the case and then deciding under which rule it should be subsumed. If the case is extraordinary, then it will not be immediately apparent what that decision should be; and the process of making it will involve some refinement of the inherited set of rules. The conclusion of this casuistic process will consist in the classification of the case—its designation as one of a kind that is covered by a particular rule. But is this not exactly what Barth forbids when he writes of the extraordinary case that 'these situations must not be classified or codified so that we may know that in certain circumstances we are confronted by the exception'?[116]

There is some reason to suppose not, for Barth himself does not hesitate to note the distinguishing characteristics of different kinds of extraordinary case. He tells us, for example, that in all cases where God commands the taking of human life, the agent is motivated by love for God, the desire to obey him, and love for the neighbour; and that he carries out the commanded act joyfully, gratefully, and resolutely, and therefore in faith that God will forgive whatever elements of sin are involved.[117] Moreover, genuine cases of such a command are rare and occur only *in extremis* after the exhaustive consideration of possible alternatives;[118] and with regard to abortion and capital punishment Barth specifies an extreme situation as one in which a choice cannot be avoided between the life of the child and the life of the mother (abortion), or between the life of a traitor and the continued existence of the state (capital punishment).[119]

However, Barth does assert that the characterization of an

---

[115] *CD* ii/2: 645–6. Barth qualifies this radical relativization of ethical tradition when, on the following page, he writes that 'the more truly it [our current answer to the question of what God commands] derives from previous ethical reflection and testing, the less will this process [of repeated criticism and reformation] be injurious to it, the more surely will it again prove its value' (ibid. 647–8).

[116] *CD* iii/4: 411.   [117] Ibid. 402, 410, 423.   [118] Ibid. 410, 421, 446–7.

[119] Ibid. 421, 446–7.

extraordinary case can never be made complete. He insists that the characteristics which he has listed are necessary but not sufficient; and that a sufficient description is impossible. We can never reach the point where analysis of the character of a situation will reveal conclusively what God commands. In his discussion of suicide he gives a reason for this. He argues that we cannot know in any final sense what occurs between the one who takes life and God;[120] and since the moral quality of such an act is decisively determined by whether or not it is an act of obedience,[121] we are never in a position to know conclusively whether a given act of life-taking was commanded by God or not. Along the same lines he argues with respect to abortion that in the extreme case where a choice must be made between the life of the child and the life of the mother, we simply cannot say that one is always to be preferred to the other. Whether or not the mother should sacrifice herself is hidden in the mystery of the encounter between her and the God who commands her.[122] Here the power of moral rules to describe an extraordinary case ceases; and from this point onward the attempt to classify and codify becomes at once futile and sinful.

Unfortunately, Barth's persistent tendency to associate system with the sinful aspiration to moral autonomy,[123] and his consequent failure to affirm unequivocally the distinction between a

---

[120] Ibid. 402, 404.

[121] Ibid. 423: 'how can there possibly be obedience, and how can the content be good and right?'   [122] Ibid. 421.

[123] This is evident in Barth's remarks on ideology in the unfinished draft of the second section of his *Dogmatics'* treatise on the command of God the Reconciler, over which he was labouring in his final years. On the one hand, he frankly affirms the human capability for conceptual organization, provided that any given organization of concepts be regarded strictly as provisional. But on the other hand, he only directly refers to 'das System' when discussing what happens when the one who exercises this ability for conceptual apprehension and organization seeks to do so independently of the living Spirit of God. Then he writes that 'there will arise at once, and at the decisive point, a distinctive numbness, hardening and rigidity, and therefore an inertia in which he will cease to be a free spirit. This comes about as he thinks he can and should ascribe to the presuppositions and sketches he has achieved by this remarkable ability, not just a provisional and transitory but a permanent normativity, not just one that is relative but one that is absolute, not just one that is human but one that is quasi-divine. His hypotheses become for him theses behind which he no longer ventures to go back with seeking, questioning, researching. He thinks that they can be thought and formulated definitively as thoughts that are not merely useful but intrinsically true and therefore binding. His ideal becomes an idol. He thinks that he knows only unshakeable principles and among them a basic principle in relation to which he must coordinate and develop them as a whole, combining them all, and with them his perceptions and concepts, into a system, making of his ideas an ideology' (*CL* 224–5).

closed and an open system that is implicit in so much of his thought, has two unhappy effects upon his characterization of extraordinary cases. First, it never attempts to be comprehensive and it sometimes manages to be superficial. In his discussion of euthanasia, for example, he alludes to the distinction between the active and the passive kinds only once; and he does so only to deny that such a distinction carries any moral weight at all. Yet in the very next sentence he begins to suggest that there might conceivably be an extraordinary case where to prolong life artificially would be an act of disobedience. And there his discussion ends.[124]

The other unhappy consequence of Barth's persistent suspicion of system is that his own implicit understanding of the character of an extraordinary case is sometimes far more discriminate than his explicit analysis reveals; and because it is largely covert, much of his discrimination is shielded from critical scrutiny. His characterization of God's extraordinary command to wage war is a case in point.[125] In *Church Dogmatics*, iii/4, Barth's overt analysis discloses, first of all, five features common to all cases where the taking of life is genuinely commanded: it is intended as an extraordinary means of protecting life; it is *ultima ratio*; it occurs in the context of a presumption in favour of not taking life; it occurs against the background of an awareness of the risk involved in interpreting the rule in an unusual fashion; and it is affirmed unconditionally, with no regard for the prospects of success, and 'in faith and therefore with a joyous and reckless determination'.[126] Beyond these features common to all extraordinary cases of the commanded taking of human life, Barth adds two mutually alternative conditions which are specific to the extraordinary case of commanded war. These are either that it be waged in fulfilment of an obligation—perhaps, but not necessarily, by treaty—to aid 'a weaker neighbour'; or in defence of the state against an attack upon its very existence and autonomy.[127] These two specific conditions are given further, negative definition by the six

---

[124] *CD* iii/4: 427.
[125] J. H. Yoder criticizes Barth at this very point for smuggling into his argument about the *Grenzfall* of commanded war elements of moral 'common sense' which have not been sufficiently exposed to the critical scrutiny of the divine Word (*Karl Barth and the Problem of War*, 70–1).
[126] *CD* iii/4: 450–64.   [127] Ibid. 461.

examples of cases of forbidden belligerency which Barth lists sub-
sequently: when a belligerent state wishes simply to expand its
dominion; when it seeks to rectify an internal situation by external
adventure; when it reckons that its honour and prestige have been
violated by another state; when it feels threatened by a shift in the
balance of power of other states; when it disapproves of affairs
internal to another state; and when it is convinced that it possesses
a historical mission or vocation to lead and rule other nations.[128]
The definition of the second condition is still further and now
positively advanced by the qualification that belligerency for the
sake of preserving the very existence of a state is commanded only
when that state has 'serious grounds' for not surrendering. And
when might that be? When 'the responsibility for the whole physical, intellectual and spiritual life of the people comprising [a
nation] and therefore their relationship with God' is bound up
with national autonomy; when this people are commissioned to
attest to something entrusted to them with national autonomy—
'something more important to them than the preservation of life
itself'.[129]

The exceptional case of a divine command to wage war receives
one final further specification in this passage of the *Dogmatics*,
when Barth remarks that he would see belligerent resistance to
'any attack on the independence, neutrality and territoriality of the
Swiss Confederation' as divinely commanded.[130] He thereby clearly
implies that he considers Switzerland to be a case where national
autonomy is constitutive of a divinely commissioned attestation.
But exactly what he means by such a commission he chooses here
to leave a mystery.

Analysis of Barth's occasional writings around the time of
World War II, however, suggests that what in this case is presented as mysterious in the *Dogmatics* is in fact little more than
curtailed explication. For these writings enable us to discover what
it was that Barth believed the Swiss had a divine commission to
attest which is more important that the preservation of life itself,
and to which national autonomy is integral: justice. Moreover, we
also learn what are the political conditions under which justice

[128] Ibid.
[129] Ibid. This divine commission is to be distinguished from the bogus claim by
a nation to be possessed of a 'historical mission' (ibid. 300, 461).
[130] Ibid. 462.

is attested: government according to a constitution which guarantees freedom for the proclamation of the Gospel of justification;
which accords limited freedom for self-expression and development
to each of a plurality of racial, linguistic, regional, social, and
confessional groups; which balances the rights of the individual
against the claims of the community; and which is probably
(social) democratic in its structures and procedures.[131]

In refusing to be overtly systematic in his characterization of
exceptional cases, Barth was basically trying hard not to do casuistry, which he believed to exemplify the (closed) ethical system
par excellence.[132] In the opening pages of *Church Dogmatics*, iii/4,
he argues that casuistry finds its pattern in the exposition of the
Torah in Rabbinical Judaism, 'with its attempt to discover in all
actual or even imaginable instances the right decision concerning
the question of the right attitude and action enjoined upon man by
God, i.e., by the text of the Torah'.[133] This understanding of casuistry as the epitome of ethical rationalism, as a necessarily closed
logical system, is something that Barth shares with most Protestant writers on ethics since the seventeenth century—including
Dietrich Bonhoeffer, Emil Brunner, and Helmut Thielicke.[134] It is,

---

[131] See Appendix 1, 'The Divine Commission of an Independent Switzerland'.

[132] We do not agree, therefore, with John Howard Yoder's assertion that Barth
rejected casuistry only as a means of manufacturing a 'good conscience' (*Karl Barth
and the Problem of War*, 60–1). He also opposed it as a self-contained method of
making moral decisions which permits the moral agent to abstract herself from
direct responsibility to the living God. This is clearly what he meant when he
wrote of Christian casuistry that it 'first arose . . . when there developed a lack of
confidence in the Spirit (who is the Lord) as the Guide, Lawgiver and Judge in
respect of Christian action' (*CD* iii/4: 7). Yoder himself virtually implies as much
when he notes how Barth's concept of *Grenzfall* plays both the negative role of
limiting the very possibility of ethics as a rational discipline (*Karl Barth and the
Problem of War*, 66–7) and the positive role of safeguarding human responsibility
(p. 68)—though he uses the word 'responsibility' here in a more existentialist and
less theological sense than Barth. [133] *CD* iii/4: 7–8.

[134] See Nigel Biggar, 'A Case for Casuistry in the Church', *Modern Theology*, 6/1
(Oct. 1989), 29–51. Bonhoeffer believed that casuistry intends to expound 'the
whole immense range of conceivable contents', of the good, and to say in advance
what would be good in every conceivable case (*Ethics*, 86). Brunner judged that 'the
error of casuistry . . . consists in deducing particular laws from a universal law in
ever greater and more scrupulous detail. . . . Casuistry tries to imprison life in a net
of "cases" as though all could be arranged beforehand' (*Divine Imperative*, 134). It
seeks to deduce the case from a general law 'in the minutest particular' (p. 138),
reckoning that 'the law in its general character logically includes within itself all
particular propositions' (p. 137). Thielicke regarded casuistry as 'predetermined by
law', and as encouraging the flight from responsible freedom to 'the security of the
functionary' (*Theological Ethics*, i: *Foundations*, ed. William H. Lazareth (Grand
Rapids: Eerdmans, 1979), 457).

however, a misconception; for casuistry has not always, or perhaps even usually, pretended to provide an absolute method of deciding what is right. Seldom has it imagined that it could capture cases by the inexorable movement of deductive logic, by the mere application of a technique.[135] Rather, if Kenneth Kirk's account is accurate,[136] casuistry has more often approximated the open, dialectical model described variously by Paul Ramsey and J. M. Brennan.[137] According to their accounts, casuistry constantly involves the modification of old rules and the generation of new ones in the attempt to give faithful expression to a given moral principle in reaction to new, morally significant data. In other words, the casuistical process is not a one-way movement from principles through rules to cases, but a dialectic in which rules provide ready-made guidance with respect to morally familiar cases while being open to adaptation in the face of unfamiliar ones. The elements of this dialectical kind of casuistry are all present in Barth's ethical thought. But his persistent identification of casuistry as the epitome of ethical rationalism prevented him from bringing them to the fore, and so robbed him of part of what is required for an explicit and coherent account of the relationship between systematic ethical deliberation about right action and the hearing of a command of God.

The other requisite is the revision of Barth's concept of the command of God. Above all, if God's command is not to be ultimately subversive of rational deliberation about right action, then it cannot be conceived as an expression of divine arbitrariness, of God's freedom to decide in a capricious and irrational manner what is his will 'now here, now there'.[138] As we have seen, there are certainly passages where Barth thinks of God's command along voluntaristic, Occamist lines, according to which moral qualities are not intrinsic to kinds of action but are posited

[135] Writing of the Roman Catholic tradition of casuistry, the major casuistical tradition in Christian ethics, James Gustafson has suggested that 'perhaps ... only the writers of the poorest manuals, the least nuanced and historically sophisticated have claimed that the gap between general principles and particular choices and actions would be closed by logic alone' (*Protestant and Roman Catholic Ethics*, 47).

[136] K. E. Kirk, *Conscience and Its Problems: An Introduction to Casuistry* (London: Longman, Green & Co., 1927), 106–29.

[137] Paul Ramsey, 'The Case of the Curious Exception', in Outka and Ramsey (eds.), *Norm and Context*; J. M. Brennan, *The Open Texture of Moral Judgements* (London: Macmillan, 1977).

[138] Barth, *Anselm: Fides quaerens intellectum* (London: SCM, 1960), 47.

by arbitrary acts of God.[139] But obviously, if human reasoning about moral matters is to have any relative validity, God's command must be the expression of a divine will that is governed by the divine *Ratio* or Wisdom, and which is therefore intelligible in principle. That is to say, it must be understood according to the tradition of which Augustine, Anselm, Aquinas, Duns Scotus, and Calvin are representatives,[140] and in which Barth places himself whenever he affirms that God's will has been decisively determined by his free decision to be for humankind in Jesus Christ. This concept of God's command still permits it to contradict the moral assumptions and conclusions of human reason, but only in so far as their actual grasp of the divine *Ratio* is mistaken, and not because their attempt to grasp it is futile in principle. There may be cases of God's commanding that are foreign, not to my understanding as such, but only to my understanding thus far. Extraordinary cases may be irregular *de facto*, but not *de jure*.

A command of God must be the expression of a divine will that is constant and therefore in principle intelligible to human moral reason. This is not to say, however, that moral reason's grasp of it, even in familiar cases, can ever be absolute. That God's will is constant does not mean that it is entirely predictable. A divine command is not exhausted in a full description of its generic features. It cannot be reduced to a moral rule; for rules cannot tell me concretely what I should do at this moment in this situation. They can tell me the kind of thing I should do, but not exactly what. So knowledge, however specific, of the character of God's commanding in this *kind* of situation will still not indicate exactly what is required of me here and now. That presents itself in terms of the particulars of the case, which necessarily elude the generic grasp of moral reason.

[139] William of Occam, *On the Four Books of the Sentences*, bk. 2, q. 19 (extract), in Idziak (ed.), *Divine Command Morality*, 55–7. Cf. *CD* iii/4: 411: 'it is not the greater or lesser cogency of human reasons which decides in this matter, but exclusively the judgement of God.'

[140] Augustine, *The City of God*, 16. 32; *De Trinitate*, 13. 10; Anselm, *De veritate*, 10; *Cur Deus homo*, 1. 12; *Monologion*, 80; *Proslogion*, 11; Aquinas, *Summa contra Gentiles*, 1. 95; *Summa theologiae*, 1a2ae, q. 19; John Duns Scotus, *The Oxford Commentary on the Four Books of the Sentences*, 3, dist. 37; Calvin, *Institutes*, 3. 23. 2. Robert Merrihew Adams is a contemporary exponent of this tradition: see 'A Modified Divine Command Theory of Ethical Wrongness', and 'Divine Command Metaethics as Necessary a Posteriori', in Paul Helm (ed.), *Divine Commands and Morality* (Oxford: Oxford University Press, 1981), 83–108, 109–19.

For example, suppose that it is characteristic of God's command that it always requires us to love our neighbour; and that in the case of our parents, it always requires that our love should take the specific form of honouring them. This rule could be specified further so as to indicate the kinds of action that honouring one's parents involves. But no matter how far it were specified, it would never amount to a prescription of what I should do here and now in order to honour my parents. That would depend upon the circumstances given at a particular time and place; and among these circumstances would be the unique history of our relationship, with its peculiar constellation of problems and possibilities.

The inconclusiveness of rules is the result of their inability to bridge the gap between the generic and the particular. Sometimes this latter is the particular way of fulfilling a rule; but, at other times, it is the particular person with regard to whom it should be fulfilled. For example, let it be granted that I am bound by the rule that I should love my neighbour. But the question arises (and not merely as a tactic of evasion): Who is my neighbour? Certainly, there are always some neighbours who are given me to love: my immediate relatives, the members of my own family, those I work with, those with whom I have regular dealings, and those who walk into my life one day and out of it the next. But there are also those to whom I could extend myself if I so choose, but who have no special claim upon my love. Sometimes I stop and reach out my hand, and sometimes I walk on past. Sometimes I am called to make a neighbour out of a particular stranger, but I am certainly not called to make a neighbour out of every stranger that comes into view. There is no rule here, but there may be a vocation.

This vocational element is, perhaps, most obvious in cases of irreducible moral dilemma, one of which is the situation where an inevitable choice must be made between the life of a mother and that of her unborn child.[141] In this case, even when all the general conditions obtain that are characteristic of a divine command to take life, we still cannot conclude that a command to abort has been issued. For there is no rule that says that in every case of this kind the life of the fetus should be taken. The mother might be ready to sacrifice herself for her child; and who are we to say that she is wrong? The point is that, here, two different courses of

---

[141] *CD* iii/4: 421.

action both have the characteristics of a divine command; and that what is actually commanded is finally determined, not by moral rules, but by personal vocation. It might be that the mother is being called to complete her life with an admirable act of self-sacrifice so that her child will be able to fulfill the destiny to which he is called. Or it might be that the mother is being called to save her own life, and the child to surrender his, so that she can perform some further service required of her. Exactly what the divine calling is in such a situation is ultimately hidden in the private dealings between these persons and God. Even though there may well be symptomatic criteria by which others can reach a reasonable judgement as to the genuineness of an alleged calling, their judgement cannot be final.

We propose, then, that a divine command should be understood, in the end, in terms of personal vocation. This is not at all to empty the command of its obligatory force, because the part that God calls me to play in his redemptive ordering of history is not something that I am free to accept or reject at will. It is not just a morally indifferent option. I am just as bound to obey my personal calling as I am bound to obey moral rules. The fact that Jonah was not obliged to go to Nineveh by any moral rule does not lessen the seriousness of his disobedience to his prophetic calling. A divine calling does oblige the one whom it addresses. It is a command.

Understood in terms of a moral vocation to do something particular here and now, the concept of hearing a divine command has the virtue of providing a theological account of the ultimate uniqueness of a moral decision. For it conceives of such a decision, not as an arbitrary choice, but as a response to a definite vocation to play a particular part in this moment of the redemptive history of the covenant between God and humankind. Moreover, as we have argued, this concept of hearing God's command also has the advantage of being compatible with the casuistic exercise of the full analytical powers of moral reason. This is so on two conditions. The first is that the command be reckoned in principle intelligible in generic terms; in which case, it will neither pretend to be a substitute for the analysis of empirical data—the facts of the case—or the formulation of moral guidance in terms of rules, nor will it preclude the formulation of rational criticism. The second condition is that casuistic deliberation about right action must be conceived as involving more than generic reasoning. It must be understood to comprise, within the terms set by generic reason, the discernment of a particular, personal vocation to do something particular here and now.

We have argued that Barth was prevented from giving an explicit account of the interaction of divine command and special ethics along these lines because of a persistent prejudice against ethical system that was strongly nourished by the traditional Protestant prejudice against casuistry. But we have also argued that all of the elements of such an account as we propose are present in Barth's thought; and, indeed, that they are sufficiently prominent to make a purely voluntarist reading of it grossly simplistic.[142]

[142] See Appendix 2, 'Ethics and Hearing God's Command'.

2

THE TRINITARIAN
DIMENSIONS OF ETHICS

I

God's command does not resound in infinite space. It acquires
form in the midst of a definite history—the history of God's relationship with humankind. It is uttered by a definite, Trinitarian
God; one who as Father decided from eternity in his Son to
reconcile to himself his sinful human creatures, in order to bring
them by his Spirit to redemption in fulfilment of the destiny ap-
pointed them in creation. Correlatively, the command of this
God is heard by definite human beings who are simultaneously
creatures, pardoned sinners, and heirs of eternal life. This definite
history does not determine the content of God's command at
any one moment, but it does give it its characteristic, three-
dimensional shape; and it is by describing this shape that special
ethics educates us to recognize the particular command that it
cannot absolutely predict.

In accordance, then, with the form of the ethical event whose
characteristics it seeks to describe, special ethics differentiates
itself into three parts: the command of God the Creator, the
command of God the Reconciler, and the command of God the
Redeemer. In reality, of course, God's command, like God himself,
is one; so we must remember that this differentiation is logical
rather than ontological. In special ethics we understand success-
ively what is actually simultaneous. Its three parts, therefore, may
be distinguished but they are not separate. Like the members of
the Trinity, they are characterized by *perichoresis*; they co-inhere.
What this means is that they are properly understood as 'stations
on a way', and that

whatever we may see and say in detail at any point on this path will by
itself never be the whole of the one divine command as it meets the acting

man in the ethical event. . . . By itself it will never be more than . . . a mere extract from his reality and therefore limited and requiring supplementation. . . . And wherever we may happen to be, we shall never be permitted to halt or rest content with this or that particular knowledge; for of itself it cannot be knowledge of the command, but has meaning and force only in its connexion with the knowledge which precedes and follows.[1]

The structure of Barth's special ethics, then, is dynamic. It comprises three 'dimensions' rather than three 'parts'. It follows that our exposition of this structure will have to strive to give an account, not only of each dimension in itself, but also of the ways in which they interrelate. That is to say, we must aspire to gain some sense of the dynamic whole.

There is, however, an obstacle that obstructs our passage: the fact that Barth died before he had completed that part of his *Church Dogmatics* which treats the command of God the Reconciler (iv/4), and before he had begun his treatise on the command of God the Redeemer. But the obstacle is not insuperable. It does mean that our account is bound to depend at certain points on an estimation of what Barth would have written, rather than what he actually wrote. Happily, however, this estimation may enjoy the status of inference and not of mere conjecture. Several factors make this possible. First is the fact that, in at least three passages in the *Church Dogmatics* as we have it, Barth outlined the whole of his ethical scheme (ss. 36, 52, and 74);[2] and, although the last of these outlines was written about twenty years after the first, it is basically the same.[3] Then there is the dynamic, perichoretical nature of Barth's ethics; which means that anticipations of what he intended to treat fully in the unwritten parts of the *Dogmatics* may be found scattered throughout the parts that he did write. Finally, we have the lectures on ethics that Barth delivered at the University of Münster between 1928 and 1929, and then repeated (with revisions) at the University of Bonn between 1930 and 1931. These present us with a complete system of ethics, formed according to the same trinitarian structure that Barth was later to use in the

---

[1] Barth, *Ethics*, trans. G. W. Bromiley (New York: Seabury, 1981), 54; *CD* iii/4: 33–4.

[2] *CD* ii/2: 549–50; iii/4: 24–6; *CL* 6–11.

[3] s. 36 is part of *KD* ii/2, originally published in 1942; s. 52 is part of *KD* iii/4, originally published in 1951; s. 74, in the form that we have it, was written in the very early 1960s.

Dogmatics. It is true that we shall have to use these lectures with circumspection, since, when he came to write the first part of his special ethics, Barth did not follow the particular lines along which the lectures unfold this trinitarian scheme. Nevertheless, used with care, they can still aid us in our attempt to project a complete outline of what Barth would have said had he lived to complete the *Dogmatics*.

One final methodological remark remains to be made before we begin to follow the path of Barth's ethics. The logical sequence of the three spheres through which we will move—from creation to reconciliation, and then to redemption—does not reflect their material order. It follows from Barth's uncompromising identification of God's being or nature with his act in Jesus Christ that the part of special ethics which focuses on the command of God the Son—the Reconciler—should enjoy a 'material primacy' in relation to the others:

That God is Lord of the covenant of grace is materially the first thing by which his being and work, and therefore his speaking and commanding, as Creator and Redeemer are also determined and stamped. . . . The core of every statement in the first and third chapters of special ethics will thus consist of statements taken from the second, from specific Christological and soteriological statements. . . . The connected history of unique and singular encounters between God and man . . . comes from God, who as Creator is Lord of this history, and from man, who as his creature is the partner of this Lord. Again it goes to God the Redeemer, who as such determines its *telos*, and to man as his child, whom he conducts to its *telos*. This 'from him' and 'to him' (Romans 11.36) are made a history (rather than a static relation), and characterized as such by the 'through him' which stands between them and is bracketed by them.

Otherwise put: the ethics of the history of completed fellowship between God and humankind—the covenant history, the history of Jesus Christ—is 'the main statement', to which the ethics of creation is 'a prologue', and the ethics of redemption 'an epilogue'.[4] It would not be unreasonable, therefore, to decide to enter Barth's special ethics by way of its central dimension. This would have the advantage of emphasizing its material primacy, which has been somewhat obscured by the relative lateness of the publication of the 1959–60 lectures on the command of God the Reconciler.

---

[4] *CL* 9–11.

However, because the command of God the Reconciler pre-supposes the command of God the Creator, it will make for a less convoluted account at this stage if we follow the logical sequence.

II

In the context of the doctrine of creation, Barth defines the task of special ethics as that of showing the degree to which 'the one command of the one God who is gracious to man in Jesus Christ is also the command of his Creator and therefore already the sanctification of the creaturely action and abstention of man'.[5] This definition makes two points. The first is that the God who meets humankind as Creator in his command

is not... a new and strange God who could require from man as his Commander something new and strange and even perhaps in conflict with what is asked of him by the God who is gracious to him in Jesus Christ. Nor is he the one God who as Creator has first a different and strange manner and intention as compared with those which in a remarkable transformation suddenly become proper to Him as He is gracious to man in Jesus Christ.[6]

God is one and his grace is one. Therefore the command of God the Creator is also the command of God's grace in Christ (God the Reconciler) and aims at human sanctification. Indeed, it is itself sanctificatory. But because the command of this grace is also the command of the Creator, it is intended for and concerns 'the whole man, and therefore his creaturely existence too'.[7] It aims at, and effects, a sanctification that includes the liberation of man to be and to behave according to 'the structure of his creatureliness'.[8] This is the second point. So, in the light of the foregoing explication, we may restate the definition to the task of special ethics in the context of the doctrine of creation as follows: to describe right human action in terms of that conformity to the given structure of their creaturely being for which God's sanctifying command liberates humans. Accordingly, the treatise on the Command of God the Creator in the *Dogmatics* (iii/4) is mainly taken up with expounding the four kinds of freedom (freedom before God, free-

---

[5] *CD* iii/4: 3.   [6] Ibid. 35.   [7] Ibid. 41.   [8] Ibid. 44.

TABLE 1. *The command of God the Creator*

1928–9 Lectures The command of God the Creator:		
s. 7 is distinctively the command of life.	s. 8 appears in the form of calling (*Beruf*).	s. 9 demands order.	s. 10 is fulfilled in faith.
1. It meets us in the fact that we live. 2. The will to live is good in so far as it is the will to live in obedience to the Creator. 3. From the affirmation of my own life to respect for life in general (including discussion of the taking of life and competition).	1. It meets us in our own definite place. 2. The circles which define life: human subjectivity, sexuality, friendship, kinship and nationality, age, guidance and endowment, death.	1. The basic ordering of the creature to the Creator. 2. The orders of creation which comprise primal testimonies to the basic order: work, marriage, family, equality, and leadership.	1, 2. i.e. in letting myself be told by the Word and Spirit of God the Father that my conduct corresponds to his will as the Creator of life.

Church Dogmatics, iii/4 (1951)

Freedom:

s. 53 before God	s. 54 in Fellowship	s. 55 for Life	s. 56 in Limitation
1. The Holy Day	1. Man and Woman (including discussion of sexuality and marriage)	1. Respect for life	1. Unique Opportunity
2. Confession	2. Parents and Children (including discussion of the family)	2. Protection of life (including discussion of the taking of life)	2. Vocation (*Beruf*)
3. Prayer	3. Near and Distant Neighbours (including discussion of the status of the nation)	3. The active life (including discussion of work and economic competition)	3. Honour (bestowed on human beings by their being commanded to do something special)

dom in fellowship, freedom for life, and freedom in limitation)[9] that correspond to the four relations that constitute human being, and which were expounded in an earlier treatise (CD iii/2).[10]

This reference to the relational constitution of human being is significant. For it has been supposed that Barth utterly repudiated the concept of the order(s) of creation,[11] or at least that he abandoned it between his Münster lectures of 1928–9 and the completion of the ethical section of the doctrine of creation in the *Church Dogmatics* (iii/4) in 1951.[12] But here in that very section some such concept is clearly operative. Right human action is defined as that which accords with the fourfold relational structure of human being. It is grounded in the ordering of human being as creaturely. So the change that took place in Barth's thinking between 1928 and 1951 was not the jettisoning of the concept of created order as such. Rather, as we shall see, it was a change in the form of that concept, combined with the refusal to call it by its usual name.

In the 1928–9 lectures 'Order' is the title of the third of four sections that comprise the treatise on the command of God the Creator. The first section identifies this command as the command to live—to affirm life; to satisfy the needs for food, love, and sleep; to be healthy, happy, individual, and powerful; to respect creaturely life in general; to protect human life as a rule; and to respect the life of others as it stands (i.e. not to engage in 'competition').[13] Then, under the title of 'Calling', the second section describes some of the 'circles' within which life is lived and which therefore characterize it as definite—human subjectivity, sexuality, friendship, kinship, age, guidance and endowment, and death.[14] The role of the third section is to discuss the specific regulation

---

[9] *CD* iii/4, ss. 53–6.

[10] *CD* iii/2, s. 44, 'Man the Creature of God'; s. 45, 'Man in His Determination as the Covenant Partner of God'; s. 46, 'Man as Soul and Body'; s. 47, 'Man in His Time'.

[11] Reinhold Niebuhr, for example, wrote of 'Karl Barth's belief that the moral life of man would possess no valid principle of guidance, if the Ten Commandments had not introduced such principles by revelation' (*The Nature and Destiny of Man*, ii: *Human Destiny* (London: Nisbet, 1943), 263).

[12] This latter supposition is not without evidence; namely, Barth's own confession to Eduard Thurneysen that he had withheld the ethical lectures of 1928 from publication because of their advocacy of the doctrine of the orders of creation (*Ethics*, p. vii).

[13] Ibid. 117–73.   [14] Ibid. 173–208.

or discipline to which the command of the Creator subjects us, in order that we might affirm life in our callings; and it is here that Barth chooses to treat what has been traditionally known as the political or civil use of the law. So its title, 'Order', refers specifically to 'the external order of our life by which we are disciplined and human life is possible as life together'. Here the affirmation of *life* becomes affirmation of the *community* of life.[15] However, it should be noted that, in spite of its identification with the political use of the law, 'order' here does not refer to the coercive order of the State, but rather to the natural order or law by which life is properly communal.[16]

Barth's discussion of this 'order' proceeds in two stages. In the first, he makes a distinction between *the* Order, which is God himself, and the orders of creation. The point of this distinction is twofold. First, it seeks to establish that the basic ordering to which we are subject is that of the subordination of human creatures to their Creator, of the subjection of our will to his, and so of our acknowledgement of God's command as God's.[17] Second, it warns that, although there exist orders of creation which are 'direct testimonies to the Word . . . primal words . . . which always *are* representatives of . . . [God's] order', our grasp of them is only relatively sure: 'very *different* names might be given than those given by us, and a very *different* analysis might be given.'[18] Therefore, 'the one who binds me is God, no one and nothing else. . . . we can point with absolute stringency to no orders to which our acts are always good when bound and always bad when not bound.'[19] Then, on the basis of these qualifications Barth proceeds, in the second stage of his discussion, to hazard a description in some detail of four orders of creation: work, marriage, family, and 'the inseparable principles' of equality and leadership.[20]

By contrast, the *Church Dogmatics* does not expound the command of God the Creator explicitly in terms of a concept of orders of creation at any point. Concepts such as those espoused by Emil Brunner and Paul Althaus are discussed, but only to explain

[15] Ibid. 58.

[16] Barth is happy here to speak of the created orders in terms of '*lex naturae*' (*Ethik*, i (Zurich: Theologischer Verlag, 1973), 366). He treats the State under the command of God the Reconciler (*Ethics*, 445–9).

[17] Barth, *Ethics*, 213 (*Ethik*, i: 362).

[18] Ibid. 215.   [19] Ibid. 214.   [20] Ibid. 216–46.

why they are unacceptable.[21] One (typically Protestant) reason that
Barth gives for this is epistemological. The concepts to which he
refers are, he believes, tied to a high estimation of the power of
human reason to apprehend the command of God the Creator
directly in 'reality'. But the fact that this reality has been created
by God does not mean that we are naturally in a position to obtain
a reliable reading of it: 'How can we know to what extent we really
have to do with God's creation, and therefore with a valid standard
for understanding the ethical event, in what we claim to recognise
here as reality?'[22] Natural reason cannot perceive 'with increasing
certainty and clarity' the order or many orders of creation, both
because 'reality' is too obscure and because natural reason is too
feeble. Besides, given that God the Creator and the God who is
gracious to humankind in Jesus Christ are one and the same, and
share one and the same intention, it follows that only when we
know about the grace of God in Jesus Christ do we know for
certain what creation is, who the Creator is, and what it means to
be the creature of this Creator. That is to say, Jesus Christ is the
noetic basis of creation. But he is also the ontic basis of our knowledge of creation in that, since creation's *raison d'être* is to act as
the external basis of God's covenant of grace with humankind in
him, he is its meaning and purpose.[23] But Barth's main objections
are not epistemological. They concern the doctrine of God, the
doctrine of redemption, and ethics. As he sees it, one problem with
available concepts of the orders of creation is that they entirely
neglect the vertical dimension for the horizontal one. In their
haste to establish 'the general truth . . . of certain laws of life and
existence', they pass right by the fundamental matter of *the* order
that obtains in the relationship between God the Creator and his
human creatures.[24] Moreover, these orders of creation are asserted
as separate from the command of the God who is gracious to
humankind in Jesus Christ. Such separation, Barth believes, must
be avoided at all costs, because it splits the unity of God and the
unity of his command, dividing the order of creation from the
orders of reconciliation and redemption, and so making it impos-
ible to maintain 'the sanctification of the whole man'.[25] Barth is
adamant that the object of redemption should be identified, not

---

[21] *CD* iii/4: 19–21.   [22] Ibid. 28.   [23] Ibid. 39, 41.   [24] Ibid. 36–8.
[25] Ibid. 37.

merely with the spiritual 'part' of human being (the soul), but with human being as 'embodied soul and besouled body'; and he asserts the ethical correlate of this, that the Christian should take the bodily dimension of human life seriously.[26]

Barth's refusal to let pass any concept of the orders of creation constructed on the basis of a supposedly direct or natural reading of reality was made on theological grounds. Nevertheless, it had a particular empirical impetus. This was acquired through Barth's experience of politics in the 1920s, when a certain concept of the orders of creation was used by the 'German Christians' to support the ideology of National Socialism. Barth alludes to this in *Church Dogmatics*, iii/4, when he accounts for N. H. Søe's repudiation of the idea of created orders in terms of his fear of 'any traces of the German theology of orders current in the twenties', and comments that this fear was 'not without good cause'.[27] Ten years earlier, he had expressed the same apprehension himself when he wrote in his *Letter to Great Britain from Switzerland* (1941) of the inadequacy of Natural Law as the basis of opposition to Nazism, because of its susceptibility to Hitlerian interpretation. 'All arguments based on Natural Law are Janus-headed,' he asserted. 'They lead to—Munich.'[28] Again, a few years later, in 1946, he wrote in *The Christian Community and the Civil Community* that Natural Law

---

[26] *CD* iii/2: 327–9. In asserting that human being comprises an integrity of both soul and body, Barth self-consciously seeks to correct what he perceives as the anti-corporeal bias of traditional theological anthropology. This he does supposedly by reference to the constitution of the humanity of Jesus. In the course of elaborating on the theme of Jesus as 'the whole man', Barth moves from describing Jesus' being to describing his behaviour in relation to others. Thus he gives us some idea of what he believed to be the ethical significance of maintaining the unity of the command of God the Creator and the command of God the Reconciler: 'And He is the one whole man in His relation to others, in what he does for them, what He gives them, what He asks of them, what He is for them and for the whole cosmos ... There is no logic here which is not as such physics, no cure of souls which is not as such bound up with cure of bodies. The man who is called by Him and who takes part in His way and work as a recipient and fellow-worker does not only receive something to consider and to will and to feel; he enters into bodily contact and fellowship. The man who comes to hear of the kingdom of God comes also to taste it. He comes to eat and to drink bodily, so that it again becomes apparent that in this bodily eating and drinking he has to do with nothing less than the hidden—in our terminology, 'inner' or 'spiritual'—savouring and tasting of the heavenly bread and power to come ... To serve Him is not only to speak to others, but also to give these others to eat and to drink' (ibid.).   [27] Ibid. 22.

[28] Karl Barth, *A Letter to Great Britain from Switzerland* (London: Sheldon Press, 1941), 17.

cannot provide 'any certain knowledge of the trustworthy standards of political decisions', or any firm and clear grounds for them.
It is, he reckoned, an arbitrary construct.[29]

There is no doubt that, between 1928 and 1951, Barth distanced
himself thoroughly from certain concepts of created orders; but
equally there is firm evidence that during the same period he
developed an alternative concept that incorporates much of what
he had said in his Münster lectures. In immediate support of
this claim, we note that in his critical discussion of Brunner
Barth strongly endorses the latter's affirmation that 'the Divine
Command is not a law which hovers above our actual existence
without any connexion with it; it is the command of the God who
has created our actual existence'.[30] We also note that, although
he sympathizes with Søe's reservations about the concept of the
orders of creation, the tone of Barth's remarks imply that he
thought that Søe had over-reacted: 'he is so afraid . . . that he . . .
will not take the slightest step.'[31] It is true that, just before these
comments on Brunner and Søe, Barth had given general approval
('It is along these lines that we certainly have to think') to
Bonhoeffer's concept of the constancy of God's commanding in
terms of divine 'mandates' that are learned from the Word of God
and are 'not laws somehow immanent in created reality and to be
established at random by the moralist'.[32] But if, by his failure to
register any reservations over the fact that Bonhoeffer's mandates
'do not emerge from reality . . . [but] descend into it',[33] Barth gives
us cause to doubt his affirmation of a concept of orders of creation,
his exposition of special ethics under the doctrine of creation
removes it. For there, although we do not find anything that
answers to the name of 'order of creation', we do find much that
corresponds to its substance. First, we meet the admission that all
three of the definite 'spheres' or relationships in which God
encounters man—Creator–creature, Reconciler–pardoned sinner,
Redeemer–child of the Father—'might very well be called orders
[*Ordnungen*]', were it not for the risk of having them misunder-

[29] Karl Barth, 'The Christian Community and the Civil Community', in
Community, State and Church, ed. and introd. Will Herberg (Gloucester, Mass.: Peter
Smith, 1968), 163–4.
[30] Emil Brunner, *The Divine Imperative*, trans. Olive Wyon (Philadelphia:
Westminster Press, 1937), 208–9. Quoted by Barth in *CD* iii/4: 20.
[31] *CD* iii/4: 22.   [32] Ibid.   [33] Ibid.

stood 'as laws, prescriptions and imperatives'.[34] This shows that, had it not been for a certain bias in the hearing of his audience, Barth would have considered it appropriate to designate the relationship between Creator and creature as an 'order of creation'. It also provides tacit confirmation of what he said in his Münster lectures, where he used *'the* order' to refer to God himself and to imply that the basic ordering of human being and action consists in the subordination (*Unterordnung*) of creatures to their Creator. More explicit confirmation appears later in the *Dogmatics*, where he argues that, if the concept of an order of creation is to have 'serious theological content', it must denote the proper relationship between Creator and human creature;[35] and where it is precisely this relationship that takes pride of place in the exposition of the command of God the Creator under the heading of 'Freedom before God'.[36]

In both the Münster lectures and the *Dogmatics*, then, there is in the context of the doctrine of creation a concept of order that refers primarily to the structured relationship between God the Creator and his human creature. But this is not the only concept of order that they share. In the Münster lectures *the* (vertical) order is represented by four orders in different kinds of (horizontal) relationship between human beings: work, marriage, family, and the inseparable principles of equality and leadership in the civil community. These secondary, horizontal orders have their equivalent in the *Dogmatics*, although conceived in much less definite terms. Whereas the first kind of freedom which the command of God the Creator effects—freedom before God—concerns human existence 'in the vertical dimension towards God',[37] the other three are about the 'horizontal' relations of human beings to their fellows, to life, and to historical finitude.

The most significant development in the way that the concept of orders of creation is used in the *Dogmatics*, as compared with the Münster lectures, is that it has become basic to the treatise of the command of God the Creator as a whole. In the lectures it provides the governing concept for only one of four sections; whereas in the

[34] Ibid. 29. In translating 'Ordnungen' (*KD* iii/4: 31) as 'orders or ordinances' A. T. Mackay obscures an important distinction that Barth later makes between 'permanent orders of creation' (*Ordnungen* or *ordines*) and 'providential ordinances' (*Anordnungen* or *ordinationes*) (*CD* iii/4: 301 (*KD* iii/4: 341)).

[35] *CD* iii/4: 38.   [36] Ibid. s. 53.   [37] Ibid. 324.

Dogmatics, whose exposition of the command of God the Creator is based upon the created relational structure of the human creature, the concept of orders of creation is predominant throughout, albeit incognito. This means that all topics are treated as specifications of the four relational structures of the human creature. So what appeared in the Münster lectures simply as 'The Command of Life' now reappears as the third species of creaturely freedom, the freedom to be and to behave according to man's constitution as soul and body; and what appeared in 1928 as the title of a major division, 'Calling' (*Der Beruf*), now gives its name to a sub-species of the freedom to live within the historical limitations of human existence (s. 56. 2, 'Vocation' (= *Der Beruf*)). Another important concomitant of the tacit predominance of a concept of the orders of creation in the *Dogmatics*' version of the first part of special ethics is that consideration of the primary order—of the creature to the Creator—moves from third place to the very front. There it undergoes considerable moral elaboration in terms of the Lord's Day, confession as the bearing of witness to the Word of God, and prayer. Since these specifically religious practices receive nothing like such special attention in the Münster lectures on the command of God the Creator, it seems that it took the years between 1928 and 1951 for Barth's conviction about the primacy of *the* ordering of the creature to the Creator to develop into a conviction (*pace* Albrecht Ritschl and Brunner) about the need for special consideration to be given in theological ethics to the specific acts whereby human creatures are responsible before God.[38]

The 1951 treatise not only differentiates itself from the Münster lectures by assigning the concept of created orders a more fundamental role. It also specifies it in different ways. In 1928 Barth had endorsed a long Christian tradition by identifying marriage and the family as created orders. But by 1951 he had become a dissenter. The drift of his dissent is indicated in his reservations about Bonhoeffer's list of the divine mandates, which includes marriage and the family.[39] These Barth describes as conceived, perhaps under the influence of 'North German patriarchalism', through 'the rigid assertion of human relationships arranged in a definite order, and the hasty assertion of their imperative character'; and he suggests that the Word of God tells us merely of

---

[38] Ibid. 48–9.   [39] Ibid. 22.

'certain constant relationships as such'.[40] It is not immediately clear from this passage exactly what Barth means by these 'constant relationships as such', although it is clear enough that he means something less definite than Bonhoeffer's mandates. What he has in mind comes to light, however, in the course of his exposition of creaturely freedom, when he furnishes us with several examples of 'constant relationships'. The most general, of course, are the four relationships that are constitutive of the being of the human creature. But the explication of the second of these relationships—between human beings and their fellows—offers more specific examples. There is the relationship between male and female. This, Barth tells us, alone rests on 'a structural and functional distinction', which is more than merely a variation on the common theme of a neutral and abstract humanity.[41] Then there is the relationship between children and parents which, although it does not rest on a structural and functional distinction, is nevertheless given and permanent: 'A man is as necessarily the child of a man and woman as he is necessarily himself a man or woman.'[42] The significance of these two examples for our discussion of Barth's reconception of the created orders is that here in 1951 (and in contrast to 1928) he prefers to speak of the constant relationship between male and female, and between children and parents, rather than of the created orders of marriage and family. In the case of marriage this is because (*pace* the Lutheran tradition) he denies it to be a universal obligation.[43] Although it is the *telos* or 'focal point' of the male–female relationship, it is nevertheless not an order of creation but a vocation.[44] The basic ground for this stance is, Barth claims, what the written Word of God has to say; for to assert the thesis that marriage is an order of creation means that 'a human tradition—later grounded in natural law—is set above Holy Scripture'.[45] It is primarily on this same ground that Barth deliberately avoids giving any role at all to the modern concept of the family as a clan. For, in spite of its having become fundamental to Christian ethics, neither the Old Testament nor the New Testament shows any interest in it.[46] But from this basic ground emerges another reason for Barth's dissent; namely, that both celibacy and a certain kind of leaving one's family are states

---

[40] Ibid.   [41] Ibid. 117.   [42] Ibid. 240.   [43] Ibid. 141, 148.
[44] Ibid. 148.   [45] Ibid. 141.   [46] Ibid. 241–2.

to which one may be called in order to bear witness to the coming kingdom.[47]

In the *Dogmatics* the first two 'horizontal' orders of creation, as designated by the Münster lectures, are made less specific. The third, 'work', receives major qualification. As in the Münster lectures, it is concerned to promote the necessary conditions of human existence. But now it is classified as but one form of the active life for which the command of God the Creator liberates humankind. It is understood to be only one of the tasks which God has imposed on his human creatures, and a subordinate one at that. For it is now conceived as 'the indispensable presupposition' of the real work of bearing witness to the coming of God's kingdom, which is the task of the Christian community.[48]

The fourth 'horizontal' order of creation, according to the 1928 lectures, is the ordering of human society in general in terms of the 'inseparable principles' of equality and leadership.[49] This entirely lacks an equivalent in the *Dogmatics*, iii/4. The natural location for such a topic would have been in the third section of 'Freedom for Fellowship' (s. 54. 3), which considers relationships with 'near and distant neighbours'. However, although the previous two sections on 'Man and Woman' (s. 55. 1) and 'Parents and Children' (s. 55. 2) both find room for a concept of the ordering of relationships in terms of superordination and subordination, this section does not. Instead, it is entirely devoted to arguing (in line with the Münster lectures) that the people or nation should not be accorded the status of a created order.[50] This absence of any discussion of the nature of political authority in the context of the doctrine of creation suggests that Barth had changed his mind since 1928. Then he had argued that the political equality of human beings and the political leadership of individuals, indicating as they do 'a severe disturbance that has already affected the relation of man to God and his neighbour', directly constitute an 'order of defense and help' and not an order of creation; but that, if they constitute an 'order of God' at all (and Barth implies that they do), then they cannot contradict the order of creation and so must have their roots in an 'order of life'.[51] But by 1951, it seems, Barth had simply come to the conclusion that

---

[47] Ibid. 147, 261.   [48] Ibid. 522–3, 515–16.   [49] Barth, *Ethics*, 243–6.
[50] In the 1928 lectures the concept of nation or people receives attention as a form of calling, not as an order of creation (ibid. 192–6).   [51] Ibid. 244.

they have no such roots. This is confirmed by his announcement, in the course of his discussion of 'near and distant neighbours', that he will consider the political form of God's command in the context of the doctrine of reconciliation.[52] He fulfilled this pledge in the final extant section of his 1959–60 lectures on 'The Command of God the Reconciler' (s. 78), to which he gave the title 'The Struggle for Human Righteousness'. In subsection 78. 2 he discusses the 'lordless powers' against which the Christian is called to revolt, and which include political absolutism. This he distinguishes from 'the problem of the government of human existence as such ... [which] the New Testament regards ... as a salutary divine ... [ordinance] which Christians should neither evade nor oppose but to which they should adjust themselves as subjects, not under compulsion, but consciously and conscientiously'.[53] He promises to consider government as such in the last subsection.[54] However, as it happens, the last subsection of s. 78 left to us ('*Fiat iustitia!*' s. 78. 4) is preoccupied with describing the style of Christian politics, and nowhere resumes discussion of political authority as such. This omission is best explained, we believe, by the incomplete state in which Barth bequeathed us the second part of his special ethics.

We have noted and described the differences between the *Dogmatics* and the Münster lectures with regard to the role of the basic order of creation and the specification of the secondary orders. It remains for us to indicate briefly one further point of divergence: namely, that in the *Dogmatics* the command of the Creator is no longer identified with the command of 'life'. Whereas in 1928 'life' was proposed as the material content or meaning of the command of the Creator[55] and therefore stood first in the order of treatment, in 1951 'life' is but one of four objects of the creaturely freedom that now comprises the content of the Creator's command. Indeed, 'life' is quite deliberately alloted third place:

Though it might have seemed logical, we have taken good care not to speak first of this simple and obvious fact [that obedience to the command of God the Creator is man's freedom to exist as a living being]. That which constitutes man as man is, of course, his existence in the vertical dimen-

---

[52] *CD* iii/4: 303.
[53] *CL* 219 (*Chr.L.* 374). Geoffrey Bromiley has misleadingly translated *Anordnung* as 'order'.
[54] ibid. [55] Barth, *Ethics*, 61, 208.

sion towards God and in the horizontal towards his fellow-men. Hence he is not first this creature or present as such. He is first for God and his fellowman, and then and for this reason he exists as this being in accordance with his determination. And his obedience to the command of God must first and supremely be understood as his right action and conduct in relation to God and his fellow-men, and only then and on this basis as his true existence in human life rightly lived as such.[56]

The upshot of this demotion is that the relativization of the value of life, already under way in 1928,[57] is heavily underscored in 1951.

III

We turn now to Barth's exposition of the command of God the Reconciler. As we have already mentioned, this forms the material heart of special ethics in the *Church Dogmatics*, with the treatises on the commands of God the Creator and God the Redeemer playing, respectively, prologue and epilogue. Although the Münster lectures share the same trinitarian structure, they do not accord material primacy to the command of the Reconciler and they present the three aspects of special ethics in a less co-inherent fashion. This is to be expected, since they were composed before Barth's study of Anselm had consolidated his Christocentric tendency.[58] But the importance of the role played in the system as a whole by the second part is only one of several points upon which the treatises of 1928–9 and 1959–60 diverge. And it is with a view to putting ourselves in the position of being able to identify these other differences that we now undertake to present a summary of the content of each treatise.

We begin, naturally, with the earlier one. This is governed by the concept of law, which indicates that the command of God is not just given to us with creaturely life itself, requiring us to affirm ourselves; it is not only the command of the Creator. As the command of the Reconciler, it comes to us as sinners. Therefore,

---

[56] *CD* iii/4: 324–5.
[57] In the Münster lectures, Barth stipulates that the will to live is good only if it is the will to live in obedience to God the Creator (*Ethics*, 124); and he asserts the possibility of the commanded taking of life in the borderline case (ibid. 145).
[58] *Anselm: Fides quaerens intellectum* was first published in 1931.

it must take the form of law, of an alien claim, of the right of a definite other. The command of God the Reconciler, then, is the law of the human being Jesus Christ; and the concrete meaning of this law is that I should be bound to my neighbour as to one whom I regard—perhaps contrary to all appearances—as the bearer of God's goodness to me, as a possible or hidden Christ. In this way I no longer live by what I am in myself but by what I am in relation to Jesus Christ, which becomes concrete in my relationship to my neighbour.[59]

Formally, the command of God the Reconciler is the command that I subject myself to 'superior direction by a specific fellowman commissioned by ... [God]'.[60] It is the command that I let my neighbour encounter me as an authority, that I let her counsel and correct me.[61] This she may do in three ways: through education, through right, and through custom. By 'education' Barth means both instruction and the formation of 'the will and character and heart as well as the understanding'.[62] By 'right' he means 'the order of human life in society that is publicly known and re-cognized and protected by public force'.[63] 'Custom' also denotes 'the order of human life in concert', though it is based, not on public acknowledgement and power, but only on 'the free consent and practice of a majority of people at a given time and place'.[64] All three belong to the order of reconciliation, which is the law of Christ among sinners, because they all have a coercive or correc-tive quality and so require a measure of self-scepticism and self-renunciation.[65]

The command of God the Reconciler is the command of law that meets me when I encounter my neighbour as the bearer of authority. To recognize my neighbour as such is to be subject to the will of God. This subjection is more than subjection to the order of creation for it means 'the conformity of the sinful and lost with him who will not let us be lost as such but who, in spite of all expectation and in defiance of all logic, loves us as such and keeps us in fellowship with himself'. Where the order of creation demands respect, the order of reconciliation demands humility. 'Humility' Barth defines as 'taking heed that we do not aspire to a purity in which we will no longer see ourselves as sinners'; and it

[59] Barth, *Ethics*, 321, 323, 329–37.   [60] Ibid. 349.   [61] Ibid. 356, 360.
[62] Ibid. 363.   [63] Ibid. 376.   [64] Ibid. 390.
[65] Ibid. 363–4, 376–8, 390, 393.

TABLE 2. *The command of God the Reconciler*

1928–9 Lectures
The command of God the Reconciler:

s. 11 is distinctively the command of law.	s. 12 appears in the form of authority.	s. 13 demands humility.	s. 14 is fulfilled in love.
1, 2. God's command is not simply given us with life itself, but also in the law or alien claim of Jesus Christ. This is the law of the concrete claim by which we are bound to our neighbour.	This authority is represented by the neighbour in the forms of: 1. Education; 2. Civil law; 3. Social custom.	1. In relation to God, this takes the form of sacrifice and conformity to the concrete and visible order of the Church. 2. In relation to human fellows, this takes the form of service and conformity to the concrete and visible order of the State.	1, 2. i.e. in letting myself be told by God's Word in Jesus Christ that I am bound to the gracious God, and through him to my neighbour.

1959–60 Lectures
Invocation: the Lord's Prayer

s. 75 Baptism (the Foundation of the Christian Life)

1. Baptism in the Holy Spirit
2. Baptism in water

s. 76 The Children and their Father

1. The Father
2. The Children
3. Invocation

s. 77 Zeal for the Honour of God

1. The Great Passion
2. The Known and Unknown God
3. Hallowed be Thy Name
4. The Precedence of the Word of God

s. 78 The Struggle for Human Righteousness

1. Revolt against Disorder
2. The Lordless Powers
3. Thy Kingdom Come
4. *Fiat Iustitia* . . .

s. ? The Lord's Supper (The Renewal of the Christian Life)

expresses itself in two kinds of self-sacrifice.[66] First, in relation to God, humble action always has the character of self-denial—the sacrificial dedication of part of one's life as a token. This order of self-denial is not, of course, the original order; but it is the kind of obedience that is 'proper to sinners who cannot be obedient in the exercise of their right to life but only in a demonstrative reduction of it'.[67] According to this order, good acts have the character of repentance. Therefore they are not proper achievements but substitute ones—improper makings-good of our infinite fault before God that we ourselves cannot make good, which are possible only on the basis of God's reconciliation of us to himself.[68] The penitent life of the reconciled sinner will be distinctive, according to Barth, in three respects: its thinking takes as its theme the miracle of God's Word of forgiveness; and its will, confessing the justice of God's judgement against it, is both broken and therefore open.[69]

The second kind of self-sacrifice through which the humility of reconciled sinners expresses itself is service to our fellows. It is necessary that this is preceded by repentance, because we cannot serve our neighbours so long as we stand in judgement over their sinfulness. Repentance is the *sine qua non* of our solidarity with others as fellow sinners.[70] Equally, it is necessary that repentance be followed by service for it to become concrete and serious.[71] The particular kind of service intended here is that of being a Christ to others, declaring to them that they are children of God in spite of everything.[72] At this point in his lectures Barth saw fit to discuss the roles of the Church and the State and the relationship between them. The Church he describes as the concrete and visible order of life by and in which people are summoned to repentance before God on the basis of accomplished reconciliation. Likewise, the State is understood as a sign of the concrete and visible order of life by which and in which we are summoned to serve the neighbour on the same basis. As service presupposes repentance, so the State presupposes the Church and shares its ultimate aim.[73]

[66] Ibid. 401–3.   [67] Ibid. 405–6.   [68] Ibid. 410–12.
[69] Ibid. 415–19.   [70] Ibid. 421–6.   [71] Ibid. 419.   [72] Ibid. 430–6.
[73] Ibid. 440–1. Our account here refers to the revised form of the 1928–9 lectures, which Barth prepared for their re-presentation at the University of Bonn in 1930–1. The original version appears in an appendix to the published lectures (*Ethics*, 517–21).

In the final subsection of the 1928–9 lectures Barth describes what he understands to be the fulfilment of the command of God the Reconciler. In this perspective, our acts are good, are obedient to the law of Christ, and occur in the acknowledgement of authority and as the work of humility, to the extent that we let ourselves be told that we are bound to God and through him to our neighbours. That we are told this and that we let ourselves be told this is the work of God and is manifest as the reality of love.[74]

In his 1959–60 lectures Barth expounds the command of God the Reconciler along very different lines. He considers several candidates for the role of governing concept here, but 'law' is not among them. Its absence bears witness to that priority of Gospel over Law that had characterized Barth's thinking ever since his work on Anselm, and which leads him now to describe the command of God emphatically as the command of grace, the law of the Gospel.[75] There is one concept prominent in the 1928–9 lectures that does receive consideration; namely, 'repentance' or 'conversion from an old manner and orientation of life, which has been overtaken and outdated in this situation, to a new one which corresponds to it better'. For a brief moment Barth muses that '[this] might undoubtedly be the concept that we need', but he quickly passes it by because, although formally clear, it is materially indefinite and does not actually tell us what conversion is.[76] According to the first version of the introductory section (s. 74), Barth originally decided to bring the ethics of reconciliation in the *Dogmatics* under the rubric of 'faithfulness'. However, by the autumn of 1960 he had changed his mind, convinced that he needed a word which better expresses the fact that God requires of human beings, not just 'a certain form of human life (which might well be construed passively) and the disposition or attitude corresponding to it', but action.[77] In the end, Barth decided upon 'invocation' or, more specifically, 'the humble and resolute, the frightened and joyful invocation of the gracious God in gratitude, praise and above all petition'. This he considered peculiarly suitable because it denotes not only an action, but one which is distinctive to humankind as the partner of God in the covenant of

---

[74] Ibid. 451.
[75] Karl Barth, *How I Changed My Mind*, ed. John Godsey (Edinburgh: St Andrew Press, 1969), 43.
[76] CL 37–8.   [77] Ibid. pp. x–xi, 42.

grace established by him, which proceeds from the fulfilment of that covenant in Jesus Christ, and which characterizes the whole of Christian life.[78]

The structure of Barth's exposition of the command of God the Reconciler, as he envisaged it under the rubric of its governing concept, is tripartite. At its centre stands a study of special themes suggested by the Lord's Prayer. Before it comes a section on baptism entitled 'The Foundation of the Christian Life'; and after it follows one on the Lord's Supper with the title of 'The Renewal of Christian Life'.

The first part (s. 75) opens with a discussion of baptism in the Holy Spirit; for this is the gracious act of God by which his work in Jesus Christ becomes a new beginning for us, turning us to faithfulness toward God and so to calling upon him. The first step in this life of faithfulness, one in which we respond freely to what God has already done in his Word, is that of asking the Christian community to administer baptism in water 'as the binding confession of . . . obedience, conversion, and hope, made in prayer for God's grace'. As prayerful petition ventured obediently in hope in Jesus Christ, this act of initiation is 'a model for all that follows'.[79]

Of the centrepiece of the ethics of reconciliation all that we have is a torso. Before he died, Barth had completed three sections (ss. 76–8), which cover only the first two petitions of the Lord's Prayer. The first, entitled 'The Children and their Father', expounds the basic meaning of invocation in terms of the relationship between human beings and God. Invocation is not just the prayer with which the creature should address his Creator. It is, more specifically, the prayer of those creatures whose gracious Creator actually permits, commands, and enables them to address him as Father and not merely as Lord. It is the prayer of God's children.[80] Invocation, then, is addressed to a God who is more than an idea or epitome of fatherhood. It is addressed to one who is 'really Father'. This, according to Barth, means several things. It means that God is 'a speaking and hearing subject, a subject that acts personally'. It means that he is the 'absolutely superior origin' of all reality distinct from himself, while being absolutely present to it. That is, he is Creator rather than mere genitor. Finally, it

---

[78] Ibid. 43.   [79] CD iv/4: 2, 213.   [80] CL 15, 19–20.

THE TRINITARIAN DIMENSIONS OF ETHICS 69

means that he is not merely sovereign, but sovereign in his love; that he acts (pre-eminently in Jesus Christ) towards his creatures in 'a free fatherly goodness'; and that therefore he should elicit not only their feeling of absolute dependence, but also their absolute respect and trust.[81]

As the divine Father is the object of invocation, so his children are its subjects. Indeed, the freedom to invoke God as Father is constitutive of being his children. This status, unlike that of creaturehood, is not something possessed by nature. It is purely the gift of the grace that addresses God's creatures in Christ and is recognized by them; and it consists in clinging to Christ, 'to what he is for them, to what they already are in him, to what they may continually become from him and through him and to him'.[82] The existence of God's children, of those who invoke the divine Father, is Christian existence. One of its characteristics is constant gratitude for 'the mystery and miracle of the free kindness of God' in addressing them as children and so in granting them the freedom to call upon him as Father, and by their constant desire to receive this grace afresh. Another is the readiness to begin again from scratch. Those who live by the grace of God are children, not masters or virtuosi. In the invocation of God everything depends on whether or not it is done 'in sheer need . . . in sheer readiness to learn . . . and in sheer helplessness'. It can be the work 'only of very weak and very little and very poor children, of those who in their littleness, weakness, and poverty can only get up and run with empty hands to their Father, appealing to him'.[83] A third characteristic of Christian existence is that it is existence in community; for the Christian calls upon 'Our Father'. Moreover, existence in the community of those who have the freedom to call upon their common Father is one that cuts across and stands out against 'all the other relations and unions that have arisen and persist both naturally and historically'.[84]

Invocation, then, is the movement in which creaturely children bring themselves to the attention of their divine Father, reminding themselves that he is their Father and they his children. It becomes an event in the lives of Christians as thanksgiving and praise and, decisively, as petition. We give thanks to God for

---

[81] Ibid. 52, 56–9. [82] Ibid. 71, 76. [83] Ibid. 77–80. [84] Ibid. 82–5.

the free gifts already given to us. We praise him as the Giver of such gifts. But we can do these things only as those who have a total need of God's giving more of them. Therefore, thanksgiving and praise can be genuine 'only in unreserved acceptance of this neediness . . . only as crying to God for His further free gifts, only as petition'. Conceived in these terms, the invocation of God is 'the primal and basic form of the whole Christian ethos'.[85]

Barth concludes his discussion of invocation by making three points. The first explicates a major implication of his choice of governing concept for expounding the command of God the Reconciler; namely, that the Christian life is a spiritual one, one 'which in its distinctiveness is from first to last conditioned and determined by that special movement and act of God in the work of the Holy Spirit'. In brief, the Christian life is 'life in awareness of the immediate presence of God'.[86] The second point is a qualification. The Christian life, life in the freedom to call upon God as Father, is certainly a very personal matter; but it is not a private one. This has already been intimated in the specification of invocation as communal, as a calling upon a common Father. Here the intimation is strengthened and extended; for the invocation of God by the Christian community is 'as such a supremely social matter, publicly social, not to say political and even cosmic'. It does not occur on an 'island of the blessed' and simply for the sake of the spiritual life of Christians. For the Christian community has been elected and separated and it lives its own strange, special existence precisely in order to carry out its mission to bear witness to the reconciliation that God has established between himself and the world in Jesus Christ.[87] Therefore, Christians

cannot cry 'Our Father' without including those with whom they do not live as yet in this union of knowledge and confession because Jesus Christ is still a stranger to them. They cannot cry it in separation from the overwhelming host of half-believers, heretics, the superstitious, and unbelievers all around them . . . In their name, then, and not just in their own, they will cry 'Our Father', as the provisional representatives and vicars of the rest; as those who now do for them what they themselves may and should do but do not yet do because they are not yet liberated and empowered and willing to do it, although they will not finally fail

[85] Ibid. 85–9.   [86] Ibid. 92.   [87] Ibid. 95, 97.

to do it when the lordship of Jesus Christ over all creation is manifested, and with it the reconciliation of the world to God that has taken place in him.[88]

Barth's final point about invocation is that, *pace* Schleiermacher, it is much more than an exercise in self-uplift. When we call upon God as Father, he hears and answers us. This means two things. First, that he lets his own work correspond to our invocation. He is not the prisoner of his own majesty in lofty isolation, but in overflowing grace freely chooses to be in genuine partnership with his children, working only in connection with their work. So, in liberating human creatures to call upon him as Father he liberates them for responsible co-operation with himself. The second significance of the fact that God actually hears and answers our prayers is that we may and must invoke him in the unconditional expectation of his corresponding action.[89]

The next section in which Barth expounds the command of God the Reconciler in terms of the Lord's Prayer (s. 77) has the title of 'Zeal for the Honour of God'. Here, under the direction of the second petition, he leads us further into what calling upon God as Father means. When Christians pray 'Hallowed be thy name', they pray that God will bring his self-declaration to its goal with the manifestation of that light which destroys all darkness; and, in so far as their prayer is genuine, it expresses their zeal for the primacy of the validity of his Word in the world, in the Church, and above all in their own hearts and lives. Christians, in other words, are marked by a definite passion, an unfulfilled desire that seeks fulfilment. This Christian passion does not displace other creaturely passions—'the . . . yearning for life, the craving for food and drink and sleep, the desire for love and hate and hate-love, the urge to have dealings with interesting and eminent people, the hankering for pleasure, power, possession, and position'—nor is it better than them. But it is distinctive.[90]

The situation in which Christians pray and are zealous for God's honour is one that is characterized by a certain ambivalence; for in it God is both known and unknown. In the world he 'may be sensed and conjectured if not recognised and known',[91] especially on the ground of the inalienable determination for himself and

---

[88] Ibid. 100–1.   [89] Ibid. 102–8.   [90] Ibid. 111–13.   [91] Ibid. 123.

orientation to himself of 'the nature of man, his human essence, in its irreversibly good creation'.[92] Nevertheless, man's ignorance of God is still very much in evidence, whether in the form of theoretical atheism, religion, or 'nostrification' (the use of God's name to serve a worldly cause), and it reaches its culmination in his ignorance of his fellow man:

He regards him as an object to whom he as subject may or may not be in relation according to his own free choice and disposal, whom he may pass by as he does so many other objects, or with whom, if this is out of the question, he may have dealings as it suits himself within the limits of what is possible for him. He does not know him as a fellow subject whom God has set unavoidably beside him, to whom he is unavoidably linked in his relation to God, so that apart from him he cannot himself be a subject, a person. He is not for him an indispensable, but in certain cases a dispensable, companion, associate, and fellow—not to mention brother. He can get along just as well without him as with him. By chance or caprice or free judgement he can just as well be to him a tyrant or slave as a free supporter, just as well a hater as an admirer, a foe as a friend, a corrupter as a helper. He can be one thing to one person and another to another, or now one thing, now another, to the same person. In relationship to his fellow man, also, he exists in total ambivalence.[93]

Ignorance of the true and living God who in divine faithfulness became human in Jesus Christ, giving himself to all others and uniting himself with them, makes it possible for people to entertain the notion that something less than faithfulness toward their fellows is an option for them.[94] But ignorance of God is by no means limited to the world. The Church, too, can display it by dealing with its living Lord as if he were neither Lord nor living. It denies his lordship when it behaves as 'the church in excess', pursuing its own glory; and when it behaves timidly as 'the church in defect' it denies that he is the *living* Lord, who by his resurrection from the dead has overcome the world that is marked and ruled by death.[95] Finally, God is both known and unknown in the life of the individual Christian, who is simultaneously righteous and sinner and in whom light and darkness are at war.[96]

It is out of this situation of ambivalence in the world, the Church, and the lives of individual Christians that the petition

---

[92] Ibid. 120.   [93] Ibid. 131.   [94] Ibid. 132.   [95] Ibid. 126, 136–7.
[96] Ibid. 142, 146–51.

'Hallowed be thy name' arises; for in it God is asked 'to make an end, a total and definitive end, of the twilight . . . to cause the sun to rise, the night to pass away completely, and the day to dawn'.[97] As such it looks 'beyond all present and future human zeal, volition, ability, and achievement to a work whose subject God alone can be and which will be that of his own volition, ability, and achievement'. Certainly, this prayer entails corresponding action on man's part; but, *pace* Luther, it deserves consideration in its own right apart from and before consideration of its ethical implications.[98] The main one of these implications is that Christians must not construe the twilight between light and darkness synthetically 'as a dialectical determination which unavoidably characterizes the meaning and course of all things, the two-sidedness, vacillation, and swing of the pendulum of all events in the world, the church, and ourselves as the natural play of thesis and antithesis . . . which like everything else may be painful in part but must be finally accepted with humour'.[99] For when we pray 'for the completed victory of light over darkness', we ask for the taking place of the unique and definitive act which we know has already taken place in Jesus Christ. So in the light of this knowledge the Christian community cannot escape 'a final profound disquiet' in face of the juxtaposition of light and darkness which dominates our present, and it can suffer it only as a disorder that is without excuse.[100]

However, if our prayer is genuine it will entail more than merely an uneasy attitude toward the persistent ambivalence of things and a yearning for its abolition. It will call forth analogous 'thoughts and words and works' of resistance. This correspondent action can only be done within the limits of human capabilities and possibilities, which prevent human agents from sharing with God the responsibility for the occurrence, success, and consequences of his work. It takes the form of the apparently little steps we have to take hour by hour 'as people of our time in what is (even in the most extraordinary case) the fairly small sphere and framework of the opportunities we are offered and the possibilities we are given, and in the fairly narrow view of our situation and problems that we usually have'. Therefore Christian action will be

---

[97] Ibid. 153.   [98] Ibid. 156–7.   [99] Ibid. 164.   [100] Ibid. 163–5.

of the nature only of 'provisional and very relative and modest resistance'.[101] In sum, what Christians are required to do in agreement with the first petition of the Lord's Prayer is to realize the precedence of the Word of God in all that they will and choose and do, and in relation to all the other creaturely factors in their lives. When they stand in this position of subordination, these factors can then assume the character of a promise pointing beyond the sphere of ambivalence.[102]

But what kinds of conduct does the precedence of God's Word entail? Barth begins his answer to this question at the level of the personal life of the individual Christian. He does so because, although he recognizes that ethical individualism is still a danger (thanks, in part, to the influence of Kierkegaard), he reckons that a greater danger is posed by the contemporary tendency to concentrate almost exclusively on external conduct, whether in the Church or in the world. For in Barth's judgement obedience without depends decisively on obedience within. At this personal level the order (*Ordnung*) in which God's Word takes precedence first of all excludes two extremes. On the one hand, it shuts out the possibility that the Christian should ever behave as though God's Word had not been spoken to him and as though God were unknown to him; and, on the other, it shuts out the possibility that he should ever be a saint, one who is determined only by his knowledge of God. In other words, it determines that the action of a Christian should be at worst not demonic, and at best not angelic. This is not to say, however, that it comprises a kind of Stoic acquiescence in the dualism of his situation. For although the Word of God addresses him on the assumption that he still exists in such a situation, it nevertheless challenges that assumption. Therefore, because he lives under God's Word, the Christian bears responsibility for declaring, in the ambivalent present and as a radical challenge to it, the Gospel of the hallowing of God's name that has already taken place in Jesus Christ and will in future be manifested in him. Therefore, he can never rest easy in the present sphere: for 'the ground beneath his feet is on fire here. He can only hurry, move and run.' Following the lead of the Word of God and accepting its discipline, the Christian must continually swim

---

[101] Ibid. 169–74.   [102] Ibid. 175–7.

against the stream that flows down to 'the ocean wastes of compromise between light and darkness'.[103]

Subordination to the Word of God implies a similar pattern of conduct for the Christian as a member of the Church. First of all, it precludes two extreme estimations of the Church: on the one hand, as Babylon, as having simply lost its knowledge of God; and, on the other, as holy, pure, and infallible, full of nothing but the knowledge of God. Then, within these boundaries it requires that Christians pray for the appearing of the one pure, holy Church, and that they will be accordingly active in resistance against the Church, and so for the Church, by striving for the precedence of God's Word.[104]

Likewise, obedience to God's Word in the world cannot take the form, on the one hand, either of principial monasticism or of a principial crusade. Both of these underrate the objective knowledge of God in the world and overrate the competence of Christians to teach the world better than it already knows. They also obscure the positive, world-affirming element in the Christian witness; and they tend to regard Christian action as divine. Therefore, neither isolation from the world nor a militant approach to it can be 'a consistent law' of the Christian's action, which is properly that of a witness. But, on the other hand, nor can obedience take the form of Christian secularism (or liberalism), except as a provisional reaction against the dogmatism of the first extreme. As a principle this underestimates the opposition of the world to God's action in Jesus Christ, jeopardizes the Christian's mission to show the world something new, obscures the fact that the Yes of the Gospel is given form by its No, and forgets that prayer for the hallowing of God's name and zeal for God's honour entails action that is 'distinctly differentiated' from that of those who neither pray thus nor have this zeal. Action that is obedient to the Word of God, then, takes the middle course between these two extremes, while maintaining the tactical freedom to take a few steps—or even to go a good way—along monastic-crusading or secularist lines. What is primarily required is not that such action should be effective, but that it should have a specific character which renders the life of the agent a text that documents the Word of God.

---

[103] Ibid. 183–7.   [104] Ibid. 190–4.

Obedient action is the action of a witness, and it is distinctive in the following respects. First, it bears the character of a movement of resistance, not against other people of the world with whom the Christian knows herself to be in solidarity, not against their interests as such, but against 'the system of the ambivalence of the knowledge and ignorance of God'. Therefore it will also be action in which the agent presents herself as one for whom God is unequivocally the God of humankind, and humankind unequivocally the humankind of God. Further, it will be action that, acknowledging the precedence of God's Word, expresses respect for the order in which God is the Lord and the human creature is the servant who must hear and obey him. Finally and decisively, the agent who is obedient to the God who has freely chosen to be for humankind eschews arbitrary vacillation between humanity and inhumanity, and is unequivocally responsible to the human fellow who is also God's child and therefore her sister or brother. She executes this responsibility by offering the neighbour 'the image of a strangely *human* person'.[105]

The third and final existing section of Barth's exposition of the command of God the Reconciler in terms of the Lord's Prayer bears the title of 'The Struggle for Human Righteousness'. Here, under the general direction of the second petition, Barth continues and concentrates his discussion of the character of obedient action in the world. We have already seen how genuine prayer that God will complete his self-manifestation is accompanied by a zeal for God's honour; how this expresses itself in the continually renewed acknowledgement of the precedence of God's Word; and how this acknowledgement issues in behaviour toward the neighbour that is characterized by a strangely unequivocal humanity. Now we learn that genuine prayer for the coming of God's kingdom—for God to cause his righteousness to appear and dwell on a new earth—is accompanied by active responsibility for the rule of human righteousness; that is, 'for the preservation and renewal, and deepening and extending, of the divinely ordained human safeguards of human rights, human freedom, and human peace on earth'. This positive responsibility takes the general, negative form of a revolt against that disorder (*Unordnung*) which consists in the cessation of the order of an obedient life of a people in fellowship with

---

[105] Ibid. 197–204. Barth's emphasis.

God, and consequently in the disruption of all human relations. The revolt that is demanded of Christians, then, is definitely not a personal revolt against certain people in defence of the freedom to live. On the contrary, Christians engage in revolt for the sake of all people, 'even, and in the last resort precisely, for those with whom they may clash', and against the general and self-incurred human plight which they share with everyone else.[106] The decisive action in this revolt is the prayer that God should cause his kingdom to come.[107] For by this prayer it is acknowledged that the institution of salutary order in human life and fellowship depends upon *God's* institution of his perfect lordship over humankind; and that therefore the basic correspondent form of obedience is the disposition of waiting for God to act.[108] But calling upon God to make his kingdom come also implies corresponding action which is none the less serious for being provisional. Genuine prayer of this kind implies a going out to meet the kingdom of God 'by seeing and grasping the possibilities which are provisionally present or which offer themselves not for divine but for human righteousness and order, by being concerned to actualise them within the limits of their weak ability and above all of their continually errant and perverted will'. This hastening toward the coming kingdom is in no way an attempt to anticipate what only God could begin and finish.[109] Human beings cannot bring in the kingdom of God, for even the most perfect human righteousness and order falls under its judgement.[110] But precisely because perfect righteousness is the work of God and because they are forbidden to attempt the impossible, Christians

are with great strictness required and with great kindness freed and empowered to do what they can do in the sphere of the relative possibilities assigned to them, to do it very imperfectly yet heartily, quietly and cheerfully. They are absolved from wasting time and energy sighing over the impassable limits of their sphere of action and thus missing the opportunities that present themselves in this sphere. They may and can and should rise up and accept responsibility to the utmost of their power for the doing of the little righteousness.[111]

Therefore, the haste of Christians consists of acting 'in the great hope of God's future' by holding 'little hopes' for the present and

---

[106] Ibid. 205–11.   [107] Ibid. 212, 261.   [108] Ibid. 212, 235.
[109] Ibid. 213.   [110] Ibid. 240.   [111] Ibid. 265.

taking 'little steps' toward actualizing 'that which in the light of the act which God has commenced and will complete can be called human right, human freedom, and human peace'.[112]

As we have already seen, this forward movement must take a predominantly negative form: we hasten toward the kingdom by revolting against disorder. Such revolt consists in opposing what Barth calls 'the lordless powers', which are human 'possibilities of life' in a state of rebellious alienation from human beings as a result of their own rebellious alienation from God. Winning a certain autonomy, even superiority, in relation to the human beings to whom they properly belong, these forces make themselves into little absolutisms. This phenomenon reinforces Barth's rejection of the Christian crusade as a way of relating to the world. For if human beings have fallen (not without responsibility and guilt) under the binding sway of 'these impalpable but supremely efficacious potencies, factors, and agents', then there can be no place 'for the formation of Christian fronts against others'. Barth discusses four species of lordless power. First come political absolutisms, in which power no longer serves the divine order and has broken loose from the rule of law (*Recht*). Then follows Mammon, 'the material possessions, property, and resources that have become the idol of man'. This is succeeded by ideologies or rigidly fixed intellectual systems that manifest themselves in slogans and propaganda. Finally, there are the *chthonic* powers, 'the spirits of the earth', which include in their number such forces as technology, fashion, sport, pleasure, and transportation.[113]

The Christian's responsibility for human righteousness usually takes the negative form of a revolt against the lordless powers that represent disorder. But it must be remembered that this negative form has a positive point. Although Christian action can never be identified with God's kingdom, being only relatively righteous, it can be analogous to it, in so far as it derives from the event of the kingdom in Jesus Christ and hastens toward its manifestation in him. The quality of being kingdom-like means that Christian action 'must in all circumstances take place with a view to people, in address to people, and with the aim of helping people'. Therefore, Christians will evaluate every cause in terms of whether and

[112] Ibid. 213, 263.   [113] Ibid. 213–33.

how far it will serve the cause of humankind. They will not be attached to any cause a priori:

In this field there can be no absolute Yes or No carrying an absolute commitment. One reason for this is that an absolute guarantee of human right and worth cannot be expected from the rule of any idea or the power of any life-form. From one standpoint or another, every idea or life-form will sooner or later prove a threat to man. Hence Christians . . . must allow themselves the liberty in certain circumstances of saying only a partial Yes or No where a total one is expected, or a total Yes or No where a partial one is expected, or of saying Yes today where they said No yesterday, and vice-versa. Their total and definitive decision is for man and not for any cause.[114]

Barth's exposition of the Christian life in terms of the Lord's Prayer ends abruptly here. We know it to be unfinished, not only because it only reached the second petition of the Lord's Prayer, but also because 'the last subsection' in which Barth had promised to discuss government as 'a salutary divine order' never appeared.[115] We are also missing, of course, the third major section of the treatise on the command of God the Reconciler, which would have borne the title of 'The Renewal of the Christian Life' and would have comprised an exposition of the Lord's Supper. Of the content of this exposition we know little more than that the Lord's Supper would have been basically conceived as 'the thanksgiving which responds to the presence of Jesus Christ in His self-sacrifice and which looks forward to His future'.[116] A letter which Barth wrote in 1963 is marginally more explicit. There he gives the Lord's Supper three dimensions, rather than two: thanksgiving for the reconciliation of the world with God that has taken place in Christ; confession that Christians are bound together as brothers and sisters who must love and assist one another as such; and affirmation of hope in Jesus Christ's final manifestation in which he will come and make all things new.[117]

Now that we have completed our summary of the 1928–9 and 1959–60 treatises on the command of God the Reconciler, we are in a position to note significant points of comparison beyond that

[114] Ibid. 265–9.   [115] Ibid. 219.   [116] *CD* iv/4: p. ix.
[117] Barth, Letter to Pastor Karl Hendrich, 22 Nov. 1963, in Karl Barth, *Letters 1961–68*, ed. Jurgen Fangmeier and Heinrich Stoevesendt, trans. G. W. Bromiley (Edinburgh: T. & T. Clark, 1981), 142–3.

of their systemic role. First, although in both cases the human hearers of the command of God the Reconciler are conceived as pardoned and reconciled sinners, the 1928–9 lectures stress their sinful condition, while the later lectures emphasize their reconciled status. So the first is dominated by the concepts of law, correction, and self-sacrifice; whereas the second is permeated by the concept of the freedom of God's children to depend upon him, and in their dependence to take action against sinful disorder. This is not to say that the theme of judgement is missing from the later treatise. God's children are naughty children who live solely by his mercy.[118] His Word of grace to humankind inevitably breaks as judgement over them, in so far as they are alienated from God and so from themselves.[119] Their imperfect works can never be more than analogous to God's kingdom.[120] Nevertheless, Barth now insists, humankind's being judged by God is neither their original and basic, nor their last and definitive, determination. It is no longer true that they are determined by their unbelief and disobedience. Nor does their existence fluctuate in the light of God's grace on the one hand, and the shadow of their sin on the other. Jesus Christ is now man's Lord. No matter how gross his sin, the grace addressed to him is greater; 'it qualifies and characterises his transgression as something that in all its gravity and horror is still an episode'.[121]

A second significant point of comparison is that, whereas the earlier treatise is mainly concerned about human conduct in relation to the human fellow, the later one focuses much more strongly on human conduct in relation to God. In the first, the form of the command of God the Reconciler is that the one who hears should obey the law of the neighbour's claim: in the second, it is primarily that God's children should call upon him. Accordingly, in 1959–60 Barth characterized the content of human obedience basically as calling upon God to complete his self-declaration and cause his kingdom to come; second, as fighting for the precedence of the Word of God; and only third, as struggling for human righteousness. In 1928–9 the first two of these characteristics are entirely absent from the description of obedience, whose realization is identified directly as love for the neighbour.

[118] CL 80, 23–4.   [119] Ibid. 15.   [120] Ibid. 265–6.   [121] Ibid. 26.

It would not be appropriate to say of the 1959–60 version that it differs from its predecessor in exalting the religious dimension over the ethical one. For that would be to speak in terms of a Kantian distinction that is fundamentally alien to Barth's programme. Nor would it be appropriate to say that the later version differs simply in exalting duties toward God over those toward the neighbour, for that would be to align it with an equally alien pietism. What is appropriate to say, however, is that the 1959–60 treatise is distinctive in emphasizing the integral dependence of active responsibility for the neighbour upon active responsibility toward God.

A third point of comparison is that the concept of invocation serves, in the 1959–60 treatise, to bring eschatological yearning right into the heart of the Christian life to an extent that is quite lacking in the Münster lectures. For we call upon God to end the twilight and bring his kingdom in. One obvious effect of this upon the description of obedient conduct is that it is couched in terms of moral (and political) dissidence: 'resistance' to disorder and 'revolt' against the lordless powers. This stands in marked contrast to the more conservative tone of the Münster lectures, where we are told that the claim of the neighbour, which mediates God's command, confronts us in the authority of civil law and social custom.

IV

When we turn to the third part of the 1928–9 lectures, it becomes dramatically clear just how far, in the 1959–60 ones, the eschatological dimension has spilled out from the epilogue and into the centre of the Christian life. For much of what Barth decided to treat there under the rubric of the command of God the Reconciler he treats here under the rubric of the command of God the Redeemer. The governing concept in this exposition is that of promise, specifically God's promise to be present as one who redeems us both from the provisional state in which we are his creatures and from the state of contradiction in which we are Christians, and to bring us to the goal of our destiny by creation. This goal is that we should not be merely creatures and therefore obedient slaves, but also members of the kingdom of the grace of

TABLE 3. *The command of God the Redeemer*

1928–9 Lectures
The command of God the Redeemer:

s. 15 is distinctively the command of promise.	s. 16 appears in the form of conscience.	s. 17 demands gratitude.	s. 18 is fulfilled in hope.
1, 2. The promise is that of God's presence as my Redeemer from the mortal state of incompleteness in which I am now his creature, and from the mortal contradiction in which I am now a Christian, into the eschatological state of being a child of God. 3. The command of this promise demands a certain 'enthusiasm', and therefore the basic eschatological act of prayer.	1. i.e. co-knowledge with God, in which we tell ourselves what God's command tells us. 2. It commands us both to wait for our future in *God*; and to hasten to our *future* in God.	1. i.e. a glad, voluntary, free readiness for what God wills of me in acknowledgement of God's gift of final unity with himself. 2. Therefore obedient conduct has the character of play (including discussion of art and humour).	1, 2. i.e. in letting myself be told that my work is done in unity with the will of God the Redeemer. This is the work of the Holy Spirit.

Christ, and so obedient children;[122] that is, those who are in 'primary and personal agreement' with God's will.[123] It is, Barth notes here in passing, 'the great presupposition' of the Lord's Prayer that we should address 'Our Father'.[124] But the capacity for such address and so for participation in a filial relationship with God is not intrinsic to nature. Rather, it comes into being in so far as we are addressed by the Word of God, Jesus Christ, who is not just the Word of him to whom we belong because without him we would not be, nor the Word of him to whom we owe ourselves because without him we would be lost, but also the Word of our Father.[125]

According to the Münster lectures, the command of God the Redeemer is distinctively the command of promise. As such it makes itself known in the form of conscience. Conscience here is defined as the human being's knowing together with God what God alone can know. It does not belong to our constitution by creation because of its judicial character; nor does it belong to our status as reconciled, for from that perspective law is not a voice within us but an alien voice that addresses us from outside. To have a conscience is to be our own judge; but, in order to be our own judge, we must be *entheoi*, in concrete fellowship with God the Redeemer—that is, children of God. For conscience is a telling ourselves what God's Word tells us. In it our voice is God's voice, not because his Word belongs to human consciousness, but because it is entrusted to us and we embrace it. Therefore our conscience is free in the sense that we are free from the character of God's command as law, having made it our own. Freedom of conscience, then, is primarily the freedom of the children of God; and we have it as we have the coming Christ—in the Holy Spirit, in prayer for God to give us the reality of sonship.[126] Secondarily, however, 'freedom of conscience' carries its more familiar meaning in that what my conscience tells me is a momentary event which is not storable and so transferable to someone else. Therefore for me to urge the pronouncements of my own conscience on others is to hinder them from hearing the only conscience they can hear—their own.[127]

Conscience takes up but also transcends the orders of creation

[122] Barth, *Ethics*, 461–3.   [123] Ibid. 467.   [124] Ibid. 464.
[125] Ibid. 466.   [126] Ibid. 475–85.   [127] Ibid. 494–5.

and the dialectic of the Christian's position in Christ's kingdom. It unsettles us by asking how far our conduct is a step toward the future promised us by God's Word, and about whether we have 'fundamentally and radically *the* hope'.[128] It proclaims the absolute future and so relativizes the present. It issues a categorical command to wait, for the future it proclaims is our future *in God*. This is a command, not to be passive, but to rest in the face of all over-hasty impatience and to engage in the basic inner work of creating the vacuum where only the name of the Lord should dwell, which is the presupposition of all obedience: 'Ripeness, readiness is all.' This 'busy waiting for the Lord' has been the valid point of mysticism, monasticism, and pietism. But conscience also issues a categorical command to hasten, for the future it proclaims is *our future* in God: 'Thus they [Christians] cannot be content with things as they are. They cannot build huts in either the kingdom of nature or that of grace as though they were to stay there. They have to march out, become pilgrims and strangers, and in these kingdoms move boldly toward the coming kingdom of glory.'[129] Obedient hastening, then, is more than simply an inner dissatisfaction with the present in the light of the future; for 'we are ordered to fight, to build, to work, to organise, to fashion things'.[130]

The command of God the Redeemer, which is distinctively the command of promise, meets us in the form of conscience. But what does it require of us? It requires gratitude for the divine giving of final unity with God. What this means specifically is 'that I am *gladly*, i.e. voluntarily and cheerfully, ready for what God wills of me in acknowledgement of what is given to me by God and as my necessary response to God's gift'.[131] The specific requirements of the commands of life and law—orderliness and humility, respectively—are not necessarily 'glad'; but in order to be a fulfilment of God's command, they must be so. For only obedience that is glad, free, and voluntary is strictly obedience. But, then, if it has this quality of freedom, grateful action can hardly be commanded simply; or, rather, it must be the requirement of a command that we ourselves affirm, a command that in the end we issue to ourselves. Like conscience, however, this

---

[128] Ibid. 487.   [129] Ibid. 487–8.   [130] Ibid. 490.
[131] Ibid. 499–500. Barth's emphasis.

freedom is present to us as promise, and is therefore less like our property than 'like lightning in a dark sky, a charisma which it is best not to grasp but rather to rejoice in when it is there and not to be surprised when it is not'.[132] Because it has the nature of participation in God's promise, present obedience is characterized by provisionality. Accordingly, it should display freedom from the seriousness with which we think we can save ourselves, and which causes us to harass both ourselves and others. We should conduct ourselves, not in earnest, but in play: 'we must not try to view our work as a solemnly serious cooperation with God on the part of those who will be or are already becoming his colleagues . . . [For] one can walk before God in full seriousness only when one realizes that God alone is fully serious.'[133] At this point, Barth introduces a discussion of art and humour as two 'possibilities of life' which the playful character of obedient action brings to light. Art is the specific external form of playful action, while humour is its universal and inner form. Both take the present with less than ultimate seriousness because they are orientated toward God's future; and both, when genuine, are characterized by the suffering of deep pain at the fact that the future is present only as future, and so at the terrible unredeemedness of our present.[134]

The command of promise requires gratitude. Human action is obedient, is good, when it is grateful, glad, playful. But in order to be truly grateful, it must be hopeful. Hope, the work of the Holy Spirit, consists in our being told, and in our letting ourselves be told, that our action is done in unity with the will of the Redeemer. In this, then, the command of promise finds its fulfilment.

From this summary, it will now be clear that the leading themes of Barth's 1928–9 exposition of the command of God the Redeemer appear in the 1959–60 exposition of the command of God the Reconciler: the relationship of human beings to God as children to their Father; and the character of obedient action as a restless waiting for, and subversive hastening towards, God's future. What are we to make of this rearrangement? What is its significance? First of all, it obviously does not mean that what was originally considered to be primarily future was later deemed to be simply present. For in both treatises the status of being a child of

---

[132] Ibid. 503.   [133] Ibid. 504–5.   [134] Ibid. 506–12.

the divine Father is at once present and future. In 1928–9 Barth speaks of it as a future that is present to those who have been addressed by God's Word, have received the promise, live in hope of coming into their inheritance, and pray.[135] In the later lectures its future quality is indicated in statements such as this: 'Christians . . . have never become but are always becoming. Even their standing . . . can never take place except between two steps in their journey.'[136] Moreover, Barth's identification in 1959–60 of prayer as the basic form of Christian action, and his refusal to grant any form of such action a status greater than that of witness to the coming kingdom, underscores its essential orientation toward the eschatological future. Nevertheless, the very transference of the treatment of the child-Father relationship from the exposition of the order of redemption to that of the order of reconciliation does have the effect of putting the stress on the *presence* of the future, on our status as children of God already established by his reconciling work in Jesus Christ. It also has the effect of changing the basic form of love for the neighbour. No longer does that love primarily take the conservative form of respecting the neighbour's authority to limit and correct one through civil law and social custom (as in the second part of the 1928–9 lectures); it now assumes the more radical, critical, and subversive shape of struggling for the humanity of the neighbour against the unruly political, economic, ideological, and *chthonic* powers that enslave him—and therefore to some extent against the neighbour himself. In the 1959–60 lectures, the integral connection between love and conflict is much more patent.

The transference of so much that had appeared in the third part of the earlier treatise to the second part of the later one exacerbates the problem of trying to identify what the content of the exposition of the command of God the Redeemer would have been in the fifth volume of the *Church Dogmatics*. Given that Barth decided at the eleventh hour to characterize the human being in relation to the Reconciler as child of God rather than as pardoned sinner,[137] how did he intend to designate the human being in relation to the

---

[135] Ibid. 472–3.   [136] *CL* 78.

[137] This alteration was a consequence of Barth's decision in the second half of 1960 to expound the heart of the Christian life in terms of themes presented by the Lord's Prayer, the first of which was the human invocation of God as Father. Before then, he had intended to characterize the human being in relation to God the Reconciler as pardoned sinner (along the lines of his Münster lectures). This he announced in the introductory section of *CD* iii/4 (pp. 25–6); and it remained his

command of the Redeemer? Obviously, we can do nothing more here than speculate, but we can do so with some reason. One reasonable guess is that Barth would have characterized human-kind in relation to God the Redeemer as future heirs of eternal life. In the Münster lectures this status is ascribed to them together with that of children of God. The inaugural thesis which stands at the head of the lectures on the command of the Redeemer has as its opening sentence: 'God's command applies to me inasmuch as, being his child, I am an heir of eternal life.'[138] Likewise, the intro-ductory section of the 1959–60 lectures identifies the human being in relation to the Redeemer 'as his child and future heir'.[139] However, Barth's last-minute decision to make invocation the governing concept of his exposition of the Reconciler had the con-sequence of identifying the reconciled human being as child of God simply. The subsection in which he expounds the status of human beings before God the Reconciler has the title of 'The Chil-dren' (s. 76. 2), and the theme of humans as heirs of eternal life receives no mention. Therefore it is reasonable to surmise that, in deciding to reconceive his exposition of the command of God the Reconciler as he did, Barth also decided to reserve the concept of heir to designate the status of humankind before God the Redeemer. The appropriateness of such a decision is obvious; for, unlike the concept of child, the concept of heir has a logical refer-ence to the future. Theologically, of course, the concept of child of God is partly eschatological. No human being is a child of God simply. She is such only in that she is always becoming such. Nevertheless, in that the human being's status as God's child is a fact that has already been established by God's Word, Jesus Christ, it is eminently suitable to play a major conceptual role in an expo-sition of the command of God the Reconciler. Equally, although the human's status as heir of eternal life is also established by God's work of reconciliation, its logical reference to the future makes it a more appropriate candidate for prominent use in an exposition of the command of God the Redeemer.

Beyond the matter of the specific characterization of human

---

declared intention even in the equivalent section of his 1959–60 lectures, where he describes the human being in relation to the Reconciler as 'the being that, in spite of its own unfaithfulness and therefore not according to its merits but by the faith-fulness of God, is a participant in his grace, is justified before God, sanctified for him, and called to his service' (CL 6–7).

[138] Barth, Ethics, 461.   [139] CL 7.

being, speculation about the content of the exposition of the command of God the Redeemer, according to the revised scheme, becomes more haphazard. The most that we can do with reason is to note of certain themes which Barth treated under the rubric of the command of the Redeemer in 1928–9 that he gave them no significant attention in the 1959–60 lectures on the command of the Reconciler, and that he would have had good reason to consider them under the rubric of the command of the Redeemer. Of these themes the two most obvious are conscience and hope. A third might be gratitude, except that it has a logically retrospective rather than prospective reference, and it does receive some attention in Barth's exposition of the Christian life as one of the modes of existence of a child of God.[140] Although we may have doubts about gratitude, we should have fewer of them about play or playfulness; for in the earlier treatise Barth defined this as a form of activity or an attitude that takes the present with a measure of lightness, because it regards God's future as more serious. According to this definition 'play' or 'playfulness' has a logical reference to the future. Finally, if we have reason to suppose that the theme of play or playfulness would have received some attention in the *Dogmatics'* version of the command of the Redeemer, then we have equal reason to suppose the same of art and humour.

V

We have completed our inspection of each of the three dimensions of Barth's ethics. In so far as it has been possible, we have identified and explored the differences between the 1928–9 and the 1959–60 versions. The point of this has not been merely to trace the development of Barth's thought. It has not been simply an exercise in intellectual history. Rather it has been an attempt to draw out the significance of the later arrangement of each treatise by contrasting it with a closely related alternative. Now the time has come to focus exclusively on the later scheme and attempt a more integrated view. This we shall do by describing the distinctive features of each of the three dimensions, taking care to indicate how each qualifies the others. On this occasion we will follow the order of material, rather than logical, priority.

[140] Ibid. 77–8.

The fact that the one God is God the Reconciler specifies God the Creator as one who loves his creatures and is committed to their cause. Such specification is not superfluous, because there is nothing in the concept of divine Creator that logically excludes his being a sadist who creates in order to tease and frustrate. So the identification of God the Creator with God the Reconciler serves to specify his command as one that treats with respect the nature and destiny of his creatures. One implication of this is that what God commands—the content of obedience—will always be in accordance with creaturely limitations. Therefore, even when human beings hasten in hope toward the eschatological future, if they hasten obediently, then they will do so only as creatures whose existence and powers are finite. They may and must hasten boldly, but their steps will still be small and their victories provisional. Because God's command respects the creatureliness of human beings, it frees them from the intolerable burden of their pretensions to divine responsibility.

The specification of God as the Reconciler also specifies his command as one that aims at—and, if obeyed, effects— sanctification, that is, liberation for life in accordance with creaturely nature. This purpose of the command presupposes the sinfulness of the human existence that it enters. Indeed, that is why God's will addresses human beings in an imperative, coercive form; for it can only encounter sinners heteronomously. So the fact that God commands at all means that what he commands cannot be a simple, naïve affirmation of the current state of human affairs. It can only be a critical affirmation. That is why God's command necessarily excludes Christian secularism as a policy, if not as a tactic.

Nevertheless, the law of God's judgement only appears alien to us in so far as we are at odds with our creaturely nature and destiny. It contradicts us in so far as we strive to be other than truly human. It opposes us for our own sake. It binds us in order to set us free. So the fact that the command of God is the command of God the Reconciler has the effect of asserting that the purpose of the law is to serve the Gospel; and of establishing that the ascetic, renunciatory element in obedience, though necessary, is strictly tactical.

The human correlate of the specification of God as Reconciler is the specification of (human) creatures as beloved of their Creator.

Only on this basis is creaturely freedom really possible. First, the prayer in which human creatures realize their freedom before God is not possible simply on the ground of creaturely need and impotence. Its other and primary condition is the freedom that God the Reconciler gives his sinful creatures to call upon him. The inner basis of the prayer (*das Gebet*) of God's creatures is the invocation (*die Anrufung*) of God's children. Second, the fellowship in which creatures realize their freedom is possible only as fellowship among covenant-partners of God. For only when human beings recognize themselves as reconciled sinners will they relinquish the moral self-righteousness that lies at the root of social strife. The inner basis of human justice is divine justification. Third, the point of respecting and protecting life is to provide the conditions necessary for human work. But human work will only realize creaturely freedom if it subordinates itself to the criterion of true humanity, which is being-for-others; for only thus can it avoid degenerating into ruthless competition and exploitation. Creaturely freedom for life, then, finds its inner basis in the service of the Christian community, which is to correspond to God's work of reconciliation in Jesus Christ. Finally, freedom within creaturely limitations depends upon the specification of human creatures as reconciled sinners. This is so in two respects. First, the freedom of the creature in respect of her temporal limits consists in her being able to regard her finite existence as a unique opportunity. This, Barth argues, becomes possible by the light of the incarnation of God and the resurrection of Jesus. Through the incarnation we see God himself making of limited human existence 'not . . . a pitiful portion but a rich dowry full of meaning and promise';[141] and through the resurrection our fear of death is supplanted by hope.[142] Second, the freedom of the creature in respect of the limits imposed on her by age, historical situation, personal aptitude, and the ordinary sphere of operation consists in her being able to believe that she has the honour of being specially commanded by God to do something in particular.[143] This she can do in the knowledge that the God who commands her is one who has become her Brother, in order to make her into a child of God.[144] That she is addressed by God the Reconciler makes of the human creature not just a specimen, but an individual.[145]

---

[141] Ibid. 571.   [142] Ibid. 594.   [143] Ibid. 607–47, 655.   [144] Ibid. 685.
[145] Ibid. 655.

The fact that the one command of God is not just the command of the Creator but also that of the Reconciler means that the one who hears it cannot obey it simply as a creature but only as a reconciled sinner. It is not possible to subordinate oneself simply to God the Creator. In order to be and behave like a creature, and to enjoy the freedom thereof, one must also subordinate oneself to God's reconciling Word in Jesus Christ. In other words, there is no human obedience, no good human action, that is not 'Christian'. In saying this, Barth adopts an Augustinian position with regard to the relationship between morality and spirituality, and to the possibility of genuine virtue among pagans. For Ausgustine, there can be no genuine virtue among unbelievers because the hierarchy of loves is such that, withoug *caritas* or love for God, all other human loves are disordered. Morality and spirituality, therefore, are inseparable. It is quite clear, and when we proceed to discuss the command of God the Creator it will become clearer, that this is Barth's position. Unlike Augustine, however, Barth is willing to entertain the possibility of subordination to the Word of God apart from explicit Christian confession. Here, he draws alongside Rahner, although instead of 'anonymous Christianity' he proposes the category of 'virtual Christianity'.[146] In this way Barth is able to affirm both the dependence of the goodness of human action upon a rightly ordered relationship with God, and the possibility of genuine virtue among (apparent) pagans; and to do so without recourse to the Thomist distinction between nature and grace or the Calvinist distinction between common and saving grace.

We turn now to the specification of God as Creator. The fact that God is Creator as well as Reconciler means that his one command aims to sanctify the human creature *as a whole*. It is not just concerned with a discrete spiritual 'part' (the 'soul'), but with human being in its spiritual, corporeal, and therefore social dimensions. Sanctification does not consist in the liberation of the human spirit from its worldly connections, but rather in the liberation which results from the right ordering of human being in all of its relations. The most basic of these is, of course, the relation of the human creature to its Creator. It is as a consequence of the rejection of the ordering of this relation, according to which

---

[146] See below, pp. 150–1 for further discussion.

God is Lord and the human creature his servant, that disorder is introduced into 'horizontal' relations in the form of the 'lordless powers'; for 'the whole meaning and soundness of the secondary and lower relationship[s] depends on the existence and order of the primary and higher'.[147] If the fact that God's command is the command of the Reconciler means that creaturely freedom can only be realized on the basis of acknowledgement of God's initiative in reordering—in 'justifying'—the relationship between himself and his creatures, then the fact that God's command is the command of the Creator means that what God's grace liberates sinful creatures for is life according to the orders of creation.

Finally, the fact that the one command of God is also the command of God the Redeemer means that neither the process of liberation from sin, nor the process of realizing the destiny of human creatures to become children of God, is yet complete. Therefore God's command cannot be such that obedience could take the form of self-complacency. Human beings, although reconciled, are still sinners and therefore continue to stand in need of contradiction and correction. Likewise, nor could obedience take the form of a kind of Stoic or Hegelian acquiescence in the ambiguous present; for the promise that God will cause his light utterly to dispel the darkness—the fact that God *is* the Redeemer—requires his creatures to revolt against the disorder that persists. The fact that the one command of God is the command of the Redeemer, as well as of the Creator and Reconciler, means that obedience to it must include moments of ascetic renunciation and prophetic rebellion, as well as moments of the glad affirmation of life.

VI

We have sought to show in general terms how each of the three dimensions shapes the form of the one command of God. In conclusion, we now attempt to show how these three dimensions shape this command in respect of a particular moral problem; and, in order that we may build on our earlier analysis,[148] we choose the problem of war.

---

[147] *CD* iii/2: 342.   [148] See above, pp. 38–40.

War as a moral problem receives its fullest consideration under the rubric of the command of God the Creator. Here Barth argues that this command always requires the protection of life (in some manner); that modern war is primarily about the acquisition and protection of material interests, and is basically 'a brutal matter of killing' as many of the enemy as possible by whatever means; and that therefore 'the inflexible negative of pacifism has almost infinite arguments in its favour and is almost overpoweringly strong'.[149] That having been said, however, Barth proceeds to describe the general features of the case where belligerency is commanded. These we have already listed in Chapter I,[150] but we will summarize them here. First, there are the five features common to all cases where the taking of life is commanded: it is intended as an extraordinary means of protecting life; it is *ultima ratio*; it presupposes a heavy presumption against the taking of life; it is resolved upon in full awareness of the risk attendant upon making an extraordinary interpretation of the rule; and it is undertaken without an eye to the prospects of success, in faith, and so in joyous and reckless determination. Then there are the two mutually alternative conditions specific to the extraordinary case of commanded war: that it be waged either out of obligation—not necessarily by formal treaty—to aid 'a weaker neighbour', or in defence of the State against an assault upon its very existence and autonomy. This last condition Barth tightens by requiring 'serious grounds' for self-defence by the State. These grounds turn out to be the preservation of the political conditions under which justice is attested: a constitution which guarantees freedom for the proclamation of the Gospel of justification; which accords a measure of freedom for self-expression and development to each of a plurality of racial, linguistic, regional, social, and confessional groups; which balances the rights of the individual against the claims of the community; and which is probably (social) democratic in its structures and procedures.

Such is the account of the moral problem of war that Barth gives under the rubric of the command of the Creator. Nothing that he says about either of the two other dimensions of God's command gainsays this account, but some of what he says does serve to qualify it in significant respects. One of the effects of the fact that God

---

[149] *CD* iii/4: 455.   [150] See above, pp. 38–40.

commands also as Reconciler is to intensify that presumption against war as the possible content of a divine command which is already established by the fact of his commanding as Creator. One of the 'prominent lines' of the command of Jesus, Barth tells us here, is the attestation of the kingdom of God 'as an end of the fixed idea of the necessary and beneficial value of force'. Because of the assurance of the fatherly care and protection of God, force directed against oneself is not to be feared but to be suffered confidently; and the use of force against others is to be renounced. The kingdom of God invalidates the friend–foe relationship, in which force is the *ultima ratio*: the disciples of Jesus are to love their enemies. Not that we have here a general rule, but only a 'prominent line' along which Jesus' command was wont to move: 'according to the sense of the New Testament we cannot be pacifists in principle, only in practice'. Nevertheless, 'we have to consider very closely whether, if we are called to discipleship, we can avoid being practical pacifists, or fail to be so'.[151]

God's commanding as Reconciler reinforces, not only the general presumption against war, but also that condition of commanded belligerency according to which Christians can only obediently fight *against* others, if in so doing they are ultimately fighting *for* them. Christians are commanded to revolt against a disorder that consists in deviation from the order 'of an obedient life of people in fellowship with God which includes as such the corresponding form—the guarantee of human right, freedom and peace—of a life of people in fellowship with one another'.[152] Therefore, they cannot fight 'strictly and seriously and primarily' against threats to 'their life and its preservation, the possibility of their life and its actualization'; for, 'as Christians they can and may refrain from revolts of this kind, and in some circumstances will have to do so'.[153] Indeed, they 'become and are free and fit for this [commanded] revolt and conflict precisely to the degree that they have left far behind them the more personal revolts and conflicts of that other kind'. The revolt demanded of Christians is not directed *against* anyone, neither against the unbeliever nor against the wicked. Rather, since they fight against the 'general and self-incurred human plight' which they share with all others,

---

[151] *CD* iv/2: 549–50.   [152] *CL* 211.   [153] Ibid. 206–7.

Christians 'rebel and fight for *all* men, even, and in the last resort precisely, for those with whom they may clash'.[154]

Beyond reinforcing two conditions of an exceptional case of commanded war, the command of God as Reconciler adds two more. The first is that a divine command to wage war can only be given to those who have abandoned the defence of their own property—whether goods in their possession, their prestige, or their very lives. This condition is implied and further informed when we are told that the call to discipleship involves a command to correspond to the break which God has made for us in Jesus Christ, not only with the dominion of force, but also with that of the possessions and worldly honour in the name of whose defence the use of force is usually invoked.[155] In other words, the command to wage war can only be addressed to those who have been freed from the lordless power of Mammon. The second condition is that, since all Christian action must have the aim of helping people rather than serving a cause,[156] war can only be commanded which has the intention of protecting concrete human lives rather than some ideology of 'life'.

Whereas God's commanding as Reconciler reinforces and augments what he commands as Creator with regard to war in terms of Christian nonconformity to the idolatrous powers presently operative in the world, we surmise that his commanding as Redeemer would have made its qualifications in terms of the promise and hope of God's consummation of his Parousia—that is, in terms of the *futurity* of the presence of God's kingdom.[157] This present age is the age 'between the times', between the resurrection of Christ and his coming again in glory. Because the resurrection stands behind us there is no place now for pessimism; but because the final, universal, and definitive revelation of God's Word in Jesus Christ has not yet occurred and because, therefore, the children of God have not yet come fully into their inheritance, there is equally no room for simple optimism. Because we live in the hope that God will cause his kingdom to come, because we act prayerfully, we cannot expect to build a world which does not stand in need of redemption; or to rid it of the longing and desire of human beings

---

[154] Ibid. 209–11.   [155] *CD* iv/2: 543–4.   [156] *CL* 266–7, 269.
[157] *CD* iv/3: 902–10.

to do wrong against others in order to secure right for themselves, 'to resist one another, to vie and quarrel'; or, therefore, to transcend the necessity of the use of force by the state as the means of containing the chaotic effects of sin. Christians cannot repudiate war absolutely.[158] However, if the futurity of the presence of God's kingdom withholds us from precluding the possibility of a divine command to wage war, it also withholds us from regarding even commanded war as anything more than a police action. In so far as a command to wage war is a command of God the Redeemer, it cannot be a command to engage in a crusade.

---

[158] Ibid. 938. Cf. 'The Christian Community in the Midst of Political Change', in Karl Barth, *Against the Stream*, ed. Ronald Gregor Smith, trans. E. M. Delacour and Stanley Godman (London: SCM, 1954), 78–9, 83–4; 'Blessed are the Meek, for They shall Inherit the Earth', in *Against the Stream*, 54; 'A Letter to Great Britain from Switzerland', in *Letter to Great Britain*, 13.

3

BIBLICAL INDICATIONS

I

In Chapter 1 we explored Barth's understanding of the relationship between the event of hearing a command of God and ethical reasoning. In Chapter 2 we sought to lay bare the three-dimensional structure of Barth's own 'special' ethics, and to gain some sense of the 'system' as a dynamic whole. Here we turn to the first of three immediate sources—or, relatively speaking, authorities—for ethics that aspire to sharpen our hearing of God's command: namely, Scripture. The second and third of these sources, the Church and the world, will be discussed, respectively, in Chapters 4 and 5.

II

To understand the role of Scripture in Barth's ethics we must first consider his doctrine of Scripture in general. The famous, and in conservative quarters infamous, concept which Barth uses to expound this doctrine is that of 'witness'. This concept has both a positive and a negative function. It affirms that, as 'the original and legitimate witness' to God's self-revelation, Scripture has that revelation as its 'basis, object, and content'.[1] In this sense, therefore, 'God Himself now says what the text says.'[2] As original and direct witness Scripture is itself the Word of God and has priority over all other writings.[3] Among authorities in dogmatics and theological ethics, then, Scripture takes pride of place.

However, if the characterization of Scripture as witness affirms that it may never be separated from God's revelation, it also denies that it may ever be identified with it.[4] A witness is not the same as

---

[1] *CD* i/2: 502, 463. [2] Ibid. 532. [3] Ibid. 502. [4] Ibid. 463.

what it attests. This denial of identity between Scripture and the Word of God is made for several reasons. The first one is to affirm the humanity of the former. The words of Scripture are human words. The biblical texts are therefore historically relative and proper matter for historical, cultural, and linguistic study. This is by no means to say, however, that their meaning may be reduced to their background. They are much more than mere expressions of the general context to which they belong; for in their context they do actually say something, they point toward something, they refer to an object.[5] To use the language of Paul Ricoeur, the meaning of these texts lies more in front of them than behind them. Therefore those who seek to understand them cannot confine themselves to the safety of historico-critical or linguistic analysis. They must venture beyond exegesis into interpretation.[6]

To some extent Barth's insistence on the 'concrete humanity' of the Bible is intended as much to dignify (obedient) humanity as to draw attention to the limitations under which the Bible operates: humanity that is free, and therefore free for obedience to God, may actually speak his Word. The Word dignifies humanity by taking on the flesh of human words.[7] This is one part of Barth's meaning. The other part—and perhaps the one that predominates—is that Scripture, being human, can err. The biblical authors, Barth tells us, 'speak as fallible, erring men like ourselves', and what they say can be subjected to all sorts of criticism, whether philosophical (weltanschaulichen), historical, ethical, religious, or theological. But the kind of error that Barth envisages here is not that of sheer untruth. Often it is the kind that any disparate collection of occasional writings is bound to manifest: for example, lacunae and overemphases.[8] Barth does at one point speak of contradictions or inconsistencies (Widersprüche)—between the Law and the prophets, John and the Synoptic evangelists, Paul and Jesus—but only as part of an argument that the Bible is not a theological system.[9] There is, however, another kind of error that Barth attributes to Scripture, and which is not just characteristic of an unsystematic nature: the limitations imposed on understanding by a particular cultural environment. 'Each in his own way and

---

[5] Ibid. 464.
[6] See T. F. Torrance, *Karl Barth: Biblical and Evangelical Theologian* (Edinburgh: T. & T. Clark, 1990), 76-7, 111.
[7] *CD* i/2: 499.   [8] Ibid. 507.   [9] Ibid. 509.

degree, they [the biblical authors] shared the culture of their age and environment, whose form and content could be contested by other ages and environments ... In the biblical view of the world and man we are constantly coming up against presuppositions which are not ours, and statements and judgements which we cannot accept.'[10] Barth provides an example of this kind of cultural stumbling-block: the failure to observe the distinction between fact and value, between history on the one hand and saga or legend on the other. For a moment it seems that Barth allows the possibility that the interpreter of the Bible might legitimately dissent from it in some fashion. Certainly, he is swift to qualify such a possibility by restricting it to matters of secondary or even peripheral importance. He makes it clear that since we cannot attach any 'final seriousness' to the fact–value distinction, we cannot regard the Bible's neglect of it as comprising a 'final difficulty'. Like others of its kind, this error is merely a point of detail.[11] Nevertheless, there still appears to be room for a measure of rightful dissent. But not for long, for Barth immediately beats a headlong retreat by arguing that, although the Bible may be erroneous in principle, it cannot be so in practice. This is because we can never be in a position to stand in judgement on it, since our own cultural views are 'neither divine nor even Solomonic'.[12] Instead of affirming the possibility of the humble and docile venturing of provisional criticism, Barth seems to propose that we offer up before the Bible a permanent *sacrificium intellectus*. The most that he allows us to do is to speak of the biblical authors' 'capacity for errors'. We may not speak of their 'errors' simply. For all practical purposes Barth's concept of biblical 'error' comprises only the limitations imposed by a lack of system. The Bible is erroneous, not in the sense that it contains falsehoods, but only in the sense that it is imperfect.

That is part of the import of Barth's distinction between the Bible and the Word of God. Another part follows closely on its heels. To say that the Bible is imperfect in the sense of 'unsystematic' is to deny that we have direct access to its meaning. Even in relation to the well-developed theologies of St Paul and St John, Barth tells us, 'we can only arrive later and by dint of much laborious construction at a certain hypothetical scheme'; and the

---

[10] Ibid. 508.   [11] Ibid. 508–9.   [12] Ibid.

process of this construction involves venturing judgements about what utterances are more central and what are more peripheral, and which are to be understood literally and which symbolically. The sense of the text in its various wholeness—its 'common order'—is not simply there for the taking;[13] it comes into being by a creative act of interpretation. Here Barth makes a point that has been strongly asserted and elaborated by contemporary theorists of hermeneutics: interpretation is not simply a matter of discovery, but also of construction.[14] Barth, however, makes it *en passant*, since the matter that really concerns him lies elsewhere. For him, understanding the Bible is much more than a process of interpretation. It comprises much more than an interpreter acting upon a text to discover or construct its meaning. It involves the interpreter being addressed through the text by what the text refers to. And in the case of the Bible this, for Barth, is pre-eminently the living reality of the God who is his Word.

The meaning of the Bible is not there for the taking because it is a personal subject who gives (or withholds) himself freely. Understanding the Bible, then, is not finally a process, but an event when what the text means—what it refers to—presents itself out of sheer grace. This is the objective side of what Barth means when he speaks of the Bible 'becoming' the Word of God by divine miracle, and of God's Word 'deciding' when Scripture should become the Word.[15] Correlatively, apprehension of the Bible's meaning—hearing the Word of God—is not, therefore, just a matter of applying the right interpretative method to the text. It is also a matter of the interpreter being rightly disposed to its referent. In order to understand what the Bible means, the interpreter must be ready to meet the Word of grace that judges and commands her. Specifically, she must be thankful, penitent, and obedient: she must approach the text in faith. But the awakening and strengthening of faith is itself a work of the Holy Spirit.

---

[13] Ibid. 509.

[14] The foremost proponent of this claim is H.-G. Gadamer, who has argued that the real meaning of the text transcends the authorial intention and original reception, since it is also always partly determined by the situation of the interpreter. Interpretation, therefore, is *productive* and not merely *reproductive* (*Truth and Method* (New York: Seabury, 1975), 263–4). The productive or creative dimension of interpretation is explored in detail by Werner Jeanrond in *Text and Interpretation as Categories of Theological Thinking* (Dublin: Gill & Macmillan, 1988).

[15] *CD* i/2: 513, 530–1.

This is the other, subjective side of the miracle by which the Bible becomes the Word of God.[16] So the distinction between the Bible and the Word of God functions, not simply to preserve God's freedom, but also to assert the theological historicity of the interpreter. That is to say, it places the interaction of biblical text and interpreter firmly in the context of the relationship between a gracious God and sinful human creatures, and thus gives an account of biblical interpretation that is thoroughly theological.

What is at stake for Barth in this distinction between the Bible and the Word of God is perhaps most clearly visible when set over and against that doctrine of Scripture which it was designed to oppose; namely, that of verbal or grammatical inspiration. Barth notes that such a doctrine was present in the early Church and characterized Protestant orthodoxy, and he regards it as expressive of the secularization of the concept of revelation. By 'secularization' here he means the tendency to take for granted the possibility of *direct*, 'natural' access to the Bible's meaning; to acknowledge the role of the Spirit in the composition of the Bible, while neglecting it in the act of right reading. To operate with a secularized concept of revelation is to imagine that the Bible can be rightly used without the free grace of God.[17] To identify the Bible with the Word of God is to encourage its use as a book of oracles, a compendium of divine knowledge.[18] It is to make it a magical instrument of human power rather than an occasion for human thankfulness, penitence, and obedience in response to the gracious power of God.

It could be said (and Barth virtually says it) that the distinction between Scripture and the Word of God is designed to subvert the *use* of Scripture. 'Use' here is intended in the specific sense of self-justifying manipulation. We may be able to master and exploit this text for ideological purposes, but we cannot master its meaning, its referent. We cannot play master and understand the text at the same time. We can only understand it by subordinating ourselves to its meaning and letting it criticize us. Here Barth anticipates a point of Gadamerian emphasis that has now become a hermeneutical truism: that the interpreter must allow the text to address and question her.[19]

In itself this is a point worth asserting. But Barth's relentless

[16] Ibid. 512.   [17] Ibid. 518–19, 521–2, 523.   [18] Ibid. 507–8.
[19] Gadamer, *Truth and Method*, 325–41.

reiteration of it exposes him to criticism. Werner Jeanrond, for example, believes that Barth tends to regard the assertion of the critical primacy of God's Word as entailing the exclusion of reflection upon hermeneutical method, since such reflection is bound to encourage the illusion that all that is required to grasp God's revelation is adequate technique. To this Jeanrond responds:

the event of God's revelation ... can, of course, never be guaranteed by any methodological consideration; however, methodological reflection can prepare the reader to act more responsibly in the process of interpretation.[20]

However, Jeanrond himself notes Barth's proposal of a three-stage method of interpretation: exegesis (*explicatio*), reflection (*meditatio*), and appropriation (*applicatio*).[21] He is also aware that Barth did not intend, by the assertion of the critical primacy of the Word, to displace literary-historical criticism of the Bible altogether, and that this comprises the first stage in his method.[22] Moreover, while the 'open' discussion of the presuppositions with which we approach a given text is a major feature of the hermeneutical methodology that Jeanrond misses in Barth, he nevertheless acknowledges that such criticism is the main function of the second stage of Barth's method.[23] Therefore, in one—and to some extent, even in Jeanrond's—sense it is not true to say that Barth simply eschewed methodological reflection upon the interpretation of the Bible—in spite of what his rhetoric sometimes seems to indicate. But it is true to say, as Jeanrond does, that Barth's hermeneutical methodology does not engage with the issue of how far the identity of the text is the legitimate creation of the historically conditioned reader, or with the subsequent issue of the possibility of a legitimate plurality of historically conditioned readings. Nevertheless, it is not obvious that Barth's failure here is attributable to theological or hermeneutical principle. We have already seen that he grants that the meaning of the Bible is in some measure a human construction; and since the limited validity of

[20] Werner Jeanrond, 'Karl Barth's Hermeneutics', in Nigel Biggar (ed.), *Reckoning with Barth* (Oxford: Mowbray, 1988), 94. Jeanrond notes major similarities in form between the hermeneutics of Barth and Gadamer and judges their common rejection of Schleiermacher to be mistaken (ibid.).

[21] Ibid. 88–9; *CD*, i/2: 722–40.

[22] Jeanrond in *Reckoning with Barth*, 85, 88–9; *CD* i/2: 722–7.

[23] *Reckoning with Barth*, 87, 88.

all human understanding is one of his most basic tenets, it would not be at all out of character for him to endorse the possibility of a range of legitimate interpretations. In the end, it is more plausible to account for Barth's failure to extend his hermeneutical methodology into the theory of reading in terms of the fact that his primary concern was to present biblical interpretation in a way that recognizes the *theological* historicity of the reader.

III

We move now from Barth's doctrine of Scripture as such to his account of the role of the Bible in ethics. The basic features of this account are determined by his general programme. Barth's central concern to preclude a self-justifying, manipulative approach to Scripture expresses itself here in his denial that the Bible is a kind of 'supernatural register or arsenal' which provides direct moral guidance like 'a box of magic cards'.[24] The same motive is operative in his warding off the spectre of autonomous casuistry by marginalizing Scripture's role as a source-book of moral rules.[25] Instead, anticipating the recent fashion by several decades, Barth brings biblical narrative to ethical centre-stage.

Here it is made to play several parts—as it is in contemporary ethical discussion.[26] Its main appearance is in the form of the history of God's covenantal relationship of grace with humankind; for this story is 'the true content and object of the biblical witness'[27] and represents the history that is the basic, theological context of the human moral agent. It gives her the basic identity of sinful creature, reconciled and being redeemed, and implies a set of right dispositions toward her divine Creator, Reconciler, and Redeemer—a set which includes gratitude, penitence, and child-like trust.

This role of narrative raises, of course, the crucial question of whether it is possible to identify rationally *the* story of the Bible. Does it not contain rather an irreducible plurality of stories?

[24] *CD* ii/2: 704. [25] Ibid. 675.
[26] For a helpful analysis of the various roles that narrative is assigned in contemporary ethical discussion, see Paul Nelson, *Narrative and Morality: A Theological Inquiry* (University Park, Pa.: Pennsylvania State University Press, 1987).
[27] *CD* ii/2: 672.

Certainly, it contains a plurality of stories—stories about different individuals and stories about the Jewish and the Christian communities in different places and at different times. And in so far as these are stories and therefore deal in the currency of the contingent, in one sense they cannot be reduced to anything else. But they can—and they do—derive their significance from the larger, common narrative framework in which they are all set: the meta-story of God's pursuit of his creatures' salvation by way of the life, death, and resurrection of his incarnate Son. That the Bible does intend to tell *a* story in this sense seems clear enough.[28]

But, even if we grant this, is not this story susceptible of a plurality of responsible readings? This is so certainly in the sense that it can bear an infinite number of instantiations: the meta-story will take a different concrete form in the case of each creature whose salvation God pursues. But it is also true that the meta-story itself can be construed differently. Some readers, for example, might prefer to substitute the word 'liberation' for 'salvation', understanding the former primarily in a socio-economic sense. But the extent to which this is a responsible reading can be the subject of rational discussion, for the text's identity is not entirely a product of the reader's interests.[29] To venture *an* account of *the* story of the Bible is not to say that another account could not be shown to be better. The venturing of a provisional judgement about the wholeness of the Bible is methodologically necessary if its ethical resources are to be used coherently,[30] and Barth was certainly wise to make it in narrative rather than conceptual terms. For narrative terms are more

---

[28] James Barr, for one, thinks so: 'the [biblical] literature is meant to be read as a story with a beginning and a progression. All "acts of God" and incidents of the story make sense because a framework of meaning has already been created by previous acts, remembered in the tradition' (*The Bible in the Modern World* (New York: Harper & Row, 1973), 147).

[29] See Jeanrond, *Text and Interpretation*, ch. 2. 3, 4, 5.

[30] James Gustafson ('The Place of Scripture in Christian Ethics: A Methodological Study', in *Theology and Christian Ethics* (Philadelphia: Pilgrim Press, 1974), 134–5) and Allen Verhey (*The Great Reversal: Ethics and the New Testament* (Grand Rapids: Eerdmans, 1984), 166) believe that such a judgement is necessary and imply that it may be rational, even if only provisional. Charles Curran, on the other hand, seems to regard it as neither possible nor necessary ('Dialogue with the Scriptures: The Role and Function of the Scriptures in Moral Theology', *Catholic Moral Theology in Dialogue* (Notre Dame, Ind.: University of Notre Dame Press, 1976), 41–7, 52–3, 55).

comprehensive of the range and diversity of biblical material, and it is generally recognized that attempts to summarize the Bible's theological or ethical meaning in terms of a single concept or theme are not successful.[31]

In Barth's ethics the Bible's primary contribution is in the form of narrative rather than of ethical principles and rules. The first and fundamental species of narrative with which it furnishes us is that of the general history of God's relationship with humankind through Jesus Christ. The ethical import of this history is that it locates the moral agent theologically, defining her basic identity as that of a sinful creature addressed by the commands of a Creator who has reconciled her to himself and is in the process of redeeming her. But the Bible is also replete with specimens of another species of ethically significant story; that is, of particular instances of direct divine commanding and human responding. Examples of the kind of event that Barth has in mind here are God's commands to Adam and Eve to be fruitful and multiply, to Noah to build the ark, to Abraham to leave Haran for the Promised Land, to Moses to approach Pharaoh, to Joseph to take Mary as his wife; and Jesus' commands to Peter and Andrew to leave their nets and become his disciples, to the rich young man to sell all he has and give it to the poor, and to Peter in the Garden of Gethsemane to put away his sword.[32] The importance of these 'historical pictures' for ethics, in Barth's eyes, is precisely not that they can be universalized into moral rules or treated as paradigms to be copied directly. Their importance is not, in the first place, moral at all. It is theological and lies in their indication of the person of the God who commands us—that is, the God who has reconciled us to himself in Jesus Christ. So when Barth speaks of the form of Christian life in terms of 'correspondence', he is not exactly speaking of simple conformity to biblical paradigms of right conduct. He is not saying that we should simply reproduce what the Gospels tell us Jesus did. He is saying rather that we

---

[31] See e.g. Barr, *The Bible in the Modern World*, 135–6; David Kelsey, *The Uses of Scripture in Recent Theology* (Philadelphia: Fortress Press, 1975), 25–9; Gustafson, 'The Place of Scripture in Christian Ethics', 134–5; Curran, 'Dialogue with the Scripture', 42, 43–4; Stanley Hauerwas, 'The Moral Authority of Scripture', in *A Community of Character* (Notre Dame, Ind.: University of Notre Dame Press, 1981), 67.   [32] *CD* ii/2: 673–5.

should correspond to the living God, whom the biblical (and pre-eminently the Gospel) stories characterize as one who acts out of grace.[33]

How does Barth specify the content of this correspondence? In his discussion of it in his 'general' ethics as the general content of God's command (*CD* ii/2, s. 37. 2) he characteristically concentrates on the vertical, religious dimension. Correspondence to God's grace, he tells us, means basically that we 'accept God's action as right' and 'adhere to the fact that the gracious God does the right'. This involves laying aside all hostility, indifference, and self-will with regard to it; responding to it 'with the burning and exclusive desire to be obedient to it'; and loving God in his action with all our heart, and soul, and strength. It also involves accepting as right the fact that we belong to God in Jesus Christ and do not have our lives on our own hands; that God never meets us except as the One who comes to the help of our misery, except apart from and against our deserts; and that 'beyond our physical and spiritual delights and desires, beyond our bondage to earth and titanic strivings, beyond our faults and virtues, beyond our good and evil work', God is our righteousness.[34]

As for the horizontal dimension of inter-human relations, Barth's explication of the content of correspondence to God's gracious action is rather thin. After a brief consideration of passages in the Epistles of the New Testament which speak of the imitation of Christ,[35] he concludes that

our aim must correspond to the distinctive aim [*Zielstrebigkeit*] of our Father in heaven, who meets both the good and the evil with the same beneficence. It must be a readiness to forgive one [an]other, to be compassionate, to bear one another's burdens and to live and help one another. It must be persistent kindness even towards persecutors of the faith. It must be a humility in which we do not look at our own things, but at the things of others. It must be a love which is directed even,—and especially—to our enemies.[36]

Four years after the publication of that part of the *Church Dogmatics* which contains his discussion of the form of Christian life as one of 'correspondence' (ii/2), Barth published a brief essay

---

[33] Ibid. 575–6.   [34] Ibid. 579–83.   [35] Ibid. 576–7.
[36] Ibid. 578. *Zielstrebigkeit* has been rendered 'aim' in the ET. It would have been better translated as 'determination' or 'single-mindedness'.

entitled 'Christian Ethics',[37] where he offers another exposition of what it means to 'correspond' to God's gracious action in the history of Jesus Christ. He proceeds as follows. Since God has dignified humankind by becoming incarnate and making himself our neighbour for our sake, we should affirm everyone as an end in themselves and not as a means to some other end. Since humankind is saved by *God's grace* alone, we should have a sober rather than an optimistic view of ourselves, and we should treat each other with patience, receiving and granting forgiveness. Since humankind *is* saved by grace, we should not regard ourselves or each other pessimistically but with hope. Since God comes to our aid by electing and calling us personally, we must take direct personal responsibility for ourselves. Since God has come to the aid of everyone, we should treat each other as fellows in need and as members of one community. Since God has glorified himself in becoming the slave of his human creatures, we should put ourselves at the disposal of others. Finally, since God's act for us is comprehensive and definitive, we should love God both in the present and in hope for the eschatological future, both in prayer and in work, both in spirit and in body, and both privately and publicly.[38]

In the 'special' ethics of the *Church Dogmatics* the concept of correspondence is little mentioned, but it is very much at work. The invocation of God in baptism, the Lord's Prayer, and the Lord's Supper answers to the command of God the Reconciler by corresponding to God's gracious action in Jesus Christ. This it does in several respects. First of all, it corresponds in that it is the fitting response. Then, more specifically, it corresponds in that to invoke God is to treat him as Father and to assume the role of child, which is to imitate the general stance or disposition of Jesus Christ in his humanity. Finally, and most specifically, to invoke God in baptism, the Lord's Prayer, and the Lord's Supper is to correspond to God in Christ by following his example and instruction. Beyond the various ways in which the 'vertical' act of invocation is itself the basic form of correspondence, there are also the different kinds of 'horizontal' action which correspond to different forms of invocation. Some of these Barth discusses in the sections

---

[37] *KD* ii/2 was published in 1942; *Christliche Ethik* in 1946.

[38] Karl Barth, 'Christian Ethics', in *God Here and Now*, trans. Paul van Buren (London: Routledge & Kegan Paul, 1964), 90–3.

of his exposition of the Lord's Prayer where the treats the first two petitions. Corresponding to the invocation of God to hallow his name—to make his self-declaration fully manifest—is the action of giving precedence to his Word over all other creaturely factors in the personal life of the individual, in the Church, and in the world; and corresponding to the invocation of God to cause his kingdom to come—to cause his righteousness to appear and dwell on a new earth under a new heaven—are the acts of revolting against the various lordless powers (political absolutism, Mammon, ideologies, and the chthonic forces) and of taking responsibility for the preservation and renewal, the deepening and extending, of the divinely ordained human safeguards of human rights, human freedom, and human peace on earth.

To correspond to God's gracious action in Christ means primarily to answer to God as Father by playing the child of God in invocation. But this crucial mode of correspondence presupposes another, in which the human being answers to God as Creator by playing the creature; and it is qualified by a third, in which the creaturely child of God answers to God as Redeemer by playing heir of eternal life.

One of the most remarkable features of Barth's concept of correspondence with the action of God in Christ is its difference from either the Roman Catholic notion of the *imitatio Christi* or the Anabaptist notion of Christian discipleship. In his exposition of what he means by 'correspondence' Barth makes almost no reference at all to the Passion of Christ and cites none of the versions of 'If any man would come after me, let him deny himself and take up his cross daily and follow me.'[39] Even in the 1928–9 lectures, where self-sacrifice is a prominent theme, he refers to this famous saying only once.[40] The later version of the treatise on the command of the Reconciler makes it implicitly clear why Barth avoids giving his concept of correspondence this focus: because he deems it inappropriate to characterize the life of God Incarnate by any one of its moments. Accordingly, he denies that the way of correspondence to God Incarnate can be identified with the way of the cross. As Barth explicitly rejects principial monasticism, so he implicitly rejects principial suffering. Self-sacrifice is not *the*

---

[39] Matt. 16: 24, Mark 8: 34, Luke 9: 23. I rely here on the index of Scripture references provided in *CL*.

[40] Mark 8: 34, in *Ethics*, trans. G. W. Bromiley (New York: Seabury 1981), 328.

principle of Christian life. There is no such thing. And for the very same reason, in spite of his belief that God's action in Jesus expels the use of coercive and lethal force to the very margins of possibility as far as God's commanding is concerned, he denies that 'following' Jesus entails principial pacifism.[41]

The methodological reason for the different moral conclusions at which Barth arrives is that, according to him, the normative 'story' to which human conduct should correspond does not comprise an extract from Jesus' life or a refrain in it, but a theological summary of it. Barth does not move from epitomical or characteristic acts of Jesus to moral prescriptions. Instead, he moves from the Bible directly to a general theological description of God's action in Christ—a judgement about *the* 'story' or meaning or message of the Bible—or to some very fundamental theological proposition, and it is from these that he draws moral conclusions. Given Barth's judgement, which is surely correct, that the Bible intends to point us to God in Christ before it tells us how to live, to speak about the law only firmly in the context of the Gospel; and given his judgement (surely also correct) that the Bible does not present us with a single theological or ethical system, his method of deriving moral propositions from theological rather than biblical ones is well conceived.

So the role that Scripture plays in Barth's ethics is not direct: he does not derive moral propositions straight from the Bible. But, for that matter, he does not derive theological propositions straight from the Bible either. In the *Church Dogmatics* the main text comprises discourse of the theological or theologico-ethical rather than an exegetical kind. Exegesis does occur, with notable regularity and sometimes at very remarkable length,[42] but invariably in the small print.[43] It therefore has the function of substantiating or grounding theological and ethical statements already formulated. But it would be quite wrong to suppose that, since exegesis is introduced only to support a given theological or ethical statement, Scripture has no creative influence over the original

---

[41] *CD* iv/2: 550.

[42] See e.g. Barth's exegetical discussion of the moral status of the 'people' or 'nation' in *CD* iii/4: 309–23.

[43] In the *Church Dogmatics* Barth consigned exegetical, historical, and critical discussion, not to foot- or endnotes, but to passages of small print, sometimes the length of a short paragraph, sometimes running for twenty or more pages, which frequently interrupt the main text.

formulation of such statements. The fact that theological or ethical propositions are presented in advance of their exegetical grounds is no sufficient reason for supposing that those grounds were marshalled only after the propositions had been formulated. But even if they had been assembled afterwards, that in itself is no reason to suppose that they are tendentious; for they may articulate an inchoate intuition that has inspired and guided the process of theological or ethical formulation. Besides, unless we are going to deny the truth of theological and ethical statements simply because they are compatible with the biblical text rather than repetitions of it or logical derivates from it, then we do not need to insist that Scripture always play a creative role in theology and theological ethics. It should be quite sufficient that sometimes its part is purely critical.

Barth's consignment of his exegesis to the small print, then, is in itself no indication of a casual, self-justifying use of Scripture in his dogmatics and ethics. Certainly, there are occasions when the moral logic of his dogmatic premises unfolds with such momentum that exegesis appears to receive short shrift. So, for example, he moves from the creation of human being in the image of the triune God, through humanity as fellow-humanity, the male-female relationship as the archetypal sphere of fellow-humanity, the disobedience of the principial self-containment and self-sufficiency of the sexes, to 'the physical, psychological and social sickness, the phenomenon of perversion, decadence and decay' that is homosexuality.[44] In his discussion of homosexuality as such, which is very brief, Barth only refers to one biblical passage, Romans 1: 25–7:

In Romans 1 Paul connected it [homosexuality] with idolatry, with changing the truth of God into a lie, with the adoration of the creature instead of the Creator (v. 25). 'For this cause God gave them up unto vile affections: for even their woman did change the natural use into that which is against nature: and likewise also the men, leaving the natural use of the woman, burned in their lust one toward another; men with men working that which is unseemly, and receiving in themselves the recompense of their error which was meet' (vv. 26–27). From the refusal to recognise God there follows the failure to appreciate man, and thus humanity without the fellow-man.[45]

---

[44] *CD* iii/4: 116–7, 165–6.   [45] Ibid. 166.

However, it is notable that Barth chose this biblical passage rather than any of the others directly relevant to the topic, for it is the only one that gives an account of the moral status of homosexuality in terms of theological anthropology.[46] Considered in that light, his selection appears less haphazard than might have been the case at first. For it may reasonably be presumed that he reckoned that the other moral condemnations and prohibitions of homosexuality in the Bible find their rationale at the level of a theological understanding of human being; and that Romans 1: 25–7, therefore, offers the most enlightening biblical statement on the matter.

Moreover, it would be a mistake to suppose that the logic by which Barth arrives at his judgement about homosexuality from his theological concept of humanity proceeds without serious regard for the witness of the Bible. For his assertion that the interrelationship between man and woman is the type and norm of fellow-humanity is explicitly grounded in Genesis 1. 27 ('So God created man in his own image, in the image of God he created him; male and female he created them'), which he interprets as meaning that human being is the image of God in that being in the differentiated relationship between man and woman mirrors the God who is not solitary but triune.[47] This interpretation he later corroborates by referring to 1 Corinthians 11: 11 ('Neither is the man without the woman, neither the woman without the man, in the Lord'), which he also uses to substantiate his inference that 'in obedience to the divine command, there is no such thing as a self-contained and self-sufficient male life or female life'.[48] So although Barth only makes direct reference to a single biblical passage in his discussion of homosexuality, his employment of Scripture there is not as casual and offhanded as it might seem at first. For it is clear that the logic by which he reaches his moral conclusion about homosexuality from theological premises is decisively directed by his exegesis of Genesis 1: 27 and his corroborative interpretation of 1 Corinthians 11: 11, and it is also clear that the conclusion itself is corroborated by Romans 1: 25–7. It remains true, however, that the level at which Scripture exercises its influence here is theological rather than directly ethical.

[46] Cf. Gen. 19; Judg. 19: 22–30; Lev. 18: 22, 20: 13; 1 Cor. 6: 9–10; 1 Tim. 1: 9–10.
[47] *CD* iii/4: 116.   [48] Ibid. 144–5, 163.

In part, this is no doubt due to Barth's concern that the Bible should not be used moralistically, simply or merely as a source-book of moral rules. But, more deeply and positively, it is surely also due to his conviction that Christian ethics should not proceed by using the Bible arbitrarily, which would be the case if it were built upon isolated and historically relative commands and prohibitions scattered throughout its diverse materials. Barth correctly judges that, in order to be coherent and rational, Christian ethics must develop under the direct control of dogmatics rather than of the Bible itself. The Bible's role is primarily that of shaping and monitoring the development of dogmatics, and only then of monitoring the movement from dogmatics to ethics.

That having been said, it must be admitted that there are moral issues other than homosexuality in relation to which Barth engages much more thoroughly in the exegesis and interpretation of relevant biblical texts. Take, for example, his treatment of divorce, in the course of which he substantiates his position with an exegesis of Mark 10: 9 and Matthew 19: 6 that is biblically circumspect; or, better, take his exegetical treatment of the claim of the 'people' or 'nation' to be a created order, which runs to over fourteen pages, most of them preoccupied with Genesis 10 and 11.[49] This suggests that there may be a third reason for Barth's comparatively thin exegetical treatment of homosexuality: that it seemed to him that the Bible's witness on this matter is unequivocal.

What are we to make, however, of Barth's discussions of other moral issues which include no exegetical consideration—indeed, no reference to Scripture—at all: for example, abortion, euthanasia, and war? Again, there are reasons why we should decline to read this fact as expressive of a casual regard for the moral authority of the Bible. Primarily, we should decline because Barth's consideration of the various species of homicide occurs only at the end of an extensive discourse on the duty to respect and protect human life. As usual, this discourse is predominantly dogmatic; but Scripture nevertheless plays a vital role in it. Its fundamental premiss is that God has unequivocally and fully sided with human life in the incarnation of his Word, Jesus Christ. From this it follows, according to Barth, that 'respect to due to it, and, with

---

[49] Ibid. 204–6, 309–23.

respect, protection against each and every callous negation and destruction'.[50] So the first contribution that Scripture makes to the general consideration of the moral status of human life is the support it gives to the doctrine of God's incarnation in Jesus Christ. But that is by no means all. It makes a second, directly ethical contribution in the form of the Sixth Commandment (Exod. 20: 13, Deut. 5: 17). Barth does not open his discussion with this for the good reason that it is negative and defensive in form, and presupposes a positive regard—a respect—for human life as a loan given by God for a special purpose. Therefore he judges that 'we shall better understand the negative expressed in this [the Sixth] command if we first turn our attention to the positive fact which, although not expressed, is undoubtedly contained in it'.[51] However, when he comes to discuss the protection of life that is entailed by respect for it, he begins with an interpretation of Exodus 20: 13. It is true that his interpretation is governed by a theological concept; namely, of human life as a loan from God whose protection by humans is properly subject to God's will and is therefore not absolute. But Barth provides convincing exegetical support for such a reading: most obviously the fact that the Sixth Commandment is clearly not a prohibition of every kind of extinction of human life by human decision and action, but only of 'murder'.[52] At this point scriptural exegesis makes its third contribution to Barth's general discussion of the moral claims of human life by substantiating what characterizes the murderous extinction of human life, and what distinguishes its legitimate or commanded taking: wilfulness, wantonness, callousness, and malice in the case of the first; rarity in the case of the second.[53]

Set against this background, the lack of any exegetical moment in Barth's treatment of abortion, euthanasia, and war becomes less grave. Its gravity is further reduced when we recall that the Bible has no direct comment to make on euthanasia, virtually none to make on abortion, and little *moral* comment to make on war. It is true that Barth's handling of war naturally depends decisively on a theology of the State, to the consideration of which the Bible has a considerable body of relevant material. But the absence of exegetical small print here may be explained by Barth's intention

---

[50] Ibid. 415–23 (abortion), 423–7 (euthanasia), 450–70 (war).
[51] Ibid. 397.   [52] Ibid. 344.   [53] Ibid. 397–400.

to reserve the full presentation of his theology of the State for
the ethical conclusion to the doctrine of reconciliation. In sum,
there are particular reasons for the lack of direct reference to the
Bible in, or of an exegetical component to, Barth's discussion of
these three moral issues.

Barth's notion of correspondence to God's action in Jesus Christ
differs from classic notions of the *imitatio Christi* and Christian
discipleship in its indirect method of moving from Scripture to
ethics. It also differs in the very low level of specificity that
characterizes its moral conclusions. In his discussion of passages
in the Epistles of the New Testament that speak of the imitation of
Christ Barth acknowledges that they speak of definite acts as well
as attitudes.[54] But he then proceeds to summarize them entirely
in terms of the latter: 'singlemindedness', 'readiness', 'kindness',
'humility', 'love'. In his essay 'Christian Ethics' there is some
exposition of the moral content of correspondence to God in
Christ in terms of action—forgiving others and putting oneself at
their disposal—but only of the most general kind. And when, in
the special ethics of the *Church Dogmatics*, Barth does stoop to
speak in terms of kinds of action, as distinct from attitudes and
manners of action, he declines to venture very far up the ladder of
specificity. The reason for this rather frustrating vagueness is, of
course, Barth's suspicion of moral rules and their proclivity to
become the legalistic heart and soul of ethics.

This prompts us to ask how Barth deals with morally prescriptive material in the Bible that appears in the form of rules or
'laws'—pre-eminently, the Decalogue and the Sermon on the
Mount. His opening move is to tell us that these should be understood in terms of the 'historical pictures' of divine commanding
and human responding that the Bible provides.[55] Barth acknowledges that these texts do not appear to be concerned with the
particular responses of particular people to *ad hoc* commands of
God, but rather with certain possible kinds of action on the part of
all people; and he also acknowledges that they appear to present
God's command in the form of general principles and rules. But,
Barth tells us, this appearance is deceptive; for the Decalogue and
the Sermon on the Mount are actually 'collections or summaries'
of particular instances of divine commanding. They comprise

[54] *CD* ii/2: 578.   [55] Ibid. 675–6.

'comprehensive demands' addressed to the people of God. In no way at all do they obscure or detract from the event of God's personal address to the individual and the individual's definite response to God, but they do set that encounter in the context of the Church. What Barth seems to mean by this is that these comprehensive demands refer us to the divine Commander as the one who has graciously elected, separated, and gathered his people, and so discloses the invariable theological 'background' or 'framework' of every individual event of encounter. But, more than this, they go some way toward specifying God's command by stating in definite, albeit general, terms 'everything which God requires from the individual'. In this sense Barth is happy to describe them as 'proclamations of law' (*Gesetzproklamationen*).[56]

Accordingly, Barth insists that the Decalogue should be interpreted as part of the whole corpus of ordinances given Moses for the concrete shaping of the people's life in the presence of God. Noting that it contains no positive commands, he describes it as serving to define the sphere of God's dealings with his people in negative terms by indicating what a member of God's people must not do under any circumstances. This definition is permanently valid: 'everything that the true God, the founder and Lord of this covenant [of grace], has commanded and forbidden, or will command and forbid, is to be found within the framework of the programme of all His decisions and purposes as contained in the Decalogue.' But the latter, he reminds us, is still only a framework, not the real history.[57]

As with the Decalogue, Barth insists that the Sermon on the Mount should be read in terms of its place in the history of divine grace, which in its case is the coming of God's kingdom in the person of Jesus Christ. So understood, the Sermon may be seen to reveal what is concealed in the Decalogue, to presuppose what it awaits. For it defines the sphere where the coming of the kingdom of God is proclaimed and heard and authentic. It sets the order that constitutes the life of the people of God in the light of its fulfilment by God in his Christ for the salvation of humankind. Therefore this life-order is to be understood as defining the sphere within which people cling to the life of obedience lived out on their behalf by Jesus and use the grace that he shows them. It

[56] Ibid. 681–3 (*KD* ii/2: 762).   [57] Ibid. 683–6.

defines the sphere in which they live with Jesus as their Lord. Unlike the Decalogue, the Sermon on the Mount clearly shows that a life lived from, and of, and with the grace of God is not just the omega but the alpha of the divine demand. Barth concedes that it denotes modes of conduct that can become possible and necessary even in their literal sense for the followers of Jesus, but he (correctly) denies that it provides a complete picture of the Christian life. It addresses only a limited range of problems, and that in predominantly negative fashion. Indeed, its design in addressing such matters is not at all to give moral guidance in the form of rules, but to give examples of Jesus' 'directions' and thereby to offer a picture of the person of Jesus himself. The primary purpose of these directions is to set 'the dark text of our lives' in the light of our fulfilment in Jesus, to have us pray with him, and thereby to have us enter with him under the order of grace.[58] But beyond this they do indicate the 'prominent lines' along which the commanding of Jesus always moved *and always moves* in relation to individuals. These lines agree that the command of Jesus always calls us 'to make a particular penetration of the front of general action and abstention of others; to cut loose from a practical recognition of the legalism determined by the dominion of worldly authorities'.[59] One of these prominent lines, for example, is the attestation of the kingdom of God as the end of 'the fixed idea of the necessary and beneficial value of force'.[60] Given faith in the fatherly protection of God, force brought against oneself is no longer to be feared but suffered confidently, and the use of force against others is to be renounced. Still, Barth forbids us to treat this or any other 'prominent line' of Jesus' commanding as a *nova lex*. We are not to use them as moral blueprints to reproduce simply and directly the biblical pictures of Christian discipleship. Certainly, the 'correlated picture' composed by the 'prominent lines' ought to impress itself upon us because the call of discipleship as it comes to us will always be shaped by it. Nevertheless, the particular context of the call here and now is not fixed by the particular content there and then. The commanding of the living Lord is not 'confined to the pictures'[61] of his previous commanding, even though there will be good reason for suspicion

---

[58] Ibid. 686–98.   [59] *CD* iv/2: 546–7.   [60] Ibid. 549–50.

[61] Ibid. 552. Geoffrey Bromiley's translation of 'eingeschloßen in die Bilder' (*KD* iv/2: 625) as 'moves only in the circle' is too loose.

if we think that what may be required of us is 'something less, easier, or more comfortable' than what was required of the biblical disciples. Therefore, for example, the 'prominent line' of the renunciation of force is not to be regarded as a general rule. It does not require Christians to be pacifists in principle, though it does imply a heavy presumption in favour of Christians being pacifists in practice.[62]

Barth prefers to describe the function of the prominent lines indicated by the Sermon on the Mount as that of making us familiar with the voice of the commanding Lord.[63] They help us to recognize the Spirit; and it is because it is 'the law of the Spirit of life' that the Sermon has permanent validity as 'a constant direction to new and particular obedience on the lines it lays down'.[64] Indeed, he writes of both the Decalogue and the Sermon on the Mount that they are 'ordinances with which a man must be familiar in order to be able to hear, and actually to hear, the decrees of God which concern his [man's] actual life . . . They prepare the way for that openness of heart which . . . has to be demonstrated and realized in a specific obedience which is always new.'[65]

Barth's treatment of the biblical texts that make ethical prescriptions in the form of rules or laws confirms what his notion of correspondence suggests: that he was inclined to see the Bible's main contribution to Christian ethics in its revelation of theological reality rather than in any direct revelation of morality.[66] In what he affirms here, if not in what he denies, Barth approximates an emphasis common in Christian ethics today.[67] Where he diverges from some instances of this emphasis is in his identification of the theological reality that the Bible reveals. For example, he shares with Thomas Ogletree the understanding that the Bible's meaning lies beyond the text in its referent. The Bible reveals primarily by indicating reality. But for Ogletree the referent of the text is a kind of natural moral law—'the constitutive structures of the life-world'

---

[62] Ibid. 550.   [63] Ibid. 552.   [64] *CD* ii/2: 669.   [65] Ibid. 700.

[66] To use Gustafson's distinction ('Christian Ethics in America', in *Christian Ethics and the Community* (Philadelphia: Pilgrim Press, 1971)).

[67] See e.g. Verhey, *The Great Reversal*, 176–7; Bruce C. Birch and Larry L. Rasmussen, *Bible and Ethics in the Christian Life* (rev. edn., Minneapolis: Augsburg, 1989), 14, 32, 161, 181, 184–6; Curran, 'Dialogue with the Scriptures', 62; Hauerwas, 'The Moral Authority of Scripture', 57–9.

which are 'more elemental than social, economic, and political arrangements as such'[68]—whereas for Barth it is the living God who has elected humanity from eternity in Jesus Christ. The significance of this difference is that, for Barth, the Bible leads to an ethics at whose heart stand acts of prayer and worship, while in Ogletree's summary of the Bible's ethical contribution specifically religious acts go entirely unmentioned.

With Stanley Hauerwas Barth agrees that the Bible contributes to Christian ethics through its basic 'story'. But whereas for Barth the biblical story is significant in its reference to the reality of the living God, for Hauerwas its importance lies immediately in its sociological function in forming the identity of the Christian community and thereby providing the rationale of its morality. As a consequence, the Bible's contribution to Christian ethics turns out to be the provision of a theological vision of reality that legitimizes a distinctively Christian ethic in which acts of prayer and worship feature only incidentally.

It has been shown that Barth conceived the Bible's primary ethical contribution as theological in content. But that in itself does not settle the question of where he stands in the debate about the Bible's role in furnishing Christian ethics with moral rules. Would he have agreed with Allen Verhey that it is simply inappropriate to enquire of Scripture at the level of moral rules?[69] Or would he have gone as far as James Childress in contending for a biblical contribution at the level of rules too?[70]

We have noted how Barth resists the use of the Bible simply as a resource-book of moral rules, and how he prefers to speak of its role as that of making us familiar with the character of God and his will—of preparing us to hear God's command—by presenting us with 'stories' of divine commanding and human responding; and we have noted his corresponding interpretation of the Decalogue and the Sermon on the Mount, not as codes of moral law, but as 'collections or summaries' of such 'stories'. However, at the same time we have also noted that Barth concedes that these 'summaries' are not haphazard but state in general terms 'everything which God requires from the individual',[71] even going so far

---

[68] Thomas Ogletree, *The Use of the Bible in Christian Ethics* (Oxford: Blackwell, 1984), 7.   [69] Verhey, *The Great Reversal*, 176–7.
[70] James Childress, 'Scripture and Christian Ethics', *Interpretation*, 34/4 (Oct. 1980), 371–80.   [71] *CD* ii/2: 682.

as to call them 'proclamations of law'.[72] If we were tempted then to think that, in spite of much that he says and with obvious reluctance, Barth ultimately recognizes that the Bible does proffer rules and, indeed, comprehensive sets of rules, then his discussion of the duty to protect human life should encourage us to succumb to the temptation.

It is true that he tells us that the duty to protect human life is not absolute, since human life is not a human property but a divine loan that may be recalled at any moment; and that his description of the rule expressed by the commandment 'Thou shalt not kill' as being subject to unpredictable exceptions is redolent of the Occamist notion of moral rules being susceptible of suspension at the divine pleasure.[73] Closer inspection, however, discovers the elements of a more rational account. Barth makes it quite explicit that God could never command the wilful, wanton, callous, or malicious taking of human life; and in that the Sixth Commandment only prohibits that species of killing, he implies that a divine command would never contradict it.[74] He thereby implicitly treats the Sixth Commandment as an absolute rule in the sense that it holds in all *appropriate* cases. Unfortunately, Barth obscures this logic by insisting that the command to protect life is unconditional—that is, applies in *all* cases—but that 'protection' has its 'inner norm' in the will of God.[75] In other, voluntarist words, God decides what protection means and involves; and although it usually means what we assume it to mean, sometimes it means something quite extraordinary (even nonsensical). This account leads Barth into the logically awkward position of having to describe instances of divine commanding to take life as unusual forms of the absolute divine command to protect it. Although this need not be logically incoherent in cases of abortion or self-defence where one life must taken if another's is to be saved, it is nonsense in other cases.

A little later, in his discussion of killing in self-defence, Barth acknowledges that the Bible not only refers us to the person of the Commander, but also presents us with moral rules. Writing of the sayings of the New Testament about not resisting evil, especially those in the Sermon on the Mount (Matt. 5: 38–42), he says that they are

---

[72] Ibid. 683.   [73] *CD* iii/4: 397–8.   [74] Ibid. 398.   [75] Ibid. 397.

among those of which it is said that 'they shall not pass away'. For they do not merely express the well-meant exaggeration of humanitarianism, nor do they simply constitute a special rule for good or particularly good Christians. They declare the simple command of God which is valid for all men in its basic and primary sense, and which is to be kept until further notice. . . . They give us the rule whereas the rest of our discussion can deal only with exceptions.[76]

Here, as elsewhere, Barth speaks of provisional rules, which are subject to 'border-line' cases and so hold only 'until further notice'. His concern, as we have already sought to explain, is to exclude a concept of ethics as a self-contained, autonomous set of logical operations, for which God is quite dispensable in practice if not in theory. However, as we have argued in Chapter 1, it would have enhanced the coherence of Barth's own account had he spoken of rules which are absolute in the sense of always holding in all appropriate cases; and had he acknowledged that such a concept of rules is quite compatible with an understanding of ethics as both rational and open.

Barth's reluctance to admit the rule-proffering role of the Bible was not, however, just an expression of his general resistance to autonomous ethics. It was also the negative side of his affirmation of the priority of the human being's relationship with the living God, of her participation in the history of God's covenant of grace, of her faithful response to Jesus Christ. Therefore, before we look to the Bible to find out what we ought to do, Barth would have us look to it to find out who God is, and therefore who we are and what set of dispositions is appropriate to our real (as opposed to delusory) identity. We should look to it first as the occasion *par excellence* for meeting God. Only then, but then certainly, may we read the Bible for moral (in the narrow sense) guidance. But even then we must not read it simply for its express moral prescriptions and prohibitions, for it also guides—and guides more inspirationally—through its stories. And when we do read the Bible for its moral rules, we must not read it as if it were a complete and comprehensive ethical system, as if its various rules did not need to be brought into coherent and mutually qualifying relationship with one another, and this at a dogmatic and not just an ethical level. For all these reasons Barth was reluctant to speak

[76] Ibid. 430.

too soon of the Bible as a source of moral rules. But once the requisite qualifications had been made and repeatedly underscored, he gingerly acknowledged that, in addition to everything else, the Bible also provides us with prescriptions and prohibitions of general validity.

In the course of our discussion of the role of the Bible in Barth's ethics we have noted how Scripture plays its part either indirectly through dogmatics, or directly but under dogmatic supervision.[77] Does this mean that Scripture is necessarily manipulated or exploited by a particular dogmatic system? Not necessarily, for it is perfectly possible for someone who seeks to make moral sense of the Bible in terms of a dogmatic system—and there is no other way of making adequate sense of it—to let Scripture question and challenge that system and its ethical implications. If the business of making moral sense of the Bible through dogmatics is performed with appropriate humility and docility, then there will be occasions when it is patent to the interpreter that the dogmatic system as it stands hinders the text from speaking its own moral language; and on such occasions the humble and docile interpreter will react by setting about the task of revising her dogmatics.

In the case of Barth's own dogmatics the basic hermeneutical principle to which it gives rise is that of the normative priority of the New Testament to the Old. Both are witness to the revelation of God in Jesus Christ, but the latter is the witness of expectation and preparation whereas the .former is the witness of recollection and accomplishment.[78] Here we have a canon within the Canon which is of impeccable Protestant pedigree, and has obvious Christological grounding. Unlike Luther, however, Barth does not correlate the Old Testament to the Law, and the New to the Gospel. The dialectic of Law and Gospel is operative in both Testaments, but in the New the priority of Gospel to Law is unequivocally established. So Barth's mutual ordering of the Testaments does not mean that the Old is surpassed in the sense of annulled or displaced. What it means is that the Old must be

[77] The propriety of the dogmatic mediation of Scripture's contribution to ethics is affirmed by one eminent biblical scholar: 'It .[the Bible] can only be read as presenting a coherent and self-consistent "message" or set of "rulings" on any subject if it is placed within some corpus of belief much more systematic and well-articulated than it is itself' (John Barton, 'The Place of the Bible in Moral Debate', *Theology* (May 1985), 206). [78] *CD* i/2: 481.

interpreted and, if need be, qualified by the New. One material example of this may be found in Barth's discussion of killing. Here he notes that the Old Testament prohibits murder but not the taking of human life as such, and that the New Testament does not contradict it. But, he says,

there can be no doubt that the protection of human life against wilful extinction has acquired in the New Testament, on the one hand through the incarnation, through the identity of the actualised kingdom of God with the Son of Man, and on the other through His crucifixion for the sins of the world, a severity and emphasis which compel us, when we ask concerning our own conduct, to push back the frontier between the *ultima ratione* [*sic*] and forbidden murder. The difference between the frequency with which the Old Testament counts on the exceptional case [of just killing] and the rarity with which it occurs in the New is quite striking even within or in spite of the basic perception common to both.[79]

Another example of the New Testament's qualification of the Old, and a stronger one, is to be found in Barth's well-known discussion of marriage. There he argues that the normative status of marriage in the Old Testament was based on 'the necessity to procreate imposed by the history of salvation prior to the appearance of the Messiah'. With the birth of the Christ, however, this necessity has fallen away, and with it the obligatory character of the married state.[80]

Although it is true to say that the New Testament acts as a canon within the Canon in Barth's ethics, it is not enough to stop there. For that would be to imply that the New Testament is a simple unit which speaks with a single, undifferentiated voice; which is not the case. We must go one step further, then, and ask, What is the canon by which the canon within the Canon is interpreted? The fullest answer to this question lies in the first three, dogmatic parts of volume iv of the *Church Dogmatics*. In summary form, it is this: the salvific work of God in Jesus Christ as broadly conceived by classical orthodoxy. In the end, for Barth, the canon by which the Bible is interpreted is the Christological 'story' as narrated by Nicaea and Chalcedon.

---

[79] *CD* iii/4: 400.   [80] Ibid. 143–4.

4

THE ECCLESIAL MATRIX
OF ETHICS AND CHARACTER

I

The Word of God commands us through Scripture, but not as we sit in splendid and decidedly ungodlike isolation. It commands us invariably in the context of the Church; and by 'Church' here is meant primarily the Christian community. That it does so is no accident, for it belongs to its very nature to create 'moral fellowship' (*sittliche Gemeinschaft*). As Barth would have it, the Word of God is the foundation of (real or true) human being, which is being in open encounter with others. Every hearer of this Word necessarily finds herself in a situation of subordination to the authority of God and subjection to his judgement. She cannot but identify herself as sinful creature. Moreover, she is forced to relinquish a certain kind of sinful stance—indeed, the basic kind.

For since the command of God is the command of his Word, and since his Word is that by which he has graciously reconciled humankind to himself in spite of their sinfulness, it necessarily undermines any inclination of the part of its hearers to assume an identity of moral self-righteousness by launching moral crusades against others. By nature it subverts the kind of moral autonomy in which 'I confront [others] . . . as one who is right, wanting to break over them as the great crisis.'[1] It overcomes the radical, absolute division which reigns in situations where 'at bottom no one understands the language of others because he is too much convinced of the soundness of his own seriously to want to understand others'.[2] By its command the Word of divine justification

---

[1] *CD* iv/1: 451.   [2] Ibid. 447.

establishes human justice in the sense of right relations between reconciled sinners.[3]

These relations consist, in the first (and negative) place, in the refusal to stand over one's fellows in final judgement. But, positively, they also consist in dialogue. For the command of God's Word judges the sinful and anti-social pretensions of his creatures in order to establish real humanity, which is human 'being in the openness of one to the other with a view to and on behalf of the other'. In practice this takes the basic form of mutual speech and hearing, the mutual offering and acceptance of the objective self as 'new and strange and different', mutual correction, and dialogue.[4]

The Word of God establishes among its hearers a fellowship of open and critical dialogue. Accordingly, it is as members of that fellowship that it addresses individuals: 'the Word of God is not spoken to individuals, but to the Church of God and to individuals in the Church.'[5] Therefore,

> it may well be the case—indeed it will always be so—that one man has the task of interfering in respect of the conduct of another, that with the great or little authority and knowledge which he has in relation to the other he must warn him very concretely and particularly about this or that mode of behaviour or act, or vice-versa spur him to do it . . . that here and now the command of God must be proclaimed by one man to another who must hear it through him; that the very case of conscience in which each must act for himself means for both that they should talk and listen to each other. It can please the Holy Spirit—and it continually pleases Him—that not merely ethical advice and direction but the very command of God should be given in a very concrete form immediately from one man to another or to many others.[6]

The kind of dialogue which mediates the command of God has several distinctive characteristics. It proceeds in the context of the

---

[3] Barth asserts a causal connection between divine justification and *political* justice in his famous essay *Rechtfertigung und Recht* (ET: 'Church and State'). He could reasonably have made this connection in terms of relational justice in so far as just political structures and policies depend on a right regard for others on the part of those who erect and formulate them, respectively. Instead, however, he argues that the divine justification of humankind supports the authority of just law by providing 'the only protection against the sophisms and excuses of man, who is always so ready to justify himself and is always secretly trying to escape from true law' ('Church and State', in *Community, State and Church*, ed. Will Herberg (Gloucester, Mass.: Peter Smith, 1968), 141).

[4] *CD* iii/2: 250–9.   [5] *CD* i/2: 588.   [6] *CD* iii/4: 9.

practice of exegesis of Scripture[7] and of prayer for the Holy Spirit's illumination.[8] It culminates in the utterance by one person to another only of a *conditional* imperative, which may or may not be taken up and fulfilled by the unconditional command of God. It is not monologue in disguise: so 'he who takes the risk of counselling must be prepared to be counselled in turn by his brother if there is need of it'.[9] Nor is it the pseudo-dialogue of those who seek peace at the cost of conviction. Sometimes it will involve vigorous conflict in which we cannot and should not spare either ourselves or others. But conflict under the Word of God will never be more than relative. It will be conflict for the sake of fellowship and therefore in fellowship.[10] Those who disagree under the Word of God may fight hard, but they may not turn their backs on each other. They must practice the forgiveness of theological and ethical sins.[11] Finally, because the conflict in Christian dialogue is not radical it may and should be creative, stimulating dialectical progress.[12] But in order to be so, the interlocutors themselves must display a virtuous dialectic of courage and humility, resolution and modesty: courage and resolution in venturing a definite imperative; humility and modesty in recognizing its questionableness.[13]

God's command addresses individuals as they engage with their contemporaries in dialogue under the Word of God in Scripture. More often, however, it addresses them as they engage with authoritative voices from the past. 'The common action of hearing and receiving', Barth writes, 'is partly contemporary: it takes place among those who belong to the same age and period of the Church. But to a much greater extent it is non-contemporary: it takes place among those who belonged to an earlier and those who belonged to a later age in the Church, between the present age and those who preceded it.'[14] To debate within the Church is to debate

---

[7] *CD* i/2: 694–5; *The Church and the Political Problem of our Day* (London: Hodder & Stoughton, 1939), 84.

[8] Barth, 'The Church between East and West', in *Against the Stream*, ed. R. G. Smith, trans. E. M. Delacour and Stanley Godman (London: SCM, 1954), 127.

[9] Barth, 'The Gift of Freedom', in *The Humanity of God* (Richmond, Va.: John Knox Press, 1960), 86–7. Cf. *CD* i/2: 860.

[10] *CD* ii/2: 716–17.   [11] Barth, 'The Gift of Freedom', 94–5.

[12] Barth, 'Political Decisions in the Unity of Faith', in *Against the Stream*, 157–8.

[13] Ibid. 160–1.   [14] *CD* i/2: 588.

in the context of a tradition which finds expression in the historic confessions and the writings of Church fathers.[15] These traditional authorities, of course, are not binding. They deserve very careful attention, but not unthinking recitation.[16] For

the *ecclesia semper reformanda* should be constantly *en route* with its own questions, asking what the Holy Spirit and the Word of God require of us today, ready to revise its whole fund of knowledge and experience. It is founded on and preserved by the Word of God alone, and therefore it must be unconditionally faithful to this foundation in order to be free and flexible.[17]

It is clear that those recent interpreters who present Barth as an unorthodox disciple of the Enlightenment—as radically 'modern'—do have a worthwhile point to make.[18] He does relativize the heteronomy of the moral tradition of the Church, and with some ambiguity he does affirm the moral autonomy of the individual—that is, the power and right to discern and interpret the moral law (here, God's command) over and against the authority of that tradition. But he only *relativizes* it. The moral tradition of the Church may not be worthy of unconditional loyalty or unqualified conformity, but it does deserve a very serious hearing. It may not be lightly dismissed. Barth is not prepared to say simply that the command of God *is* mediated by ecclesial tradition. But he does seem to argue that we should approach it with something of an initial presumption that that is the case. Barth's attitude of critical loyalty to the Church's moral tradition under the Word of God characterizes him more as Protestant than as modern; although in his advocacy of open dialogue within that tradition, and in his ecumenical concept of it as plural, his Protestant character takes on a distinctly modern hue.

---

[15] Barth, 'The Gift of Freedom', 87, 94–5.

[16] Ibid. 93; 'The Christian Understanding of Revelation', in *Against the Stream*, 234.   [17] 'The Christian Understanding of Revelation', 234.

[18] See e.g. Trutz Rendtorff, *Theorie des Christentums: Historisch-theologisch Studien zu seiner neuzeitlichen Verfassung* (Gütersloh: Mohr, 1972). John Macken, SJ, rightly criticizes Rendtorff and other Idealist reinterpreters of Barth for disregarding Barth's insistence that human autonomy consists in responsiveness to the Word of God (*The Autonomy Theme in the 'Church Dogmatics'* (Cambridge: Cambridge University Press, 1990), 132, 133, 140).

II

Because of the crucial importance of the concept of personal encounter in Barth's theology, the ethical role of the Christian Church that receives most direct attention is that of making dialogue with others basic to the process of moral deliberation. But it is not the only ethical role that Barth attributes to the Church. Another one is that of comprising a school for the formation of character. This is a controversial assertion which will need some extensive justification; for there are some who doubt that Barth's ethics has any secure place for character and its formation at all.

Stanley Hauerwas, for example, argued in one of his earliest books, *Character and the Christian Life*, that Protestant ethics have tended to conceive of the human self as 'passive and atomistic', lacking duration and continuity, the capacity for growth, and a genuine power of self-determination.[19] This he attributed to the tendency to construe the moral life in terms of obedience to God's commands; for 'the logic of commands is the logic of imperatives directed to specific cases and practices', and it therefore obscures the fact that 'what is at stake in most of our decisions is not the act itself, but the kind of person we will be'.[20] In other words, because Protestant ethics is dominated by the concept of obedience to divine commands it neglects the dimension of moral character, which Hauerwas defined as the 'qualification of a man's self-agency through his beliefs, intentions, and actions, by which a man acquires a moral history befitting his nature as a self-determining being'.[21] On this score Hauerwas rated Barth relatively highly, showing that, in contrast to Bultmann, he does at least affirm the importance of the idea of character.[22] Nevertheless, in *Character and the Christian Life*, Hauerwas found Barth deficient in three major respects: in failing to show how and in what sense Christ forms the character of Christians;[23] in holding back from specifying Christian character in detail;[24] and in preferring to speak of the Christian life in terms of the repetition of the action

---

[19] Stanley Hauerwas, *Character and the Christian Life* (San Antonio: Trinity University Press, 1975), 3.
[20] Ibid. 8.   [21] Ibid. 13.   [22] Ibid. 157.   [23] Ibid. 171, 176.
[24] Ibid. 141, 141 n. 40, 157.

of obedience to God's commanding, rather than in terms of the development of character.[25]

Against this last criticism William Werpehowski has defended Barth in such a way as to move Hauerwas to revise his judgement. In his article 'Command and History in the Ethics of Karl Barth' Werpehowski argues that Barth's concentration on acts of obedience to God's command did not prevent him from providing a coherent account of the 'growth-in-continuity' of the self—the development of moral character—in terms of a theological concept of history. According to this concept, the character of the self and its growth are understood primarily in terms of its relationship with God.[26] In a recent essay Hauerwas has declared himself 'almost' convinced by Werpehowski that Barth's concentration upon divine command and human act does not entail a concept of the self as lacking continuity.[27] Nevertheless, Hauerwas's other original reservations persist. Although he has taken Werpehowski's point that the theological history of relationship with God *includes* and is *mediated by* secular history,[28] Hauerwas continues to find Barth's ethic haunted by an abstractness 'that gives his account of the moral life an aura of unreality'.[29] This abstractness he finds in Barth's characteristic tendency to avoid discussing normative ethical concepts (e.g. honour) in concrete terms, and also in his tendency not to provide an account of the means (e.g. the Christian community) by which character is formed.[30]

With a view to assessing Hauerwas's criticisms—and, indeed, Werpehowski's apology—we proceed now to present our own

---

[25] Ibid. 175, 175 n. 139, 176. In the new introduction to the 3rd printing of *Character and the Christian Life* (1985) Hauerwas withdraws none of his original criticisms. He does acknowledge, however, that Barth describes the Christian life in terms of the metaphor of 'journey' as well as in terms of hearing divine commands; and so he implies that a concept of the growth of character holds a more prominent place in Barth's ethics than he had thought at first (p. xxviii).

[26] William Werpehowski, 'Command and History in the Ethics of Karl Barth', *Journal of Religious Ethics*, 9/2 (Autumn 1981), 303.

[27] Stanley Hauerwas, 'On Honour: By Way of a Comparison of Barth and Trollope', in Nigel Biggar (ed.), *Reckoning with Barth* (Oxford: Mowbray, 1988), 148–9.

[28] Werpehowski, 'Command and History', 304–5; Hauerwas, 'On Honour', 147–8. The point that Werpehowski makes here is the subject of considerable explication by Ingolf Dalferth in his essay 'Karl Barth's Eschatological Realism', in S. W. Sykes (ed.), *Karl Barth: Centenary Essays* (Cambridge: Cambridge University Press, 1989), esp. 27–42.

[29] Hauerwas, 'On Honour', 147, 149.   [30] Ibid. 155, 169.

account of Barth's concept of character and its development. The first thing to be said is that the act of responding to God's command does not fill the whole of Barth's ethical stage. It may be the climax but it is not the whole story. In addition to acts of response, there are attitudes or dispositions. Indeed, as we have sought to show in Chapter 1, the main purpose of ethics in Barth's eyes is to dispose the human agent to hear and obey God's command by disclosing the theological history in which she stands, its implications for her self-understanding, and so her posture with regard to external reality. Symptomatic of this is the frequency with which Barth's ethical thinking expresses itself in dispositional language and the prominent part played throughout by such dispositions as openness, gratefulness, joy, courage, and modesty. Especially notable is the extent to which these dispositions function as criteria for judging whether an act is an act of obedience to an extraordinary command of God. Accordingly, whether or not someone is commanded to kill himself, in order to avoid betraying his friends and his cause and his faith, will be partly indicated by whether or not God gives him the freedom to do it 'joyfully, resolutely and with a good rather than a doubtful conscience'.[31] And again, whether or not someone stands in the rare situation of being commanded to have an abortion will be signalled in part by her capacity to venture such an act resolutely and joyfully.[32] Similarly, only those who have been granted freedom from 'the mere impulse of self-preservation, the mere instinct, emotion, interest and arbitrariness of primitive self-defense. . . . [and] the anxious assertion of their rights' could be divinely commissioned to oppose an unjust assailant with lethal force.[33] The criteriological decisiveness of disposition in Barth's ethics is made most dramatically clear, perhaps, in his famous judgement that, since the conspirators in von Stauffenberg's plot against Hitler's life were not disposed to act with absolute disregard for their own lives, they had 'no clear and categorical command from God to do it'.[34]

It is certainly not true, then, that Barth's conception of moral agency is simply atomistic, being exhausted in the event of hearing God's command and in the act of response to it. The responsive act, of course, is decisive. But it does not occur in a vacuum. Its

[31] *CD* iii/4: 412.   [32] Ibid. 423.   [33] Ibid. 435–6.   [34] Ibid. 449.

occurrence is considerably determined and its nature formed by the interplay of the set of dispositions that characterize the agent at the moment of action. Therefore it comprises a moment in a history; for the set of dispositions out of which I act in the situation before me now has been shaped and confirmed by the acts in which I have responded to similar situations in the past. As Barth puts it: 'There are no ... neutral points in time ... And in my present action, I in some sense recapitulate all my past, and anticipate my future conduct.... [T]his present decision stands in unbroken continuity with all my earlier decisions.'[35] It is noteworthy that although he acknowledges that an act in the present has a past which it 'recapitulates', Barth does not specify here how this takes place. He says only that it does so 'in some sense'. It could be argued that the past bears upon an act here and now simply through the range of objective possibilities open to the agent and determined in part by her previous acts. But the range of objective possibilities is determined in part by the set of subjective dispositions that characterize the would-be agent. The kind of person I am, with certain strengths and weaknesses, certain inclinations and aversions, makes me able to grasp some possibilities and not others. My subjective dispositions determine what is objectively possible *for me*. This Barth alludes to when he writes that

[a]s I reach the frontier and cross into the future, I am not a mere cipher, a blank sheet of paper. I am gifted and burdened, freed and enslaved, enriched and impoverished, credited and committed, strengthened and weakened, inclined, directed and determined, by the many earlier transitions I have made in the past and right up to this point. I am what all my past life has made me.... Whatever I may be and do and experience now, and whatever I shall be and do and experience after this Now, the prejudices and assumptions which I have brought from the past are in varying degrees significant for this Now and will continue to be so for my future.[36]

However, although Barth admits a concept of historically formed moral disposition, he nevertheless tends to avoid discrete discussion of it. The reason for this is his acute wariness of any way of thinking about the moral agent that leaves any room at all for supposing her being to be absolute. Barth is unwilling to let us forget even for a moment that the moral agent is always to some

---

[35] *CD* ii/2: 659.   [36] *CD* iii/2: 533.

extent constituted by her relationships. For this reason he prefers to speak of human being as a history rather than a state. For the idea of a state involves the idea of 'something completely insulated within the state in question', whereas the history of a being begins when 'something other than itself and transcending its own nature encounters it, approaches it and determines its being in the nature proper to it so that it is compelled and enabled to transcend itself in response and in relation to this new factor'.[37]

This is not at all to say that Barth reduces human being to the sum of its relations. There is undoubtedly a self which suffers encounter and which is the subject of its history: '[t]he concept of history . . . is introduced and achieved when something happens to *a being in a certain state.*'[38] Nevertheless, Barth is very keen not to speak about the human subject in such a way as to appear to condone the commonly received notion of an independent entity—an absolute substance—which simply 'possesses' certain 'properties'. Hence his reluctance to dwell on moral disposition, virtues, and character as such, and his correlative tendency to focus on the relationship of the human subject with what it encounters, whether actively conceived in terms of the subject's response or passively in terms of the object's impact.

In the Münster lectures on ethics, for example, Barth concludes each of the three parts of special ethics with a section on the kinds of human conduct in which God's command is fulfilled, and he says of these sections that, 'understood with a pinch of salt, this is our equivalent of teaching about "virtues"'.[39] The 'pinch of salt' here is revealing; for it refers to Barth's insistence that, although these 'virtues' describe 'a real attitude and action on man's part', they describe 'one which is in no sense man's own achievement, but which . . . is in the strictest sense a work, or rather *the* work of God on man'.[40] Here, the 'virtues' of faith, hope, and love may be human properties, but only in the sense of gifts. Indeed, in these lectures Barth makes a rather stronger claim when he writes that '[g]ood means *sanctified by God*'; that 'human action is good in so far as God sanctifies it'; and that '*sanctified* man . . . is the predicate and not the subject of the statements of theological ethics'.[41] The causation of good human conduct is not to be conceived in mech-

[37] Ibid. 158.   [38] Ibid. Author's emphasis.
[39] Barth, *Ethics*, trans. G. W. Bromiley (New York: Seabury, 1981), 61.
[40] Ibid. 59.   [41] Ibid. 16, 17, 54. Barth's emphases.

anical terms: for it is not the case that, once set in motion, human virtue thereafter proceeds under its own momentum. The gift here is not detachable from the Giver. Human virtue should not be thought of as possessed in any simple or absolute fashion. Rather, it is best understood as the symptom of a dynamic relationship with God. Only strictly in the context of the divine–human relationship was Barth willing to countenance talk of human 'virtue'. In his insistence on this point he may fairly be understood to be trying to take seriously the moral implications of St Paul's doctrine of participation in Christ, according to which 'there are Christians only in Christ and not in themselves'.[42]

Barth's caution with regard to talking about human virtue persisted, and was perhaps a little stronger, in the *Church Dogmatics*. There none of the three parts of special ethics were structured so as to culminate in the discussion of a peculiarly appropriate 'virtue'. Certainly, the first part is governed by the concept of freedom, which may be considered as a kind of a human disposition. But the second and crucial part of special ethics is governed by the concept of invocation, which was chosen deliberately because it refers to an action rather than 'a certain form of human life (which might be construed passively) and the disposition or attitude corresponding to it'.[43] Moreover, on the one occasion in the *Dogmatics* when Barth does discuss 'virtue' directly and explicitly, he does so under the rubric of 'vocation' and in terms of personal aptitude rather than moral goodness.[44]

Nevertheless, in the *Dogmatics* Barth remained willing to speak of human goodness and virtuous dispositions, subject to the condition laid down in the 1928–9 lectures: that the sanctificatory consequences of God's revelation to, and work in, humankind are not considered separately from that revelation and work themselves. The holy man must not be treated independently of the holy God. This is axiomatic for Barth's ethical programme in the

---

[42] Ibid. 14. Equally, Barth may be understood to be trying to take seriously the moral implications of Luther's doctrine of faith. In a discussion about the relationship between dogmatics and ethics, Barth complains of the ethics of Thomas Venatorius of Nuremberg (who was, ironically, a Lutheran) that 'faith is now understood as *virtus*, as the power of love and life in its "possessor" . . . The faith which was capable of being represented in this way was obviously something quite different from the true Reformation concept of faith as justifying solely by the power of its object' (*CD* i/2: 784).

[43] *CL* 42.   [44] *CD* iii/4: 624–6.

Dogmatics, according to which ethics and dogmatics must together comprise a unity:

What theology has to learn and teach with regard to the holy man can be derived only from the one book. In this book it is, of course, very emphatically a question of the holy man as well. But in this book the holy man has no independent existence. Therefore he never becomes an independent object of thought. He exists only in the course of the existence of the holy God and of the study of His speech and action.[45]

The full impact of this crucial methodological stipulation upon the concept of moral disposition becomes most clear in Barth's brief discussion of character in the *Church Dogmatics*, iii/4. Here character is defined as 'the particular form of life' which a person is commanded to attain: 'Character is the particular form in which each is commanded to be. It is his nature as disciplined by his being from God—disciplined in the sense of ordered, directed, restrained but also extended in its limits.'[46] It may not be immediately obvious that this is a *moral* concept at all, if what is moral is thought to be expressible always in terms of rules which bind universally in appropriate cases. Certainly, Barth speaks of character in terms which might be considered more vocational than moral:

No one should make more of himself than he is. Not all human possibilities are the possibilities of all, even though they may seem desirable to all. . . . On the other hand, no one should make less of himself than he is . . . Again—and this is perhaps the most urgent point—no one should try to be or pretend to be different from what he is. We must be careful not to become enamoured of the roles which we see others play even if they seem to be finer and more interesting than our own. We must play our own part, and this alone. A genuine chorister is better than a false soloist, and an honest pupil than a supposed master on his own responsibility; and in any case there are no good or less good roles before God but only the right ones as individually assigned by Him.[47]

However, as we have already seen, Barth does not recognize a fundamental distinction between the moral and the vocational. Certainly, he affirms that God's commanding may be expressed in terms of rules to a certain extent. So, for example, we may say that God always commands the preservation of the life of an unborn

---

[45] *CD* i/2: 790.   [46] *CD* iii/4: 388.   [47] Ibid. 388–9.

child except in rare cases where its life is pitted against its mother's. However, in such a case we cannot say that God always commands that the life of the child be taken. Here there is no rule. 'We cannot and must not maintain, on the basis of the command-ment,' Barth tells us, 'that the life and health of the mother must always be saved at the expense of the life of the child. There may well be mothers who for their part are ready to take any risk for their unborn children, and how can we forbid them to do so?'[48] But the fact that there is no rule does not mean that the decision is arbitrary and morally indifferent. One way or another, according to Barth, the mother is addressed by a divine calling which obliges just as much as any divinely sanctioned rule. The question of whether or not to obey this calling is a question of right or wrong. Obedience to a unique personal vocation is a moral matter. So the fact that 'character' is a matter of the unique form of life to which each individual is called by God does not make it amoral. God's calling has the form of a command. It obliges.

Now that we have clarified the moral status of Barth's concept of character, we may proceed to explore its relationship to the concept of moral disposition. The first thing to be said is that the divine call to a particular character occurs within, rather than apart from, the specific moral boundaries drawn by our knowledge of what God always commands. As we observed in Chapter 1, the event of the divine command—which is at heart a divine vocation—occurs in the space defined by moral rules. So the moral act of obedience to a unique divine calling presupposes conformity to the full array of such rules; and for Barth, as we have seen, these concern kinds of disposition at least as often as kinds of action. But if this concept of character presupposes a particular set of right moral dispositions, it also relativizes it. For it finds the heart of moral life, not in the inculcation of a set of normative dis-positions, but in the following of a highly personal but none the less obligatory vocation. One implication of this for the formation of moral dispositions is that it should not be regarded as a task to be undertaken directly and in abstraction from an individual's peculiar calling. For moral dispositions grow precisely as the indi-vidual engages concretely with the particular moral tasks that his vocation presents to him. Another implication is that moral

[48] Ibid. 421.

formation always lies in front of the moral agent, and never simply behind him. Each human being is called by his Creator to make of his life a particular and unique service. The fulfilment of this service comprises the moral character he is commanded to be, and its requirements determine at each point who he should become.[49] An individual, then, never already possesses his character but is always in the process of acquiring it in the course of the history of his life. Character is 'original' or 'natural' in the sense that it is the aim of our lives given us by our Creator from the beginning. But it is neither original nor natural in the sense that it is simply a given property, something to which we can appeal in order to claim exemption from all sorts of challenges and readjustments. Character is given primarily as an end, a *telos*, and not even as one whose nature may be fully grasped in advance:

It is to be noted that for all its distinctness the original character of each, as the discipline of his nature and distinctive moulding of his course of life in the sense described, is necessarily open, because his origin, the divine address and therefore the Thou as which man stands before God is not a dead but itself a living being and event. God lives, speaks and guides, and therefore man lives before God and his character has a novelty, in which his particularity is never merely present but always in process of coming, and will only be fully seen by man in the eternal consummation. If a man regards his character as a final magnitude which he can survey and dispose, and conducts himself accordingly—'I am made that way!' —he is again confusing it with his nature and himself, his soul and his small ego. The Thou–I, the soul that lives by the Spirit of God, the real self, is for all its continuity, discipline and moulding continually on the way to new shores, and will only have and know itself, take itself seriously and express itself on this voyage. For who really knows himself? Who has not continually to discover himself? Who will ever cease to do this? In this respect, too, we must consider the truth that 'it doth not yet appear what we shall be' (I Jn. 3. 2).[50]

This suggests that it is not quite enough to say that moral character is teleological in the sense that it is the unique end to which each human creature is called. Individual vocation needs to be located in the larger history of the redemption of all things, which will find its end in 'the eternal consummation'. Indeed, were it not for this location, character would have no hope of ever

---

[49] Ibid. 389–90.   [50] Ibid. 389.

finally acquiring its *esse*. Moral character is not only teleological but eschatological. The fulfilment of our reconciliation with God, and so of our divine vocation, lies in front of us, not behind us, and in God's hands, not ours. We *are* the children of God only as we trust the promise that he *shall* make us so. We possess our character as Christian, sanctified, holy, and therefore moral, only in hope. Our moral character is given, but only in faith.[51] In practice, therefore, it depends on acts of invocation in which we call upon God to make his future into our present.

Although it is true, as we have seen, that Barth recognizes the formative impact of the past upon the present, there is no doubt that his emphasis falls heavily upon the openness of the present to the future. The present may be defined by the past, but it is not imprisoned by it. It might seem that this orientation toward the future reflects an existentialist confidence in the capacity of the human agent to choose and realize himself afresh each moment.[52] But the real reason for it is theological, especially soteriological, and presupposes human impotence and the power of divine grace. For it is because the fulfilment of humankind's redemption lies in God's future that sinful humans are constantly being called and commanded and enabled by God to use the present to break free from their past. Because salvation is extrinsic to humankind, as regards its origin, it necessarily encounters humans in the form of judgement—in the critical form of a divine command.[53] It necessarily challenges them to change radically. As Barth writes of the call to Christian discipleship:

no matter how or when it is issued to a man, or whether it comes to him for the first time or as a second or third or hundredth confirmation, [it] is always the summons to take in faith . . . a definite first step. This step . . . is distinguished from every other step that he may take by the fact that in relation to the whole of his previous life and thinking and judgement it involves a right-about turn and therefore a complete break and new beginning. To follow Jesus means to go beyond oneself in a specific action and attitude, and therefore to turn one's back upon oneself, to leave oneself behind. . . . [I]t can never be a question of a routine continuation or repetition of what has hitherto been our customary practice. It always involves the decision of a new day; the seizing of a new opportunity which

---

[51] *CD* i/2: 784. Cf. *Ethics*, 34–6.   [52] See e.g. *CD* iii/4: 5–6.
[53] *CD* ii/2: 645.

was not present yesterday but is now given in and with the call of Jesus. Inevitably the man who is called by Jesus renounces and turns away from himself as he was yesterday.[54]

Were we to take a passage such as this at face value, then we would have to conclude that for Barth the past has simply a negative significance: it is that which we are called to leave behind us. There is, however, reason to read it as rhetoric. This is supplied by the fact that Barth provides us with other, more measured passages, where we are exhorted, not simply to abandon the past at every turn, but rather to subject it repeatedly to critical reflection:

What ought we to do? If the What? is seriously meant, every answer that we and others may have given is continually questioned again. It is not, of course, dismissed and effaced. We are never *tabula rasa*, and we cannot and must not try to make ourselves such. Integral to the humility in which we must ask what we are to do according to the divine command is the sober recognition that we always come from the school of the divine command and that we have not been in vain to that school, always bringing with us all kinds of more or less well-founded hypotheses and convictions that the command of God demands from us. ... If we ask seriously: What ought we to do?, the What? necessarily means that we are not complacent about ourselves, that we do not anticipate the answer in view of the continuity of our previous works, that under the guise and pretext of the What? we do not secretly ask: How can I progress further on the right path which I am, of course, already treading? ... When we honestly ask: *What* ought we to do?, we approach God as those who are ignorant in and with all that they already know, and stand in dire need of divine instruction and conversion. We are then ready, with a view to our next decision, to bracket and hold in reserve all that we think we know concerning the rightness and goodness of our past and present actions, all the rules and axioms, however good, all the inner and outer laws and necessities under which we have hitherto placed ourselves and perhaps do so again.[55]

'And perhaps do so again.' What we bring from the past, the moral wisdom which we have accumulated, the character we have formed, *may* prove valid again today. Indeed, the more often it has been exposed to critical reflection, 'the more surely will it again prove its value'.[56] We have not been to the school of the divine command in vain. Nevertheless, its reliability can never be more than provisional; and in the face of 'the great possibility of

[54] *CD* iv/2: 538.   [55] *CD* ii/2: 645–6.   [56] Ibid. 648.

the grace of God, that our own life and understanding can be made new and different', we need 'a complete openness'.[57]

For Barth, the formation of good character depends precisely upon our refusal to take the 'goodness' of our character as given. Indeed, it consists essentially in our *repeated obedience* to the command of God's grace and so to 'the discipline of the new beginning of our life and understanding'. There is continuity and growth in the moral life of the Christian, but only epiphenomenally, only as a by-product of our repeated obedience: 'The principle of necessary repetition and renewal, and not a law of stability, is the law of spiritual growth and continuity of our life.'[58] Our moral character exists only as it grows, and it grows only so long as we are engaged in taking the next step into God's future.

From the foregoing account it should be clear that Hauerwas is mistaken to suppose that, in speaking of the Christian life primarily in terms of the repetition of the action of obedience to God's command, Barth excludes the concept of the development of character. Werpehowski is quite correct to argue that Barth provides space for it in the larger context of a theological concept of history, making it strictly contingent upon the historically defined relationship between the human agent and God. It might be objected here, however, that Barth does not really have a concept of the *history* of such a relationship; for 'history' denotes the present as in some sense the culmination or, at least, the accumulation of the past, whereas Barth is forever insisting that in relationship to God the human task is always to return to the beginning. This objection, of course, is the same as that levelled by Hauerwas against Barth's concept of character; and our response here is the same as it was there. In his insistence that our duty in relation to God is always to start again, Barth was not at all denying that our relationship with God is formed by our past—that it has (in one sense) a particular history. Rather, he was asserting that we cannot presume upon the goodness or, at least, the sufficient goodness of what we bring from the past; and that, therefore, we must constantly start again in the sense of regularly laying all that we have accumulated open to divine judgement. Some—perhaps all—of it may pass muster. It may prove reliable enough to build upon. There may be progress, but only so long as our readiness to

---

[57] Ibid. 647.   [58] Ibid.

obey God's command and accept his judgement here and now is greater than our confidence in what we have achieved so far. For us to start again does not at all mean that we should always return to the same place, but that in different places we should be careful to return to the same posture—specifically, to our knees. Indeed, to begin again is the precondition of our progress, and so of our having (in another sense) a history.[59]

We have found Hauerwas's third criticism wanting. But how should we assess his second one, that Barth's discussion of Christian character hovers at a frustrating level of abstraction? To some extent this amounts to a complaint that Barth is not a novelist, and it is accordingly unfair.[60] Of course, a novel by Trollope would be more useful in the moral education of the young than selections from the *Church Dogmatics* on, for example, character or joy or honour. Of course, credible stories in which virtue is made attractive and vice ugly are more effective in fostering love for the good than tomes of systematic ethical discourse. Systematic ethics is generally a critical discipline, examining precisely what moral educational material takes for granted—for example, the order of moral authorities, ethical method, and moral norms. It is not primarily designed to inspire, to move its audience to love and hate rightly. So Barth must be readily forgiven for not doing something that he never intended to do. Moreover, he even deserves some credit for writing theological ethics in a manner that sometimes displays a remarkably fine feeling for the texture of moral life as lived in the flesh. Take, for example, his discourse on vocation in the final section of the first part of special ethics in the *Church Dogmatics*.[61]

Nevertheless, Hauerwas's complaint is not entirely wide of the mark. Barth does tend to discuss Christian character in rather

---

[59] James Gustafson proposes two ideal types of concept of the moral self. According to one, which he attributes to Schleiermacher, '[t]he self in its action expresses the personal history that it has accumulated through its past experiences and associations'; and according to the other, which he attributes to Kant, Barth, and the existentialists, 'the self in its action is a free self undetermined by its phenomenal history, facing an imperative or a command of God, an open present and future, and acting out of this freedom to determine the future' (*Christ and the Moral Life* (Chicago: University of Chicago Press, 1968), 93). Although we agree with Gustafson that Barth's stress lies on the indeterminateness of the moral self, we contend that it is qualified by a ready acknowledgement that such openness to the future is historically defined.

[60] Hauerwas, 'On Honour', 167.   [61] *CD* iii/4, s. 56. 2.

abstract terms. He never provides illustrative stories or cases. This Hauerwas originally attributed to the predominance in Barth's ethics of the concept of hearing God's command, and so he read it as evidence of the absence of a secure place for a concept of character. We have argued, however, that the concepts of hearing God's command and of moral character are quite compatible. So we are inclined to look for an explanation elsewhere. It could be argued that Barth's failure to depict the moral life of the Christian in detail may be accounted for simply in terms of the nature of his primary intentions and concerns. It could be argued, then, that in general Barth's main intention was to write a systematic theology, and that his main intention with regard to ethics was to build it strictly within the framework of that theology. Accordingly, his driving ethical concern was to derive basic ethical concepts from, or at least to ensure their qualification by, the tenets of Christian dogma; and not to depict the concrete texture of Christian life. In other words, the claim could be made that Barth deliberately limited his ethical scope to the level of general concepts, leaving to others the task of filling in the detail.

This would be a plausible argument, were it not for three contrary facts. The first is that Barth nowhere acknowledges a deliberate, economic restriction of his ethical scope. He never gives the impression of having said anything less than needed to be said. The second is that, at least in the first part of the *Dogmatics'* special ethics, he does avert his gaze from the theological ground of ethics and the religious heart of morality to deal with particular moral problems (albeit not very specifically). Then, third and most important, we know of one reason of principle why Barth would have deliberately eschewed depicting the Christian life in detail: his methodological axiom that, since Christian life has no independent existence, it should not become an independent object of thought.[62] The motive behind Barth's espousal of this principle is the belief that even to think of Christian life apart from the dynamic relationship with God that constitutes it is bound to lead to the supposition that such life is ontically absolute. There is no need to suppose that Barth held that thinking about something in abstraction from its relations of dependence ensues, by logical necessity, in the attribution to it of ontic independence.

[62] *CD* i/2: 790.

Barth's point need only be that, given certain human or cultural tendencies, such a movement is virtually certain. This is not adequately answered by pointing out that it is perfectly possible in general to consider something under one of its aspects without losing sight of the others. For Barth is not commenting on thinking in general, but on thinking about human goodness in particular, and his implicit premiss is that in respect of this particular object of thought (modern) human beings are especially susceptible of delusions of grandeur. A more pertinent answer to his position would seem to be that, even if the risk of distortion were as high as Barth believed it to be, the appropriate response would be to bracket any discrete description of the moral shape of Christian life with severe reminders that such a description has been abstracted from its primary religious substance—the dynamic relationship of the Christian subject to God in Christ. The fact that human thought is inclined to let the horizontal dimension obscure the vertical one surely calls for vigilance against intellectual myopia in considering the former, not for a policy of always refusing to regard it except from a safely remote distance.

There remains Hauerwas's first criticism, that Barth fails to show how and in what sense the moral character of Christians is formed. What Hauerwas has in mind here is only alluded to in *Character and the Christian Life*. There he speaks of character as comprising beliefs and reasons which order our desires and affections, and through them our actions;[63] and he thereby implies that it is formed at the level of beliefs and reasons. In the new introduction which he wrote in 1985, Hauerwas expressed some regret over the 'intellectualism' of this account.[64] But even in the original text there are hints of other dimensions. He tells us, for example, that 'to have Christian character is to have our "seeing" of the world directed by the fundamental symbols of the language of faith'; and that this character is not formed by 'logical deduction', but by 'association with the community that embodies the language, rituals, and moral practices from which this particular [i.e. the Christian] form of life grows'.[65] The aesthetic and communal dimensions of the formation of Christian character, to which these statements refer, receive fuller attention in other parts of

[63] Hauerwas, *Character*, 202–3. [64] Hauerwas, *Character* (1985), p. xxi.
[65] Hauerwas, *Character*, 203, 210.

Hauerwas's work.[66] There, their significance becomes clearer. In drawing attention to the aesthetic dimension, Hauerwas seeks to express several interrelated concerns. One is to assert that moral thinking proceeds more often by way of imagination than of logical deduction. Another correlative purpose is to point out that prior to particular moral beliefs and reasons there is 'story'. By 'story' Hauerwas refers to a basic vision or 'reading' of reality and in particular to the agent's corresponding understanding of herself and the meaning of her action. Usually, though often only implicitly, when he speaks of 'story' Hauerwas means the biblical history of salvation, especially as it finds its epitome in the story of Jesus. His advocacy of the ethical role of 'story' is designed partly to correct the intellectualist misunderstanding of ethics as a basically conceptual and logical affair; partly to exalt narrative over propositions as an effective means of moral education; but above all to encourage the Christian Church to think and act morally in accordance with its own identity as given it by its own peculiar 'story'. Hauerwas's purpose in drawing attention to the communal dimension of character-formation is to affirm both the community-relative nature of moral values and the socially embodied nature of their communication. Long before an individual receives explicit moral instruction (if she ever does), she has already been formed morally by the language, the rituals, and the moral practices of the community of which she is a member and in which she has been brought up.

It is true that Barth does not offer an explicit theory of how Christian character is formed. Nevertheless, he does give an implicit account which recognizes many of Hauerwas's concerns, albeit in theological rather than sociological terms. According to this implicit account, the moral character of the Christian is formed as she hears and responds to God's command. But the capacity for such hearing is itself formed by a growing understanding of the Word of God written; and for Barth, as we have already seen, Scripture consists primarily in the story of God's covenant of

---

[66] See e.g. 'The Significance of Vision: Toward an Aesthetic Ethic' and 'The Self as Story', in *Vision and Virtue* (Notre Dame, Ind.: Fides Press, 1974); 'A Story-Formed Community: Reflections on *Watership Down*' and 'Character, Narrative, and Growth in the Christian Life', in *A Community of Character* (Notre Dame, Ind.: University of Notre Dame Press, 1981); and *The Peaceable Kingdom* (Notre Dame, Ind.: University of Notre Dame Press, 1983), 24–34.

grace with humankind and only secondarily in moral prescriptions. For Barth, as for Hauerwas, this story finds its epitome in
the story of Jesus Christ, though in a subtly different version.
Barth's version in the first place is Nicaean and Chalcedonian,
whereas Hauerwas's is primarily Anabaptist.[67] One ethical consequence of this, which redounds to Barth's credit, is that he gives
far more prominence to the moral normativity of Jesus' relationship with his divine Father. Hauerwas has complained that ethics
which begin with Christology tend to ignore or use selectively the
life of the man Jesus.[68] This is not obviously true in the case of
Barth; for in both the *Ethics* and the *Church Dogmatics* broad
characterizations of Jesus' life play a vital role in the construction
of the crucial part of special ethics. In the *Ethics* Jesus' moral
significance is described in terms of self-sacrificial humility and
love, and in the *Dogmatics* in terms of invocation, zeal for the
primacy of God's Word, and revolt against the lordless powers.
Ironically, Hauerwas's own characterization of Jesus' life in the
very specific terms of non-violent love is, if anything, more selective than Barth's.[69]

The primary role of the biblical or, rather, evangelical story
in Barth's ethics is the same as in Hauerwas's: to ensure that
Christian ethics is genuinely Christian. Both are concerned that
questions of right conduct should be addressed by the Church in
terms strictly governed by her basic theological convictions; and
therefore that prior to the prescription of right action there is the
correct description of the existential predicament of the moral
agent. Moral rules are only ultimately intelligible in terms of the
'story' of the human condition and the part that the human agent
plays in it.

Barth also shares with Hauerwas the aim of correcting that
understanding of ethics which sees it as basically a conceptual and
logical affair. He constantly derides ethics in so far as it is taken to
be a merely theoretical exercise. But unlike Hauerwas, his main
aim in this is not to promote the moral role of imagination but

---

[67] Hauerwas insists that his emphasis on the ethical significance of Jesus' life 'as
depicted by the early church' is not expressive of a 'low' Christology (*Peaceable
Kingdom*, 75). But, when compared to Barth's reading of Jesus' ethical significance,
it is clear that that is exactly what it is. If Hauerwas holds to a 'high' Christology,
then he has chosen to neglect its ethical import.

[68] Ibid. 72–3.   [69] Ibid. 76–81.

rather to assert that at heart the moral life consists in responding to the address of a reality beyond ourselves; that is, to the obliging call of the God who has loved us from eternity in Jesus Christ. In attacking ethical intellectualism Barth is mainly concerned to denounce the illusion that the human moral agent stands alone and supreme in the empire of her own moral consciousness. Nevertheless, in denying that the Bible may be regarded in the first place as a compendium of moral rules, in bringing to the fore the moral authority of the stories of discipleship in the Gospels, and in instructing us to make our lives 'correspondent' or 'analogous' to these biblical 'pictures', Barth implicitly provides an important ethical role for imagination.

Barth shows no interest, however, in asserting the pedagogical advantages of morally veridical stories over sheerly prescriptive material. His account of ethics could easily support such an assertion, but Barth himself nowhere makes it. This lack of attention to the instruments of moral education could be attributed to Barth's refusal, on erroneous principle, to be distracted from the business of conceiving the moral life strictly in terms of the religious relationship. But whereas it is reasonable to expect an exponent of theological ethics to describe as closely as possible the universal features of the moral life that ensues from a right relationship with God, it would perhaps be less reasonable to expect him to make comparative practical judgements about the efficacy of particular means of moral education. Somewhere the brief of the theologian must cease, and that of the moral educationalist or psychologist begin.

We come, at last, to the role of the Church in moral formation. As with the topic of moral formation in general, Barth does not address this directly. His attention is fixed firmly on the primary and irreducible theological cause of moral formation: active response to God's command. Nevertheless, it is implicitly clear that the Church plays an important mediating role. For the command of God addresses us through Scripture as it is interpreted in preaching and in the counsel of our fellow hearers, past and present. Moreover, it also addresses us in baptism and the Lord's Supper. As we have already argued, God's command does not communicate itself to us in a vacuum, but through the medium of the Church—through the traditions of interpretation of the biblical 'story', through contemporary preaching and fraternal counsel, and through liturgical rites. All of these help to form us into the kind of people who are able to hear the voice of God. However, unless the preparation that the Church gives us culminates in our own acts of response, it will all have been in vain. For ultimately, according to Barth, what decides our character is not the Church's preparation, but our active response to God—which takes the basic and central forms of our submission to baptism, our continual calling upon God to establish his kingdom, and our regular participation in the Lord's Supper.

In contemporary Christian ethics the emphasis placed on the *social* formation of moral character is very marked indeed. As a corrective to an earlier, individualistic preoccupation with moral decision-making, that is certainly to be welcomed. But in much contemporary discussion this new emphasis is exaggerated to the point where the transcendent God and the individual's relationship to him disappears from view. The sociological dimension so eclipses the theological that the authors of one popular textbook, for example, can tell us simply and without qualification that '[c]ommunity is the chief architect of character'.[70] Set against this kind of thinking, the virtue of Barth's position is stark. For, on the one hand, he is able to affirm the importance of the Christian community as the place where we may expect to hear God's command and as the school in which we are trained to discern the tones of his voice. But on the other hand, Barth never lets us forget that the community is no more absolute than the individual; and that moral character is formed, not simply as the individual is shaped by tradition and custom, but as she responds to the command of God's Word that reaches her through—and often in spite of—her social context. No one may fairly accuse Barth of neglecting the ethical roles of the Christian community; and no one would dare to accuse him of allowing the Christian community to eclipse the living God.

[70] Bruce C. Birch and Larry L. Rasmussen, *Bible and Ethics in the Christian Life* (rev. edn., Minneapolis: Augsburg, 1989), 81.

5

EAVESDROPPING IN
THE WORLD

It is not difficult to understand why some suppose that Barth finds nothing of any ethical worth outside of strictly Christian circles. His relentless insistence that ethics be firmly grounded in Christian dogmatics, that dogmatics begin with the recognition that Jesus Christ is the Word of God, and that this Word is heard through Scripture in the Church, is enough to make this supposition intelligible. It makes immediately plausible the claims which are made by one such as George Forell, who writes that 'Barth completely denies the validity of all other [i.e. non-theological] ethical approaches' and that Barth's own approach 'makes any substantive discussion between Christians and other human beings involved in moral decisions impossible'.[1]

Such a reading of Barth is understandable. But it is as mistaken as it is superficial. It is mistaken to a considerable extent because it fails to take into account Barth's understanding of the 'Church' and of its relationship with the 'World'. In particular it assumes that Barth's ecclesiology is stereotypically sectarian, distinguishing between Church and World as between Light and Darkness. Little could be further from the truth. For although Barth is vigorous in his insistence that the Christian Church should strive to be faithful to its peculiar identity, he is no less vigorous in insisting that it has a duty to listen carefully to voices on the other side of its own walls: 'In the narrow corner in which we have our place and task we cannot but eavesdrop in the world at large.'[2]

Indeed, such eavesdropping is essential to the Church's Christian identity. For, like Christians, the Christian Church exists only eschatologically. The 'real' Church exists only in Christ and is

---

[1] G. W. Forell, 'Can We Endorse the Barthian Ethics?', *Dialog*, 3 (Winter 1964), 55–6. [2] *CD* iv/3: 117.

made visible here and now only as it hears God's Word, accepts his forgiving love, submits to his judgement, answers his call, and calls upon him to make himself known universally. The Christian character of the Church is contingent upon its response to the Word of God in faith, repentance, obedience, and hope, and so upon the grace of God in the work of his Spirit.[3] The Church is *iustus*, holy, and Christian, but only by faith. Therefore it is at the same time *peccator*. There is therefore ignorance of God within the Church as well as outside it, and one of the main forms this takes is that of the denial of God's lordship by the Church's excessive pretensions:[4]

The real Church therefore lives as if constantly held and sustained over an abyss. When it imagines it can find comfort and encouragement in itself it is certainly not the real Church. The real Church lives on the comfort and exhortation which it is allowed to receive despite the folly and perversity of man.... It lives by allowing itself to be shamed by His [its Lord's] goodness. It lives only in so far as its own religiosity and pious habits, its whole ritual, ordinary as well as extraordinary, are constantly being reduced to dust and ashes in the fire of His Word and Spirit.[5]

Accordingly, what distinguishes the members of this Church from others is not their superior virtue—'those who are gathered together in the real Church are lost sinners, and hence neither religious virtuosi nor a moral elite'—but the fact that 'they are more aware of the extent of human guilt before God, are more aware than others of the indissoluble solidarity of all men as sinners'.[6] In so far as the members of the Church hear God's Word and believe that God has reconciled them to himself out of sheer love, they cannot continue to regard others, whether inside or

---

[3] Barth's ecclesiology has been subject to repeated criticism that it dissolves the being of the Church into discontinuous events of response to God's Word. See e.g. Lesslie Newbigin, *The Household of God* (London: SCM, 1953), 50; Heinrich Fries, 'Kirche als Ereignis: Zu Karl Barths Lehre von der Kirche', *Catholica*, 11 (1957), 81–108; and Trutz Rendtorff, *Theorie des Christentums* (Gütersloh: Mohr, 1972), 178. This deserves a response along the same lines as the one we made in Ch. 4 to the charge that Barth does inadequate justice to the moral continuity of the human subject in her acts—that is, to her moral character. The assertion that ecclesial being is decisively constituted by its acts of response to the Word of God in no way denies the existence of a continuous subject. All that it denies is that this subject is essentially closed and static. [4] *CL* 132–42.
[5] Barth, 'The Real Church', in *Against the Stream*, ed. R. G. Smith, trans. E. M. Delacour and Stanley Godman (London: SCM, 1954), 67–8. [6] Ibid. 67.

outside the Church, as their moral inferiors. On the contrary, they are bound to relate to them in 'moral fellowship' and are free to treat them with love.[7]

When Barth speaks of 'solidarity' or 'fellowship' with others, or when he speaks of 'love' for others, what he has in mind above all else is the practice and attitude of 'openness'. But this openness, like solidarity, fellowship, and love, is not grounded exclusively or even primarily in the Church's acknowledgement of her continuing participation in common sinfulness. It is also, mainly, and positively grounded in the true or 'real' humanity in which she participates by faith and hope in Christ. As we have already noted, real human being is being in encounter, and therefore 'being in the openness of one to the other with a view to and on behalf of the other'.[8] This openness subsists in the practice of one looking the other in the eye and so of letting the other look him in the eye, and its fulfilment requires the mutual speech and hearing by which both enter into a common life in which 'they continually have to take each other into practical account'.[9] To participate in real humanity, then, is to be free from the sin of pride in which the human creature, pretending to godlike moral wisdom, gives himself over to the ideological thinking and strife 'in which at bottom no one understands the language of others because he is too much convinced of the soundness of his own seriously to want to understand the others'.[10] So if the Christian Church is to be true to its calling and identity, it is bound to regard its own moral wisdom with proper creaturely modesty, acknowledging its partiality and consequent need of constant dialectical correction.[11] At least for this reason, it must approach outsiders with a readiness to listen, perchance to learn.

However, it is not only because the members of the Church are sinners and because they are called to participate in real humanity that they should be open to outsiders. A further reason also lies in the fact that those outside the Church may yet be found inside; for 'there are no last who might not be found among the first'.[12] In the case of both Christians and non-Christians their destiny lies in front of them. As the former have not yet arrived, so the latter might yet set out. So

---

[7] Ibid. 70.   [8] CD iii/2: 250.   [9] Ibid. 253.   [10] CD iv/1: 447.
[11] CD ii/2: 727; i/1: 207.   [12] CD iii/4: 484.

as Christians and therefore as those who are called we are constrained to be absolutely open in respect of all other men without exception, exercising towards them the same openness as that in which alone, because the event of our calling can never be behind us in such a way that it is not also before us, we can see and understand ourselves as those who are called. . . . No man who is called does not also have to see and understand himself as one who still has to be called and therefore as one who stands alongside and in solidarity with the uncalled. Is it not inevitable, then, that our self-understanding as Christians should constrain us on this side, together with our knowledge of the existence of Jesus Christ in its universal significance, to an openness towards others in which we reckon with the fact that they are what we ourselves still are even as Christians, namely those who are not called but are still to be called? For all the seriousness with which we must distinguish between Christians and non-Christians, we can never think in terms of a rigid separation. All that is possible is a genuinely unlimited openness of the called in relation to the uncalled, and unlimited readiness to see in the aliens of today the brothers of tomorrow.[13]

This is not to say that Christians should try to pass the non-Christian off as 'really a Christian . . . in view of certain brighter aspects of his character', for this would be the death of Christian responsibility in relation to him. But

the fact remains that in the existence of these others there is something which has to be taken more seriously, and indeed infinitely more seriously from the qualitative standpoint, than their blatant non-Christianity in one form or another, namely the fact that, no matter who or what they are or how they live, their vocation is before them no less surely than that Jesus Christ has died and risen again for them. This is something of unconditional significance. It is the one sure thing we know concerning them. Anything we know concerning the fact that they are not called and not Christians can finally be only a matter of more or less well-founded conjecture. And even where we think we can be most sure of the facts, the reference can only be to what they are or are not provisionally. Unconditional significance attaches only to the fact that we have always to see and understand them as those who are still to be called.[14]

Here Barth bases the moral imperative of openness to outsiders on the limited capacity for spiritual discernment available to human beings. In other words, he argues that because non-Christians deserve the benefit of doubt, they should be treated as potential

[13] *CD* iv/3: 493–4.   [14] Ibid. 493.

brothers. But there are other occasions when he argues more extra-
vagantly along soteriologically universalist lines that Christians
should treat others as 'virtual' (*virtuell*), and not just potential,
brothers.[15] He makes the stronger claim that the universal significance of the existence of Jesus Christ is not merely that all are
subject to the same calling, but that all share the same status of
actually having been reconciled to God. The only difference between Christians and non-Christians, according to this argument,
is one of awareness: Christians already realize that they and everyone else have been reconciled to God, whereas non-Christians do
not—yet. Accordingly, the Church should be seen as the vanguard
of all humankind, not just the lifeboat for some, and its members
should be regarded as

merely provisional representatives and heralds for all who do not yet
know, have not yet heard, cannot yet grasp that the reconciliation of the
world with God has also been effected for them, that the order [of life:
Lebensordnung] rooted in this event has also come into force for them.
They cannot yet live in the light of this knowledge. Or are they perhaps
already doing so, to the shame of Christians themselves? . . . [T]hat order
[of life] operates for all whether they are aware of it or not, since the
reconciliation of the world with God took place for all.[16]

---

[15] *CL* 21–2 (*Chr. L.* 31).

[16] Barth, 'The Real Church', 71 ('Die wirkliche Kirche', in *Christliche Gemeinde
im Wechsel der Staatsordnungen: Dokumente der Ungarnreise, 1948* (Zollikon-Zurich:
Evangelischer Verlag AG, 1948), 24). Cf. *CD* i/2: 422–6. These are the terms in
which Karl Heinz Peschke, SVD, understands Barth when he writes that 'in
[Barth's] mind, the word of God does not only come to man in the historical revelation of holy scripture but also in the revelation given to every man by the working
of the Holy Spirit. This is possible because the effects of the redemption in Christ
are not limited to the baptized only. The grace of Christ is present and at work
everywhere, though it is not everywhere known as such and among non-Christians
it is less efficacious than among Christians.' Peschke concludes that, for Barth,
natural ethics and Christian ethics find unity in a 'Christologic universalism'
('Karl Barth in Confrontation with Natural Non-Christian Ethics', *South-East Asia
Journal of Theology*, 11 (Autumn 1969), 24). Even if this reading were not selective,
Peschke's conclusion would still require qualification. It does not necessarily follow
from the universal operation of the grace of Christ that 'natural ethics' should
be sanctioned indiscriminately and wedded in any wholesale fashion to Christian
ethics; for even according to Peschke's account, the grace of Christ is less than fully
efficacious among non-Christians. Moreover, even if Peschke's conclusion did
follow necessarily from his account, it could hardly be attributed to Barth. For
nowhere can he be found to admit a source or criterion of truth for theological
ethics that is equal to the Word of God attested in the Bible. John Macken's
comment on Christof Gestrich's argument that Barth might have recognized the
'world' as an independent representative of Christ (*Neuzeitlichen Denken und die*

Here Barth espouses something akin to Karl Rahner's 'anonymous Christianity', except that where Rahner wishes to establish it as a condition elected by some, Barth appears to propose it as one determined for all.[17] In so doing he not only sets divine grace at odds with the formal freedom that is a fundamental constituent of human dignity, but also reduces Christian responsibility in relation to the non-Christian to that of heralding the inevitable.[18] Still, whatever the problems occasioned by this last rationale, it is clear that, according to Barth, the lordship of Christ does manifest itself outside of the Christian Church:

in all ages the will of God has been fulfilled outside the Church as well. Indeed, to the shame of the Church it has often been better fulfilled outside the Church than in it. This is ... because Jesus, as the One who has risen from the dead and sits at the right hand of God, is in fact the Lord of the whole World, who has His servants even where His name is not yet or no longer known and praised.[19]

Accordingly, the Church must be open to hearing God's Word issuing forth from the lips of the apparently indifferent and godless; for 'it may be that the Lord has bidden those outside the Church to say something important to the Church. The Church therefore has every reason not to ignore the questions and warnings of the outside world.'[20] So, far from espousing a kind of sectarianism, Barth actually proposes a remarkably extrovert ecclesiology and warrants Hans Urs von Balthasar's judgement that he is 'as open to the world as any theologian could be'.[21]

Spaltung der dialektischen Theologie: Zur Frage der natürlichen Theologie, Beiträge zur historischen Theologie 52 (Tübingen: Mohr, 1977), 217–19) could equally be made of Peschke's: 'it too evidently overthrows the fundamental thrust of Barth's theology to which he bore witness to the end. It would establish a source of truth for theology alongside and equal to the proclamation of the Word of God in the Church' (*The Autonomy Theme in the 'Church Dogmatics'* (Cambridge: Cambridge University Press, 1990), 140). Macken's own discussion of Barth's position with regard to 'true words *extra muros ecclesiae*' suffers from too exclusive a focus on only one of the several rationales he offers; namely, the irresistible cosmic sovereignty of Christ (*The Autonomy Theme*, 63–6).

[17] Karl Rahner, 'Anonymous Christians', in *Theological Investigations*, (London: Darton, Longman, & Todd, 1969): 'it would be wrong to go so far as to declare every man, whether he accept the grace or not, an "anonymous Christian"' (p. 394).

[18] *CL* 21. [19] *CD* ii/2: 569.

[20] Barth, 'The Christian Understanding of Revelation', in *Against the Stream*, 228–9.

[21] Hans Urs von Balthasar, *The Theology of Karl Barth*, trans. J. Drury (New York: Anchor, 1972), 157.

What, then, is the impact of Barth's advocacy of ecclesial openness upon his ethics? Obviously, it means that Barth is quite
willing to give credit to non-Christian ethical thought where he
thinks it is due. So, for example, he endorses Luther's description
of Hammurabi as 'an exponent of the order of God'.[22] He praises
the achievement of the Greeks in grasping—'to a certain degree'—
through their concept of *eros* the fact that real human being is
'free, radically open, willing, spontaneous, joyful, cheerful and
gregarious'.[23] He acknowledges that Rousseau had theoretical and
practical insights about politics which have an affinity with his
own characterization of Christian political thought and action.[24]
He credits Kant with expressing 'the essential concern of Christian ethics' by pointing out that the concept of what is pleasing or
useful cannot of itself produce the concept of what is obligatory,
and he endorses Kant's definition of the ethical as that which may
be expressed in terms of a universal law.[25] And he confesses that
the insight that capital punishment should not be maintained
as part of the normal order of a national community has been
adopted 'far more readily and energetically by the children of the
world than by the children of light'.[26]

Some have been suspicious of Barth's willingness to give credit
to non-Christian ethical thought. N. H. Søe, for example, urged
greater caution than he felt Barth had shown in affirming that God
can also grant those outside the walls of the Church the capacity to
speak 'true words';[27] and in indirect criticism of Barth he stressed
the need for secular concepts to be 'transformed, translated into
Christian thinking' before being adopted by the Church.[28] But Søe
really need not have worried, for Barth does not advocate a supine,
indiscriminate openness. Indeed, he uses a distinctly aggressive
metaphor to describe the relation of Christian dogmatics to 'secular' or 'general' or 'philosophical' ethics, namely, 'annexation'.
Barth's choice of this metaphor was careful. For, on the one hand,
as he uses it, it makes sense of the openness of theological ethics
by implying that when it invades the territory of general ethics,

---

[22] *Karl Barth's Table Talk*, ed. John D. Godsey, Scottish Journal of Theology
Occasional Papers No. 10 (Edinburgh: Oliver & Boyd, 1963), 75.
[23] *CD* ii/2: 650, 656.   [24] *CD* iii/2: 283.
[25] Barth, 'The Christian Community and the Civil Community', in *Community,
State and Church*, ed. Will Herberg (Gloucester, Mass.: Peter Smith, 1968), 180–1.
[26] *CD* iii/4: 445–6.   [27] *CD* iv/3: 113–35.
[28] N. H. Søe, 'The Three "Uses" of the Law', in Gene Outka and Paul Ramsey
(eds.), *Norm and Context in Christian Ethics* (London: SCM, 1968), 318–19.

it behaves like the Israelites on entering Canaan; that is, it is recovering land that originally belonged to it. Since all ethics have their real origin and meaning in the command of the grace of God in Jesus Christ; and since, therefore, the Whence and Whither of theological ethics is not finally and properly alien to 'philosophical' ethics, theological ethics 'will be absolutely open to all that it can learn from general human ethical enquiry and reply. It can be absolutely open because it has nothing to fear from this quarter.'[29] Because the lordship of Christ is effective, albeit covertly, even in the very midst of human spiritual rebellion, the Christian moralist may expect to hear God's command objectively spoken by non-Christians in spite of their own subjective, spiritual disposition. There is a 'rule of truth imposed on all men as such by the divine wisdom active and revealed in Jesus Christ'.[30]

However, if 'annexation', as Barth uses it, signifies the recovery of what properly belongs to oneself, something basically congenial rather than alien, it nevertheless also signifies its incorporation into a larger, imperial whole. Theological ethics is the subject of annexation, and 'general' ethics the object. Theological ethics dictates the terms. It may be ready to learn, 'but it must always be absolutely resolved to stick to its own colours'.[31] It may take up 'the legitimate problems and concerns and motives and assertions of every other ethics as such', but only after testing them in the light of 'its own superior principle'. It agrees with other ethics only in so far as they are aware, explicitly or implicitly, of their origin and basis in God's command. If theological ethics is comprehensive, it remains 'fundamentally critical'.[32] Annexation involves the contradiction of the authority of the 'so-called ... original inhabitants of the land'.[33] Or, more constructively, it involves their contradiction for the sake of their conversion.[34]

---

[29] CD ii/2: 524.   [30] Ibid. 523.   [31] Ibid. 524.
[32] Ibid. 527.   [33] Ibid. 520.
[34] Barth's concept of the relationship between theological and 'philosophical' ethics in terms of 'annexation' implies that, although Scripture may be the former's peculiar formal criterion, it is not its only source. Therefore, we believe that Hugo Meynell was wrong to read Barth as one who adopted an extreme version of the *sola Scriptura* principle which asserts that whatever is not explicit in Scripture is absolutely against it, thereby rejecting the assumption, 'common to the majority of Fathers and Schoolmen, and to the classical Protestant theologians of the 16th and 17th centuries, that while Scripture is the paradigm against which Christians must test all speculation about God, it need not necessarily be the source of it' (*Grace versus Nature: Studies in Karl Barth's Church Dogmatics* (London: SCM, 1965), 158, 162, 165).

It might be objected that this description of the relationship between 'theological ethics' and 'philosophical ethics' is too crude; that it treats as real ethical systems what are in fact merely ideal types; that it fails to do justice to the complex interrelations between them; and, in particular, that it obscures the subtle *dependence* of theological ethics upon philosophical concepts. Such an objection is not cogent. For Barth has no interest in denying that theological ethics employs philosophical concepts and is therefore dependent on philosophy in a certain sense. His own ethics depends heavily, for example, on the relational concept of the person as expounded by the Jewish philosopher Martin Buber; and he exhibited no embarrassment whatsoever over this fact. Barth's concern was not to deny the inevitable indebtedness of 'theology' to 'philosophy' at a secondary level and in piecemeal fashion. Rather, it was to insist that, in its own self-explication, theological ethics must remain true to its own axioms, its own peculiar convictions about the fundamental nature of reality. Barth was not calling theological ethics to self-sufficiency, but rather to critical consciousness in its inevitable borrowings. What he wanted was that material drawn from non-theological sources should be refashioned in such a way that it is made to recognize, at least tacitly, its proper basis in the sanctifying command of God. In particular, this means that such material should acknowledge the real situation of human beings. It should acknowledge the history of the relationship with God in which they stand and which gives them their most basic identity as sinful creatures who have been reconciled to God by grace and await the completion of their redemption. It should acknowledge that human beings are really human only by faith and hope in Jesus Christ.[35]

One crucial implication of this is that theological ethics will not tie itself 'unreservedly and finally' to any particular 'philosophical' ethic *as a system*. It will be critical, selective, and eclectic.[36] Accordingly, although Barth endorses Kant's principle of universalizability and his assertion that what is obligatory is a logical category distinct from that of what is pleasing, he takes issues with Kant at several crucial points. He argues, for example, that in so far as what is obligatory is the content of a command of God the Creator, 'we cannot refuse absolutely to interpret it also as

<hr />

[35] Ibid. 541, 545.   [36] Cf. *CD* i/2: 735.

that which is supremely [*im eminenten Sinn*] pleasing and useful and valuable'; and that therefore Christian ethics cannot share Kant's purely negative view of eudemonism or utilitarianism.[37] Barth also argues against Kant's concept of moral autonomy that it contradicts the phenomenon of moral obligation, that is, of being absolutely subject to an imperative; and he contends that an adequate concept of obligation must see it as something which is immediately (though not ultimately) heteronomous, something which confronts our will with an absolute authority that is not our own.[38]

Barth's account of the relation of theological ethics to non-theological ethics corresponds to his doctrine of the analogy of faith. According to this, the world as we experience it is to be conceived—and invariably reconceived—in terms of its fundamental relationship with the Word of God.[39] In the course of this reconception some of what we have thought to be our experience will be proven true and relocated, and some will be exposed as false and discarded. It is in order to prevent the uncritical assimilation of commonly accepted experience or wisdom, whose basic presuppositions deny that human beings stand in a theological history, that Barth offers an alternative to the *analogia entis*. In assimilating 'natural factors'—as it constantly does—the Word of God has to remove 'their original character as alien elements' and give them a new nature, in order to make them serviceable.[40] Thus Barth readily affirms general revelation while rejecting natural theology. Only with the eyes of faith is it possible to see the world and to read human experience properly. Only from the perspective of the Word of God can one know what is and what is not truly 'natural'. But from that perspective there is nature to be seen. There are, for example, the 'natural' relational structures between Creator and creature, man and woman, parent and child. There is

[37] *CD* ii/2: 650, 652.   [38] Ibid. 651, 667; iii/2: 422–3.
[39] That Barth intended 'empirical' reality to be incorporated within, not displaced by, his vision of theological reality has been noted by Hans Frei ('An Afterword: Eberhard Busch's Biography of Karl Barth', in H. Martin Rumscheidt (ed.), *Karl Barth in Review: Posthumous Works Reviewed and Assessed* (Pittsburgh: Pickwick Press, 1981), 114) and William Werpehowski ('Command and History in the Ethics of Karl Barth', *Journal of Religious Ethics*, 9/2 (1981), 304) and argued at some length by Ingolf Dalferth ('Karl Barth's Eschatological Realism', in S. W. Sykes (ed.), *Karl Barth* (Cambridge: Cambridge University Press, 1989)).
[40] *CD* i/2: 682. Cf. *CD* ii/1: 224–36.

the 'primal' experience of 'the truly breath-taking dialectic' which arises in the encounter between male and female.[41] And there is 'the very nature of love and marriage which calls for permanence'.[42]

In principle, then, Barth's theological ethics is inclusive of the data of human 'experience', although it retains the right to challenge what that is assumed to be. Accordingly, Barth insists that a properly theological anthropology will not simply repudiate 'the phenomena of the human recognisable to every human eye and every thinking mind'.[43] But it will qualify and order such 'general knowledge' with a necessarily theological account of real human being—that is, human being as creature, pardoned sinner, and child of the Father.[44]

However, Barth has come under considerable and sustained criticism for failing to take the consideration of empirical data sufficiently seriously in his discussion of moral problems—a charge that has much in common with Hauerwas's complaint about the frustrating 'abstractness' of Barth's ethics. Reinhold Niebuhr criticized Barth's refusal to make very specific moral judgements, and described his theology as outlining 'the final pinnacle of Christian faith and hope' while obscuring 'the foothills where human life must be lived'.[45] Charles West has noted, in relation to social and economic questions, how Barth ignores 'the vast body of social scientific literature . . . which might enlighten him as to the actual human situation he confronts', and how he seems to have left 'an empty space in his thought between his theological insight and social reality'.[46] Robert Willis has asserted, with regard to Barth's treatment of vocation and work, that it betrays 'an inadequate sensitivity to the complexity and subtlety of the empirical factors that shape the context within which man's work is carried on'; and has suggested that the cogency of Barth's analysis of the conditions of a justifiable war might have been improved had it been assisted by the insights of political science.[47] John H. Yoder also made this last point when he criticized Barth for his lack of

---

[41] *CD* iii/4: 119–20.   [42] Ibid. 207.   [43] *CD* iii/2: 199.
[44] *CD* iii/4: 43.
[45] Reinhold Niebuhr, 'We are Men and Not God', *Christian Century*, 65/43 (27 Oct. 1948), 1138–40.
[46] Charles C. West, *Communism and the Theologians* (Philadelphia: Westminster Press, 1958), 186 n. 1, 188–9, 285–7.
[47] Robert E. Willis, *The Ethics of Karl Barth* (Leiden: E. J. Brill, 1971), 383, 390. Cf. 381–91, 418–20, 428–33.

social psychological 'realism' in designating justifiable war as a *Grenzfall*, while agreeing that the State should prepare for the possibility of war.[48] Charles Curran has complained that Barth's theological approach to the morality of homosexual acts 'does not give enough importance or place to human knowledge in general, let alone the specific empirical sciences of psychology and psychiatry'; and, indeed, that his 'Christological monism' 'prevents any way into the ethical problem from the viewpoint of philosophy and human wisdom'.[49] And, more recently, with respect to his discussion of authority in the Church, Stephen Sykes has implicitly rebuked Barth for not advancing his theological assertions in terms of sociological realities.[50]

Several of Barth's critics on this matter have offered explanations for the weakness of his empirical analysis. Niebuhr attributed it partly to his 'realized eschatology', according to which confidence in the present victory of Christ removes the need to care for the world.[51] However, although it is conceivable that such confidence in divine sovereignty could be used to justify the abandonment of human responsibility and so of the need to think about how to be responsible, it will be clear to anyone who has more than a passing knowledge of Barth's life and thought that he did not use it thus. Indeed, in the very address to which Niebuhr's remarks refer, Barth made his appeal to the presence of Christ's triumph, not to annul human responsibility for the world, but to define it as the limited responsibility of creatures rather than the ultimate responsibility of an Atlas.

Charles West picked up another of Niebuhr's explanations when he attributed Barth's neglect of empirical data to a 'doctrine of all-embracing grace' which causes him to trivialize the phenomenon of moral perplexity and so to neglect the need for the 'difficult empirical analysis of real human situations'.[52] Neither Niebuhr nor West spells out this explanation, so it is not entirely clear what the causal connection between this doctrine and the failure to

---

[48] John H. Yoder, *Karl Barth and the Problem of War* (Nashville: Abingdon, 1970), 106.

[49] Charles Curran, *Catholic Moral Theology in Dialogue* (Notre Dame, Ind.: University of Notre Dame Press, 1976), 190, 192.

[50] S. W. Sykes, 'Authority and Openness in the Church', in Sykes (ed.), *Karl Barth*, 83–4.

[51] Niebuhr, 'We are Men and Not God', 1138–9.

[52] West, *Communism and the Theologians*, 313–14.

advert to moral perplexity is supposed to be. We may take it, however, that allusion is being made to Barth's conviction that the main ethical problem is not so much how we can *know* what God's command is, but rather whether we will *obey* it. It is true that Barth does appear confident that God's command will be crystal clear to those who, intent upon obeying it, really want to hear it. But there is no reason why close empirical analysis could not be regarded as one of the necessary marks of an earnest willingness to hear.

Robert Willis has offered a third explanation. Acknowledging that Barth, in principle, invests the empirical data provided by the behavioural and social sciences with a relative significance, Willis argues that his capacity to make adequate use of such data was seriously impaired by the uncertainty that attends the ontic independence of creation from God and the relationship of empirical knowledge with the knowledge of faith in his theology.[53] It is true, as we made clear in the Introduction to this study, that Barth's affirmation of the ontic independence of creation is ambiguous. Even so, we are more inclined to attribute the empirical weakness of his ethics to the cause of this ambiguity than to the ambiguity itself; and this cause we find in the methodological principle that what has no independent existence should not become an independent object of thought. Barth adopted such a principle because he was inclined to believe that, in order to avoid the illusion of human autarky, we must keep our attention focused on the human creature in its religious connection, and avoid making more than a passing glance at it in its other, secular connections. However, Barth's own tripartite differentiation of his special ethics implies that he recognized the possibility of considering separately the parts of an ontic whole, without obscuring their status as parts; and, as we have seen, in one of his less defensive moments he himself granted that the empirical or phenomenological study of human affairs has its own place *within* the overarching terms set by theological anthropology. The fact that, in practice, he failed to draw much upon the empirical sciences may be attributed partly to the lingering influence of his erroneous methodological principle, which was sustained by his acute sensitivity to the tendency of

[53] Willis, *Ethics of Karl Barth*, 329, 428–33.

the horizontal dimension to eclipse the vertical one in human thinking.

This, however, is not the whole story. For there is also reason to attribute the empirical poverty of Barth's ethics to a certain understanding of the division of theological labour. There is evidence that Barth conceived the specific task of the theological ethicist as that of drawing out the ethical implications of dogmatics, and that he considered the business of the close analysis of particular moral problems as the province of another kind of ethicist. At one point in the *Dogmatics* he distinguishes between what he calls 'theological' and 'Christian' ethics. Whereas theological ethics is concerned with formulating and expounding basic principles, Christian ethics undertakes the 'actual handling of the problems of human life' with tacit reference to basic, theological principles.[54] If we take this distinction seriously, then the instances of Barth's grappling with particular moral problems in the *Church Dogmatics* should be regarded merely as attempts to advance the specification of the moral import of dogmatics as far as possible, and not as intentionally complete accounts. The problem with this explanation is that Barth refers so rarely to this distinction between 'theological' and 'Christian' ethics; and at no point in his exposition of 'special ethics' does he give any indication that he considered himself to be providing less than full treatment. Moreover, the fact that Barth was sometimes wont to present theological premises as producing by themselves moral conclusions that, in fact, far outstrip what deductive logic warrants suggests that he was inclined to regard dogmatics as ethically self-sufficient.[55] In the end, there does seem to be a large measure of ambiguity about Barth's basic intention. Sometimes, it seems to be the modest one of deriving a general ethical framework from dogmatic grounds. But, at other times, it appears to be the more grandiose (and ill-conceived) one of deriving the full content of ethics from dogmatics. In the first case, empirical knowledge finds its own proper space within the knowledge of faith; but in the second, the knowledge of faith displaces it entirely.

[54] *CD* ii/2: 542. Cf. the discussion of the relation between 'Christian theological ethics' and 'Christian philosophical ethics' in *Ethics*, trans. G. W. Bromiley (New York: Seabury, 1981), 27, 23.

[55] See Appendix 4, 'The Political Application of the *Analogia Fidei*'.

Our conclusion, then, is that there are several causes of the poverty of empirical analysis in Barth's ethics, not all of them consistent with one another. First, there is the erroneous methodological principle that what is not ontically independent should not become an independent object of thought. Then there is the overambitious conception of the task of theological ethics, according to which it can manage sufficiently well without referring to empirical data at all. And, finally, there is the more modest understanding of the purpose of theological ethics; namely, to derive an ethical framework from dogmatic premises, within which it is the task of another ethical discipline ('Christian ethics') to interpret empirical data properly. The extent to which this empirical poverty renders Barth's ethics defective depends upon which of its causes becomes the focus of attention. If it is either of the first two, then Barth's neglect of empirical data appears as a major flaw. But if attention rests on the third, then it appears less a problem than a limitation. Since Barth never expressly denied theological ethics' need of empirical analysis, since he did expressly allow for it in principle,[56] and since this concession is consistent with his more modest reading of the purpose of theological ethics, we do not believe that his (relative) neglect of empirical data in practice should be regarded as a fundamental defect.

The proponents of Liberation theology would probably disagree. They would argue that empirical analysis is where ethics should begin; that the economic, social, and political situation in which the ethicist finds herself should set her agenda; and, in this sense, that she should be responsive to the concrete moral demands that press upon her in her very choice of questions to examine. Taken as a plea for moral theologians to be politically responsible in their thinking, this argument has force. But can the ethicist ever simply begin with the situation in which she finds herself? Does she not always and necessarily come already armed with a particular moral vision, a particular concept of human well-being, a particular set of moral principles and rules, without which she could not begin to read the situation in moral terms at all? And, if she is a Christian, has she not come by this ethical apparatus necessarily (if not sufficiently) by tracing the moral implications of her theological

---

[56] Willis, West, and Yoder all agree on this. See Willis, *Ethics of Karl Barth*, 329–31, 385, 446; West, *Communism and the Theologians*, 314–20; and Yoder, *Karl Barth and the Problem of War*, 48–9.

convictions about the basic nature of reality? In sum, was not Barth correct in insisting that the Christian ethicist arrive at the necessary task of empirical analysis by way of a theologically derived ethical framework? It may well be—indeed, it is the case— that ethics cannot live by deduction alone. But, equally, nor can it live without it.

CONCLUSION: KARL BARTH AND CHRISTIAN ETHICS TODAY

There are a number of points at which Barth's ethics deserves criticism. But they are often not the ones that have tended to receive it. An exception to this rule is the element of determinism in Barth's account of the relation of divine grace in Christ to the human subject. Although this is strictly a feature of anthropology, it has implications which bear quite directly on ethics. In making persistent error ultimately impossible, it removes the deep and mysterious seriousness of human moral responsibility, and accordingly diminishes human dignity. It reduces the distinction between the status of the Christian and the status of the non-Christian merely to one of different stages in an inexorable process; and it thereby robs the mission of the Christian Church of any sense of urgency, if not of its purpose altogether. The fact that Barth never expressly endorsed these implications, and implicitly contradicted them, stands to his credit; but it does not make his espousal of the premiss anything less of a problem.

However, the assertion that God's grace in Christ is such that creaturely being cannot ultimately be insubordinate to creaturely order should be distinguished from the far more acceptable claim that creaturely being cannot be substantially free and truly itself without being subordinate, and that it cannot be subordinate apart from 'Christian' faith in some guise or other. And this, in turn, should be distinguished from the claim that there is no creaturely being as such outside of Christ. Although Barth sometimes seems to assert the latter, there are good reasons to suppose that he meant to assert, not that there is no human *esse* apart from Christ, but that apart from Christ there is no human *bene esse*. In so far as he recognized the fact—provisional, if not ultimate—of sin, he could not logically have meant anything else. Creaturely being is not displaced by 'Christian' conduct in Barth's ethics. Nature is not abolished by grace; it is perfected by it. God's grace in Christ orders the human soul in accordance with its creaturely nature. And if, ultimately, it *must* do so, this is not by ontological necessity, but rather by the utter strength of God's love, which cannot fail to exhaust human resistance.

Therefore, those critics are mistaken who have attributed the scant attention paid in Barth's ethics to empirical data, and its consequently abstract quality, to an alleged Christological eclipse of creaturely being. Both of these features have, as we have seen, other causes: the mistaken methodological principle that what has no independent existence should not become an independent object of thought; the overestimation of dogmatics as ethically self-sufficient; and the division of ethical labour between 'theological' ethics and 'Christian' ethics. We have argued that this last reason provides some justification for Barth's empirical weakness and saves it from becoming a fundamental flaw. For a measure of abstractness and withholding from empirical analysis is quite appropriate to a form of theological ethics whose modest purpose is to explicate the moral implications of dogmatic tenets. However, Barth was not always careful to observe the division of labour and to restrict himself to doing 'theological' ethics. At times he sought not only to derive general moral principles from theological tenets but also to apply them in making particular moral judgements. On those occasions, then, his neglect of empirical data does become a defect and not merely a limitation.

In so far as Barth understood himself to be doing 'theological' as distinct from 'Christian' ethics another feature of his ethics that has attracted critical attention could be justified: namely: the absence of whole-hearted engagement in the rational specification of rules and their application to cases. However, although it is arguable that the division of ethical labour was a cause of this, it certainly was not the only one. Also operative was the misconception of casuistry as the epitome of the closed, rationalistic ethical system, which allows no room for the highly individual, vocational dimension of moral deliberation.

This assertion of the role of vocation is one of the most salient and creditable features of Barth's ethics. Obviously, it has the beneficial effect of obstructing any tendency of an ethic to degenerate into legalism, through its emphasis on the significance for moral deliberation of historically contingent factors in the case

confronting the moral agent.[1] But, more specifically, among these
contingencies it includes and brings to the fore the agent's sense
of her own personal vocation. For Barth, this consists primarily
in a calling to a particular act of service—a particular contribution to the history of the redemption of the world—that only
the individual addressed is in a position (in terms of time, place,
skills, and disposition) to perform. But it could—and should—be
expanded to comprise the agent's reading of her own moral development and the tasks that it currently sets: the moral weaknesses
about which she must be vigilant and against which she must
struggle; and the moral strengths which she must nurture, and
which she must be alert for opportunities to exercise.

A major theological correlate of this concept of vocation is the
intimate presence of the living God to the individual human creature. Indeed, this correlate is one of the most distinctive features
of Barth's theological ethics, which is characterized by a remarkable confidence in, and focus upon, the activity of the Holy Spirit.[2]
Nevertheless, this pneumatological emphasis is carefully qualified—
and to a greater degree than many of Barth's critics have recognized—by the definite Trinitarian scheme in which it occurs. As
a result, the obliging call—the command—of the Spirit is defined
as a call to creaturely order and eschatological destiny. It liberates,
certainly; but it liberates for life that fulfils the teleological structure of creaturely being. Moreover, the Spirit's call is informed as
to the nature of such life by the prototypical instance presented in
Jesus Christ. Thus, in Barth's ethics, the Spirit's freedom is governed and ordered by God's Word incarnate and therefore also,
as original witness to this, by the Word written. During the long
course of its history, Christian ethics has not always displayed
such balance.

That the Spirit's call is to fulfil the structure of creaturely being
clearly implies that, contrary to its popular reputation, Barth's
ethics does in fact espouse what could reasonably be called a
version of natural law. It thinks of human creatures as being 'free'

---

[1] By 'legalism' is meant here that view of the making of moral judgements which
exaggerates the fixed nature of moral rules and the capacity of a system of such
rules to be comprehensive, while underplaying their need to adapt in the face of
moral cases that have novel features which are morally significant.

[2] On this point, it is worth noting that Barth associated the emergence of
casuistry in the early Church with a loss of confidence in the counsel of the Holy
Spirit (CD iii/4: 7).

in childlike friendship with God, in fellowship with other human beings, and in respect for life. That is to say, it considers that there exist certain 'goods' or states of being in which human beings flourish. Barth's method of identifying these human goods by way of reflection upon the written Word, Christologically interpreted, is responsible for his unequivocal emphasis upon the primacy of the good of friendship with God, and has more theological integrity than typical Thomist theories of natural law. But in treating Christ as the sole source of knowledge, rather than the basic criterion by which to sift a range of sources, Barth restricted his resources and consequently arrived at a list of goods that is far from complete. Had he permitted himself to reflect not only on Christology and Scripture, but also on Christian Tradition (especially the Thomist stream) and on the basic reasons for human action, he might have extended his list to include such candidates as, for example, knowledge of the truth and aesthetic experience.

Barth's understanding of the manner in which Scripture indicates the Spirit's command is relatively sophisticated. He openly recognizes the necessary role of dogmatic construction in mediating between the Scriptures and the identification of those goods and principles of conduct that invariably inform the Spirit's commanding. In so doing, he locates the authority of the Bible in ethics primarily, not at the level of its expressly moral pronouncements, but rather at the theological level of its attestation of God's salvific acts and so of his benevolence toward humankind. On the one hand, he relativizes the authority of particular moral statements in the Bible by making them subject to the possibility of criticism at the hands of an ethical system derived from dogmatic premises. But, on the other hand, he asserts the Bible's authority over dogmatics by acknowledging the venturesome character of dogmatic construction and its revisability in the light of a demonstrably better interpretation of what the biblical tradition is saying. Apart from our *interpreting* it, both dogmatically and ethically, the Bible cannot help us in discerning the Spirit's command; and yet, if we would discern that command, then it is the *Bible*, first and foremost, that we must interpret.

Barth was not a biblicist. He did not understand the Bible's authority as consisting in the undifferentiated truthfulness of all its statements. Indeed, he was prepared to admit the Bible's cultural limitations—and even its fallibility, albeit only in principle—at a secondary level. Nevertheless, as regards its basic theological vision of reality—and especially as that vision is focused in the story of the birth, life, death, resurrection, and ascension of Jesus Christ—Barth was perfectly confident in the Bible's veracity, and so in its authority. It was his main ethical purpose—and his most valuable ethical achievement—to fashion an account of the moral life in terms of this vision. However, it must be said that his account suffers from the rather vague terms in which he articulates Jesus' moral significance—a vagueness attributable to its derivation more from Christology than from the historical situation of early first-century Palestine.

Barth's, of course, is not the only ethics that speaks in theological terms. But it is, perhaps, unique in the ethical seriousness with which it takes both God as one who is actively engaged in personal relationship with his human creatures, and the human moral agent as one whose basic identity is given in that relationship. His is a theological ethic that is peculiar in its stress upon the fundamental importance of 'religious' acts for the formation and maintenance of moral character.[3] Certainly, Barth's concentration on right conduct toward God does result in a rather frustrating lack of specificity in much of his discussion of right conduct toward fellow humans. However, as a corrective to the perennial tendency to dissolve the vertical into the horizontal—whether psychological, social, or political—such rhetorical imbalance has an enduring validity. Moreover, in Barth's case, the stress upon specifically religious conduct does not at all issue in a world-neglecting pietism. On the contrary, he conceives it so that it necessarily finds horizontal expression in a dissident engagement with the world that is characterized by modesty, cheerfulness, and resilience. Barth's is a religious waiting that requires secular hastening and renders it humane.

[3] Given Barth's critique of 'religion' (*CD* i/2, s. 17, 'The Revelation of God as the Abolition of Religion'), we must explain our use of the word 'religious' here. We mean by it that which is more or less consciously related to God, and not (as with Barth) that which aspires in pious form to master God. We might have used, instead, the word 'spiritual', but chose not to because of its connotation of a thoroughly un-Barthian body–spirit dualism. With regard to our assertion of the peculiarity and importance of the 'religious' emphasis in Barth's ethics, it is pertinent to note Stephen Sykes's astute suggestion of 'the strange thought that we might . . . be able to treat this formidable Calvinist dogmatician as a spiritual writer' ('Authority and Openness in the Church', in S. W. Sykes (ed.), *Karl Barth* (Cambridge: Cambridge University Press, 1989), 83).

In conclusion, let us turn directly to the question, 'How should Christian moralists today respond to Barth's ethics?' The answer, in brief, is that they should discard some of its features, adopt others, and in three important respects move beyond it.

No contemporary Christian ethic should incorporate Barth's soteriological determinism or his misconception of casuistry, for reasons already made plain. Nor should it share his loss of nerve with regard to the practice of judging certain moral statements in the Bible to be mistaken. If, after long and searching and charitable consideration, we simply cannot find a certain biblical statement (e.g. that wives should be subordinate to their husbands) reasonable; and if what is 'reasonable' in this case is duly informed by a Christian vision of theological and moral reality, then we are bound to judge that statement to be wrong. Certainly, we should regard our judgement as provisional and leave it open to correction, but until it has been corrected we must own it. To do otherwise would be an irresponsible abandonment of intelligence. Besides, to admit that particular biblical statements are mistaken, or even to doubt the validity of certain principles espoused by particular biblical voices or traditions, is not necessarily to deny that the Bible is a moral authority, even in some sense the primary moral authority. For in order to be authoritative, a person or an institution or a body of literature does not have to be infallible. It needs only to have a proven—and, in some respects, a unique—grasp of truths that are basic to a particular field of knowledge, together with proven skill in discerning some of their implications.

Among the elements of Barth's ethics that contemporary Christian moralists would be wise to adopt are these: the concept of a personal vocation that finally determines moral duty in a concrete situation; the Christological information of the description of natural law or basic human goods; recognition of the complex interrelationship between Scripture, dogmatics, and ethics; and the importance of 'religious' acts or practices for the formation of moral character.

One respect in which a contemporary ethic needs to go beyond Barth is in determining the moral significance of Jesus Christ, not only by way of an analysis of Christology, but also through close scrutiny of the particular political, social, religious, and moral circumstances to which Jesus was responding. We cannot expect to have a very precise knowledge of what Jesus intended by what he did and said, without reference to his historical context. And it seems reasonable to suppose both that Jesus' moral intentions are relevant to a consideration of his moral significance, and that it is possible to determine, with some degree of accuracy, what those intentions were.

Second, while contemporary moralists would do well to take on board what Barth has gleaned from Christ as a moral source, and so to fortify themselves with specifically Christian criteria, they should then proceed to fulfil Barth's programme by critically availing themselves of the full range of ethical sources—including Christian, other religious, and philosophical traditions.

Finally, Christian moralists today must either be more disciplined than Barth in restricting themselves to the modest task of identifying the general ethical principles implied by dogmatic tenets, or take greater pains in coming to grips with the relevant empirical data before trying to apply those principles to them.

Karl Barth's legacy to contemporary Christian ethics is, predictably, a mixed one. Nevertheless, within its limitations and among its flaws there is much of worth to be found. Barth's word may not be the last one, but it is none the less authoritative; and this Christian moralist considers himself much the wiser for having sat at his feet for a while.

APPENDIX 1

THE DIVINE COMMISSION
OF AN INDEPENDENT SWITZERLAND

In Barth's occasional writings around the time of World War II we learn, first, that the preservation of the specific political character of Switzerland is a Christian duty,[1] and that therefore the Church should support the Swiss State in the event of need for the belligerent defence of its 'legal administration' (*Rechtsordnung*) against National Socialist Germany.[2] The rationale for this assertion is threefold. First, the Swiss order of political life (*Lebensordnung*) offers the Christian Church an assured place, where its Gospel can be proclaimed and believed in internal and external freedom.[3] Therefore her order of political life exists on the foundation, in the atmosphere, and within the range of the Church;[4] and in this sense, it has a 'göttlichen Grunde' (divine ground).[5] It is quite clear, however, that Barth does not regard the polity of Switzerland as itself divine; neither does he deem it to be Christian as such, nor does he equate it with the Church.[6] Rather, he makes the relation of the Swiss State to the Church analogous to that of the Christian to her unbelieving spouse, as described by Paul in his First Epistle to the Corinthians, 7: 12–14: as the unbeliever is sanctified by the believer because he has consented to live with her, so the Swiss State is sanctified by the Church, with which it has consented to live and whose witness it has consented to receive. Therefore, although the Swiss State cannot be described as Christian, it can be described as one confronted with the Gospel of Christ and as 'ein von ihm in exemplarischer Weise in Anspruch genommen Staatswesen' (a form of state claimed by it in an exemplary fashion).[7]

---

[1] Barth, 'Im Namen Gottes des Allmächtigen!', in *Eine schweizer Stimme, 1938–45* (Zollikon-Zurich: Evangelischer Verlag AG, 1945), 229.

[2] Barth, 'Church and State', in *Community, State and Church*, ed. Will Herberg (Gloucester, Mass.: Peter Smith, 1968), 143 (*Rechtfertigung und Recht*, Theologische Studien 1 (Zollikon-Zurich: Evangelischer Verlag AG, 1944), 42).

[3] Barth, 'Unsere Kirche und die Schweiz in der heutigen Zeit', in *Eine schweizer Stimme*, 165. Although Barth does not specify here that he means *Lebensordnung* in a political sense, it is clear from what follows that that is, indeed, what he intends.

[4] Barth, 'Im Namen', 207.   [5] Ibid. 232.

[6] Ibid. 205; Barth, 'Verheißung und Verantwortung der christlichen Gemeinde im heutigen Zeitgeschehen', in *Eine schweizer Stimme*, 312.

[7] Barth, 'Im Namen', 207–8.

Second, as a Confederation (*Eidgenoßenschaft*) the Swiss polity is based, not on common national, historical, linguistic, geographical, economic, or ideological grounds, but on an oath (*Eid*); that is, a commitment taken under the call of God and in responsibility before him.[8] Switzerland, therefore, represents in its very constitution the realization of the possibility of a political community which transcends racial, national, economic, and ideological interests. As such it has a mission (*Sendung*) to other peoples.[9] In particular, it represents the hope for a European order, once embodied in the Holy Roman Empire, in which the rights and liberties of its constitutive peoples are guaranteed against attempts by an aggressive and imperialist state (*Machtstaat*) to impose its hegemony.[10] Because of its significance as the hope of European community, Switzerland should maintain its military neutrality, Barth argues, in order to be a means of communication between warring nations.[11] For the very same reason, however, it must also preserve itself against the hegemony of Nazi Germany; for, although 'für alle und wider niemand' (for all and against no one), Switzerland must be against those who, by disturbing the peace and trampling on justice, show themselves to be 'gegen alle' (against all).[12]

Third, because it permits the proclamation of the Gospel and is therefore based upon it, witnesses to it, and reflects it, Switzerland's order of political life (*Lebensform*) constitutes a just State (*Rechten Staat*).[13] This is because human justice is founded upon and maintained by divine justification, since the divine justification of sinful men provides 'the only protection against the sophisms and excuses of man, who is always so ready to justify himself' at the expense of others.[14] As a just State, Switzerland affirms human dignity;[15] and it does so specifically by being 'einer durch das Recht verbundenen Gemeinschaft freier Volker von freier Menschen' (a community of free peoples composed of free persons and united in a confederation by law).[16] By means of this law each constitutive group and each of its members is assured of the freedom to live and grow and act, provided that they respect and co-operate with other such groups—whether linguistic, regional, social, or confessional—and their members. The making and maintenance of law is subject immediately to common deliberation and common decision, but ultimately to the freely formed and expressed conviction and judgement of each.

The Swiss political order is just, then, because it provides for both

---

[8] Ibid. 202–3, 205.   [9] Barth, 'Unsere Kirche', 166.
[10] Barth, 'Im Namen', 209–10.
[11] Barth, 'Unsere Kirche', 166; 'First Letter to French Protestants', in *A Letter to Great Britain from Switzerland*, trans. E. H. Gordon and G. Hill (London: Sheldon Press, 1941), 31.   [12] Barth, 'Im Namen', 210.
[13] Ibid. 211.   [14] Barth, 'Church and State', 146, 141.
[15] Barth, 'Unsere Kirche', 176.   [16] Barth, 'Im Namen', 209.

individual freedom and social responsibility.[17] Indeed, it is the fundamental characteristic of the just State that it seeks to order power by law and so to balance the rights of the community against those of the individual, personal freedom against common responsibility.[18] Based on law and standing between tyranny and anarchy, collectivism and individualism, the just State resists the rule of naked power and so prevents the subjugation of the weaker by the stronger.[19] As a constitutional or legitimate State (*Rechtsstaat*), it contradicts political absolutism in the concrete form of the totalitarian State (*Totalstaat*), and so opposes 'the demonism of politics' wherein man is made to serve the State, not the State man.[20]

It is quite true that Barth reckons 'democracy' to be a poor title for such a political arrangement as this, where it is properly not 'the people' who govern but rather 'das Recht und die Pflicht der Gemeinschaft und der Freiheit' (the claim and duty of the community and of freedom).[21] Nevertheless, it is both implicitly and explicitly clear that what Barth describes as the just State is what is loosely and generally called 'democracy'. At one point, for example, he exclaims that democracy bestows 'the power and blessing of justice, of freedom and of responsibility';[22] and at another he refers to democratic law or justice (*demokratischen Recht*) as 'that heavenly gift' (*Gottesgabe*).[23] Further, he argues that for Christians the fulfilment of political duty means, not mere passive subjection, but 'responsible choice of authority, responsible decision about the validity of laws, responsible care for their maintenance'. Therefore, he suggests that it is no accident that 'in the course of time "democratic" states have come into being, states, that is, which are based upon the responsible activity of their citizens'; and, further, that the democratic conception of the State is 'a

[17] Barth, 'Unsere Kirche', 165.

[18] Barth, 'A Letter to American Christians', in *The Church and the War* (New York: Macmillan, 1944), 23, 39; 'The Christian Community in the Midst of Political Change', in *Against the Stream*, ed. R. G. Smith, trans. E. M. Delacour and Stanley Godman (London: SCM, 1954), 80; 'From a Discussion in Budapest on the Morning of April 1, 1948', in *Against the Stream*, 95.

[19] Barth, 'The Christian Community and the Civil Community', in *Community*, 162; 'Unsere Kirche', 174.

[20] Barth, 'The Christian Community and the Civil Community', 172 (*Christengemeinde und Bürgergemeinde*, Theologische Studien 20 (Zollikon-Zurich: Evangelischer Verlag AG, 1946), 26); *CL* 219–20; 'The Churches of Europe in the Face of War', in *The Church and the War*, 5 ('Die protestantischen Kirchen in Europa: Ihre Gegenwart und ihre Zukunft', in *Eine schweizer Stimme*, 256); 'The Christian Community and the Civil Community', 174.

[21] Barth, 'Unsere Kirche', 165.

[22] Barth, *The Church and the Political Problem of Our Day* (London: Hodder & Stoughton, 1939), 70.

[23] Barth, 'First Letter to French Protestants', 40 ('Ein Brief nach Frankreich', in *Eine schweizer Stimme*, 116).

justifiable expansion' (*legitimer Auslegung*) of the thought of the New Testament.[24]

But the just State, according to Barth, is not merely democratic: it is also *social* democratic. The proper function of the State, and the definitive function of the just State, is to discriminate right from wrong in a given human community and to check the irruption into it of the chaos which sin entails.[25] Yet, to this negative function of restraining wickedness Barth adds a further positive one; namely, the promotion of peace and of social democracy.[26] Therefore he asserts that the Christian concept of the just State tends, not only toward order over tyranny and anarchy, nor only toward democracy over aristocratic or monarchical dictatorship, but also toward socialism over untrammelled capitalism.[27] The just State concerns itself not merely with justice but with social justice. Accordingly, Barth may be found in 1941 urging the government of wartime Switzerland to admit the Social Democratic Party into its ranks, and to address the problem of the growing disparity between an economically comfortable minority and a non-propertied and low-paid majority which was immediately vulnerable to the effects of rapid price-inflation.[28]

To our understanding of Barth's concept of the just State there remain to be added two important qualifications: first, that there will always be a distinction between the just State and the kingdom of God; and, second, that the just State need not be democratic. First, since the State exists 'between the times', between the resurrection and the Second Coming of Jesus Christ, it can never be perfect.[29] In this present, sinful age when we cannot expect to build a world which does not need or hope for redemption, not even a just State is free from the temptation 'to become at least a little Leviathan'; nor is it without sin.[30] On the contrary, 'it requires and will always require restoration'.[31] Consequently, even a just State cannot hope to achieve more than 'an external, relative and provisional humanisation of Man's existence'.[32] It is only a provisional order. At best, then, it

---

[24] Barth, 'Church and State', 144–5 (*Rechtfertigung*, 44).

[25] Barth, 'A Letter to Great Britain from Switzerland', in *Letter to Great Britain from Switzerland*, 13; 'First Letter to French Protestants', 34; 'The Christian Community and the Civil Community', 155; 'The Christian Community in the Midst of Political Change', 80–1; *CD* ii/2: 720–2.

[26] *CD* iii/4: 456–9. See Appendix 3, 'The *Opus Proprium* of the State'.

[27] Barth, 'A Letter to American Christians', 39; 'The Christian Community and the Civil Community', 173.   [28] Barth, 'Im Namen', 219–21.

[29] Barth, 'The Christian Community in the Midst of Political Change', 81, 83; 'From a Discussion in Budapest', 96.

[30] Barth, 'Church and State', 148; 'The Christian Community in the Midst of Political Change', 84; *CL*, 221.

[31] Barth, *The Church and the Political Problem*, 77.

[32] Barth, 'The Christian Community and the Civil Community', 161.

will constitute 'an allegory ... a correspondence and an analogue to the kingdom of God'; reflecting it, but never exactly being it.[33]

Strictly speaking, then, no State can be properly called 'just', if by that one means something absolute and direct. On this account, John Howard Yoder criticizes the translations of *Rechtfertigung und Recht* and *Christengemeinde und Bürgergemeinde* in the collection edited by Will Herberg:[34]

Herberg's texts consistently translate *Rechtsstaat* in ways which contribute to reinforcing a wrong concept. Sometimes it is rendered 'legitimate state' and sometimes 'just state'. For each of these, a different German expression would be used. Each of these fosters the idea of ruling that certain other states are *unjust* or *illegitimate*, and the state we approve is somehow positively righteous. This is not what *Rechtsstaat* means.... What is meant is that a state is thought of as recognising, implementing and being bound by some thinkable *justice* beyond itself and its arbitrary judgements. The 'justice-state' is the modest, self-limiting state. It will still not be just or righteous; but it has set its moral limits. The alternative to *Rechtsstaat* is not 'unjust state' or 'illegitimate state' but arbitrary authority.[35]

Yoder is correct in arguing that *Rechtsstaat* means a State which recognizes the claims of justice upon it and is committed to its implementation. A *Rechtsstaat* is a State which *intends* justice; not one which enjoys identity with it. However, this absolute intention does manifest itself in the relatively effective rule of law over power by which the rights of the individual are balanced against the claims of the community. The intention is made visible in political forms. As Yoder himself puts it, 'it can be measured in the formal commitments of both persons and structures'.[36] For that reason, it is appropriate to translate *Rechtsstaat* as 'constitutional state',[37] and *Staat des Rechts* as 'law-state'.[38] But if the opposite of *Rechtsstaat* is 'arbitrary authority'—anarchy or tyranny— then the *Rechtsstaat* itself is 'legitimate authority'.[39] Although the *Rechtsstaat* will never be perfectly just either in form or substance, its intention of justice—expressed with greater or lesser success in the constitutional and legal forms that govern and shape its political practice—and its concomitant legitimacy make it sufficiently distinguishable from the *Unrechtsstaat*,[40] and especially from

---

[33] Ibid. 169–71.

[34] Barth, *Community*. *Rechtfertigung und Recht* was translated by G. Ronald Howe under the title of 'Church and State'. *Christengemeinde und Bürgergemeinde* was translated by Stanley Godman under the title of 'The Christian Community and the Civil Community'.

[35] John H. Yoder, *Karl Barth and the Problem of War* (Nashville: Abingdon, 1970), 95 n. 1, 125 n. 5.   [36] Ibid. 50.

[37] Barth, *Community*, 172. Instead of this rendering, Yoder mentions that of 'legitimate state', of which I can find no instance.   [38] Ibid. 124.

[39] Barth, 'The Churches of Europe in the Face of War', 5; *Community*, 172.

[40] Barth, *Community*, 119, 143 (*Rechtfertigung*, 19, 42).

its tyrannical form, the *Totalstaat*.[41] And this visible distinction between order and caprice, between government and tyranny, between freedom and anarchy, between community and collectivism, between personal rights and individualism, is a *moral* distinction, albeit a relative one; a distinction between the morally better and the morally worse and, in that sense, between just (*rechte*) and unjust (*unrechte*) States.[42] The absolute intentional distinction between States expresses itself in a relative moral one. Therefore, 'in the better kind of state' (*in jenem jeweils "Besseren", im jeweils rechten Staat*) we are able to glimpse the purpose or intention of the divine ordinance.[43] On these grounds, then, we judge Yoder to be incorrect when he denies that *Rechtsstaat* implies 'the idea of ruling that certain other states are unjust or illegitimate, and the state we approve is somehow positively righteous'. A State which is a *Rechtsstaat* may be only relatively *recht*, but it is positively so; and that is how it can be 'better' than a State which is an *Unrechtsstaat* and therefore *unrecht*.[44]

Still, the *Rechtsstaat* will never be anything other than 'better'; it will never be the 'best'. And if, 'between the times', the *Rechtsstaat* will never be the kingdom of God, nor will it always be a democracy. *All* political forms and systems have their limitations, and no one political concept—even that of democracy—can be played off against all others as *the* Christian concept of the *Rechtsstaat*.[45] The form of State most approximate to the Christian concept may equally well assume the form of a monarchy or aristocracy or 'occasionally even . . . of a dictatorship', as that of a democracy. No democracy as such is immune from degeneration into anarchy or tyranny and from becoming thereby an *Unrechtsstaat*.[46] The order, justice, and freedom absolutely required by the Christian concept of the State can be frustrated under the better, democratic form of government, and can be honoured even under the worse, dictatorial one[47]—provided that such dictatorship is limited and provisional, not totalitarian.[48]

---

[41] Barth, 'The Churches of Europe in the Face of War', 5 (*Eine schweizer Stimme*, 256).

[42] Barth, 'The Christian Community and the Civil Community', 162: 'the just and the unjust State, that is . . . the better and worse.' Also p. 164: 'if in the political sphere the better stands alongside the worse, if there were and still are good as well as bad states.' (*Christengemeinde*, 18: 'neben dem Schlechteren auch ein Besseres neben dem unrechten auch einen rechten Staat').

[43] Ibid. 164 (*Christengemeinde*, 18).

[44] Robert Willis agrees: 'Although the distinctions between the various political orders are relative, they are nevertheless real and important' (*The Ethics of Karl Barth* (Leiden: E. J. Brill, 1971), 399–400).

[45] Barth, 'The Christian Community and the Civil Community', 161.

[46] Ibid. 181 (*Christengemeinde*, 36).

[47] Barth, 'A Letter to American Christians', 39–40.

[48] Barth, 'The Christian Community and the Civil Community', 174.

Nevertheless, the Christian concept of the *Rechtsstaat* tends toward democracy;[49] it tends 'on the whole towards the form of state, which, if it is not actually realized in the so-called "democracies", is at any rate more or less honestly clearly intended and desired'.[50] Therefore, 'the assertion that all forms of government are equally compatible or incompatible with the Gospel is not only outworn but false.... [I]t is not true that a Christian can endorse, or seek after a mobocracy or a dictatorship as readily as a democracy.'[51]

We are now in a position to complete our account of why Barth considered Switzerland's way of political life to be dignified with a divine commission and thus worthy of belligerent defence. Barth held that Switzerland was in receipt of a divine commission primarily because he judged that the Swiss State was a *Rechtsstaat* in the sense described above. He made this judgement because that State allowed itself to be confronted by the Gospel of divine justification, and thereby showed that it genuinely intended justice. Its constitutionality, its (social) democratic structures and procedures, its balancing of the rights of the individual against the claims of the community, its pluralism, and its representation of the memory and hope of such a political order for Europe as a whole—all these Barth deemed to be expressions of its intention of justice. Because Switzerland is a *Rechtsstaat*, its national autonomy is bound up with a divine commission to attest to divine justification and therefore to real human justice; and because of this connection, argued Barth, God commands the armed defence of Switzerland in the event of Nazi aggression.

The accuracy of this account is confirmed by the two main features of Nazism which, according to Barth, made armed resistance to it the subject of a divine command. First was Nazism's essential and deliberate hostility to the Christian Gospel and its Church,[52] and therefore to 'the Christian presupposition of Western culture'.[53] Herein lies the significance of what Barth regarded as Nazism's most characteristic feature: anti-Semitism. 'Anti-semitism means rejection of the *grace* of God'; for 'he who rejects and persecutes the Jews rejects and persecutes Him who died for the sins of the Jews'.[54] It also means the rejection of Western culture's Christian ground; for

---

[49] Barth, 'A Letter to American Christians', 39.

[50] Barth, 'The Christian Community and the Civil Community', 182 (*Christengemeinde*, 36).   [51] Barth, 'Church and State', 144 n. 34.

[52] Barth, 'Verheißung und Verantwortung der christlichen Gemeinde im heutigen Zeitgeschehen', 320; 'First Letter to French Protestants', 32; 'A Letter to American Christians', 21.

[53] Barth, 'The Churches of Europe in the Face of War', 6.

[54] Barth, *The Church and the Political Problem*, 51.

the existence of the Jew probably is the symbol of the objective metaphysical fact . . . that the Christian root of Western culture is still alive. . . . [T]he Jew is witness to the continuing vitality of the Old and New Testament revelation, by virtue of which Western culture . . . is separated as by an abyss from the inherent Godlessness of National Socialism.[55]

Second, and as a consequence of this, Nazism is 'inherently inhuman'.[56] Indeed, it has 'raised inhumanity to a principle, a system and a method'.[57] In its pure violence and arbitrariness, in its fundamental denial of political freedom and responsibility, in its systematic corruption of justice, in its suppression of the press and of the political opposition, in its making elections fraudulent, in its organized terrorism, and in its annihilation of 'incurables', Nazism proved itself to be the supreme destruction of all order, justice, freedom, and authority; the 'dissolution of the just state [rechten Staates]'; 'anarchy tempered by tyranny, or tyranny tempered by anarchy, but . . . certainly no State'.[58] The Nazi anti-state is not merely a dictatorship, but a quasi-religious totalitarian dictatorship which claims the souls as well as the bodies of men, demanding not only outward obeisance but also 'die Gleichschaltung der Gewissen, die Fugsamkeit und also die Unfreiheit jedes Wortes und jedes Gedankens' (the conformity of conscience, the tractability and captivity of every word and thought).[59] Claiming for itself absolute, divine power, this anti-state is as such also an anti-church.[60] The defence of Switzerland against Nazism would be a defence of the Rechtsstaat against the Unrechtsstaat; and what Barth says here of Switzerland's defence, he says also of the Allied war effort.[61] The war against Nazi Germany is 'the cause of the whole Church and of Christendom'.[62] It is not merely a necessary evil, but

a righteous [rechten] war, which God does not simply allow, but which he commands us to wage. . . . We deeply deplore that war must be waged today. But we have no reason to say that it ought not to be waged; no reason to hinder those who are responsible for its conduct; no reason to avoid cooperating in its conduct. Rather we have every reason to acknowledge that this war must be waged, and indeed waged with determination and vigour; we have every reason to devote ourselves wholly to it.[63]

Nevertheless, the Allies, though relatively more righteous than the Axis powers, are not without some responsibility for the outbreak of war; and

---

[55] Barth, 'The Churches of Europe in the Face of War', 5.   [56] Ibid. 6.
[57] Barth, 'The Germans and Ourselves', in The Only Way (New York: Philosophical Library, 1947), 69.
[58] Barth, 'Im Namen', 213; The Church and the Political Problem, 53–5; 'Second Letter to the French Protestants', in Letter to Great Britain from Switzerland, 46–7.
[59] Barth, The Church and the Political Problem, 38, 40, 41; 'Unsere Kirche', 160.
[60] Barth, The Church and the Political Problem, 48.
[61] Barth, 'A Letter to American Christians', 25.
[62] Barth, 'A Letter to Great Britain', 2.   [63] Ibid. 4–5.

they are no more 'Christian' as peoples than the Germans. The Allied cause, then, is not the *causa Dei*, and the Allies are not the Lord's own warriors. The war against Hitler is not a crusade of the just against the unjust; nor the execution of divine vengeance upon the guilty. Instead, it is simply a police action to restore human order and justice, and to defend humanity against the irruption of open inhumanity; and it is fought for the benefit also of the Nazis, in whom the Allies should recognize themselves 'as only slightly less visible and palpable disturbers of the peace'.[64]

[64] Barth, 'A Letter to American Christians', 25–7; 'First Letter to French Protestants', 33–6; 'The Germans and Ourselves', 89.

APPENDIX 2

ETHICS AND HEARING GOD'S COMMAND

In our account of the relationship in Barth's thought between the concept of hearing God's command and rational deliberation about moral matters, we agree with William Werpehowski that Barth did go a long way toward closing the gap between preliminary ethics and the human response to the divine command, and that he did not do so simply by means of a concept of intuition. We part company with him, however, in arguing that Barth closed the gap largely by extending the operations of moral reasoning in practice far beyond its proper sphere in principle. Werpehowski takes Barth's rejection of casuistry at its face value and does not consider the casuistic form of his special ethics.[1]

On this point Robert Willis is much closer to the mark when he writes that 'in special ethics, the process of rational deliberation occupies a place of definite importance, in contrast to its virtual exclusion in Barth's general discussion of theological ethics as the command of God'.[2] But whereas Willis denies that Barth's special ethics provides 'a set of principles or rules that are "applied" ethically by being introduced into specific contexts' (p. 425), we believe that it does, although the application is either vague or haphazard.

Further, while Willis concludes that, for Barth, 'an emphasis on the command and obedience does not and cannot exclude rational deliberation' (p. 335), he judges that Barth simply failed to provide a coherent account of their relationship (pp. 424–7) and attributes this to his initial formulation of the command against the immediate background of the total ontological determination of the human being by God's eternal election of Man through his reconciling action in Christ (pp. 423–4). Although we agree that Barth failed to provide a coherent account of the relationship between hearing God's command and rational deliberation, we do not agree that his failure was simple; for we have found in his writing substantial adumbrations of such an account. Nor are we convinced that the influence of Barth's doctrine of election upon his doctrine

[1] William Werpehowski, 'Command and History in the Ethics of Karl Barth', *Journal of Religious Ethics*, 9/2 (1981), 310–14.

[2] Robert Willis, *The Ethics of Karl Barth* (Leiden: E. J. Brill, 1971), 424.

of God's command should bear as much of the responsibility as Willis reckons. For it does not follow of logical necessity from the fact that our destiny as human beings has been determined by God's election of us in Jesus Christ that the command of God should bear upon us with an absolute definiteness; and it is quite clear from the early pages of the first volume of the *Dogmatics* that is devoted to special ethics that Barth's immediate intention in telling us that the divine command is absolutely self-interpreted and so 'leaves nothing to human choice or preference' is to protect the personal responsibility of the human being to God by precluding the intrusion of casuistry.[3]

[3] *CD* iii/4. 12.

APPENDIX 3

THE *OPUS PROPRIUM* OF THE STATE

John H. Yoder notes a shift in Barth's view of the State between 'Church and State' (1938) and *CD* iii/4 (1951).[1] In the former, the use of the threat of force is definitive of the State: its business is simply 'the administration of the law which is based on force [*Gewalt*]'.[2] In the latter, the exercise of power (*Gewalt*) does not belong to the essence of the State, but is only its *opus alienum*; its *opus proprium* here is the fashioning of peace—and the fashioning of peace 'as the fashioning of the state for democracy and of democracy for social democracy'.[3] Yoder follows A. T. van Leeuwan[4] when he comments: 'This change is, to be sure, more in perspective than in content. "Justification and Justice" [= 'Church and State'] does not say that the state is devoted exclusively to the use of force, but that is the central problem which is actually dealt with. The *Church Dogmatics* does not say that the sword is forbidden to the state but calls it an *opus alienum*, a work foreign to the state's real calling. The two texts are not strictly contradictory, but the accent has shifted.' On the contrary, they are contradictory. For, in 'Church and State' Barth explicitly denied the state a positive welfare function: 'The state as state knows nothing of the Spirit, bears the sword, and at the best, as seen in Romans 13, it does not wield it in vain. It, too, must leave to God the question of what must be done for man's welfare, in addition to the administration of the law which is based on force'.[5] It is true that, several pages later, we read that 'the state will realize its own potentialities, and thus will be a just state, in proportion as it ... actively grants freedom to the Church [to proclaim divine justification]. ... The right of the Church to liberty means the foundation, the maintenance, the restoration of everything—certainly of all human law. Wherever this right is recognised ... there we shall find a legitimate human authority and an equally legitimate human independence ... and

---

[1] John H. Yoder, *Karl Barth and the Problem of War* (Nashville: Abingdon, 1970, 97–8.

[2] Barth, 'Church and State', in *Community, State and Church*, ed. Will Herberg (Gloucester, Mass.: Peter Smith, 1968), 132 (*Rechtfertigung und Recht* (Zollikon-Zurich: Evangelischer Verlag AG, 1944), 31).

[3] *CD* iii/4: 456–9 (*KD* iii/4: 522).

[4] A. T. van Leeuwan, 'Oorlog als ultima ratio', *Wendig* (Jan. 1953), 628.

[5] Barth, *Community*, 132.

the true order of human affairs—the justice, wisdom and peace, equity and care for human welfare which are necessary to that true order—will arise'.[6] Still, Barth here did not attribute to the State any *direct* responsibility for fostering human welfare. Indeed, he argued that human welfare is fostered precisely·when the State attends to its *other*, proper function of actively granting the Church freedom to proclaim divine justification. By the time of his 'Im Namen Gottes des Allmächtigen!' (1941), however, Barth had reverted to the position that he had held in his 1928–9 lectures on ethics at the University of Münster, in which the state was accredited with a direct and positive responsibility for social welfare.[7]

Why Barth took the position that he did in 'Church and State' is not clear. Certainly, his political intention in this piece was to stiffen Swiss resolve in the face of Germany's annexation of Austria,[8] and this might explain his emphasis on the State's task of maintaining justice. But it does not explain his denial of its welfare function.

---

[6] Ibid. 147–8.

[7] Barth, *Eine schweizer Stimme, 1938–45* (Zollikon-Zurich: Evangelischer Verlag AG, 1945), 219–21; cf. *Ethics*, trans. G. W. Bromiley (New York: Seabury, 1981), 445–9.

[8] Eberhard Busch, *Karl Barth: His Life from Letters and Autobiographical Texts*, trans. John Bowden (Philadelphia: Fortress Press, 1976), 287.

by a definite Christology, according to which the event of reconciliation is one in which humankind is set on the way to authentic co-humanity: 'one is not free, then, to derive any or every possibility by analogy.'[7] But Willis himself criticizes Barth for drawing inconsistent conclusions.[8] For, on the one hand, Barth finds Christological justification for constitutional democracy;[9] while, on the other, he argues that totalitarianism is, to some degree, an image of God's grace.[10]

Yoder eventually concludes that, by his political analogues of the Church in 'The Christian Community and the Civil Community', Barth intended only casual illustrations of an analogical method that was never meant as 'a reliable, casuistically foolproof process of ethical deliberation', but only as 'one quite fitting form in which the social critic can clothe his witness'.[11] To some extent this is correct. For Barth made it quite explicit that the political guidelines in 'The Christian Community and the Civil Community' were 'merely intended to illustrate how the Church can make decisions on a Christian basis in the political sphere ... to illuminate the analogical but extremely concrete relationship between the Christian gospel and certain political decisions and modes of behaviour'.[12] However, there is no evidence that Barth intended his illustrations to be taken with anything less than seriousness. Therefore the elusiveness that characterizes the logic by which many of them are derived from theological premisses is fair game for the criticism that has been levelled at it. Barth was not mistaken in supposing that (some) Christological and ecclesiological tenets have moral or political implications. But he was mistaken in sometimes supposing them to be far more direct and specific than, in fact, they are.

[7] Robert E. Willis, *The Ethics of Karl Barth* (Leiden: E. J. Brill, 1971), 402.
[8] Ibid.   [9] Barth, *Community*, 171–9.
[10] Karl Barth and Johannes Hamel, *How to Serve God in a Marxist Land*, trans. Thomas Wieser (New York: Associated Press, 1959), 58.
[11] Yoder, *Karl Barth and the Problem of War*, 128.
[12] Barth, *Community*, 179.

separate the legislative, executive, and judicial powers; that open government and diplomacy is 'the inevitable political corollary' (*die notwendige politische Entsprechung*) of the fact that the Church lives from God's self-revelation; that from the freedom of the Word of God and the possibility of the human word being the free vehicle of this Word one arrives, 'by process of analogy' (*Sie muß das Gleichnis wagen*), at the right to freedom of speech; that since the members of the Church do not rule, but serve, 'therefore' they can only regard as diseased all political ruling that is not primarily a form of service; that since the Church is ecumenical or catholic, it resists mere parochial politics; and, finally, that 'the political analogy' of the eternity of divine mercy and the transience of divine wrath and judgement is the legitimacy of political violence only *ultima ratione*.[2]

This attempt to derive political principles directly from theological premisses has been heavily criticized. Both Brunner and Thielicke have complained that it employs a method of analogy that can be used to arrive at just about any conclusion whatsoever.[3] Will Herberg, citing Brunner, has agreed with this judgement and suggested that Barth was really framing Christological arguments to support conclusions 'already reached on other grounds'.[4] Along similar lines, Yoder has argued that 'it is quite possible to use analogy for illustrating, reinforcing, and demonstrating that which we consider desirable. But to *prove* anything, i.e. to provide a ground for guidance and clarification within a context of disagreement, the method of analogy is useless.'[5] Russell Palmer, after noting that Barth's Christological grounding of ethical principles is more successful at a general than a specific level, has concluded with Brunner and Thielicke that his use of analogy is 'essentially arbitrary': 'analogy as a device for deriving ethics from the Word of God is simply not a reliable guide. There is no way to control or check it.' Then, concurring with Herberg and Yoder, he writes: 'it would appear that what Barth actually does is to start with a certain ethical judgement, and then find justification for it via some more or less fanciful parallel with some feature of the Christian message.'[6]

Willis defends Barth here by arguing that his use of analogy is regulated

[2] Barth, 'The Christian Community and the Civil Community', in *Community*, 168–80.
[3] Helmut Thielicke, *Theological Ethics* (Grand Rapids: Eerdmans, 1979), i. 275; Emil Brunner, *Dogmatics*, ii: *The Christian Doctrine of Creation and Redemption*, trans. Olive Wyon (London: Lutterworth Press, 1952), 319.
[4] Will Herberg, 'The Social Philosophy of Karl Barth', in Barth, *Community*, 33–6.
[5] John H. Yoder, *Karl Barth and the Problem of War* (Nashville: Abingdon, 1970), 100.
[6] Russell W. Palmer, 'Methodological Weaknesses in Barth's Approach to Ethics', *Journal of Religious Thought*, 26/1 (1969), 78–80.

by a definite Christology, according to which the event of reconciliation is one in which humankind is set on the way to authentic co-humanity: 'one is not free, then, to derive any or every possibility by analogy'.[7] But Willis himself criticizes Barth for drawing inconsistent conclusions.[8] For, on the one hand, Barth finds Christological justification for constitutional democracy;[9] while, on the other, he argues that totalitarianism is, to some degree, an image of God's grace.[10]

Yoder eventually concludes that, by his political analogues of the Church in 'The Christian Community and the Civil Community', Barth intended only casual illustrations of an analogical method that was never meant as 'a reliable, casuistically foolproof process of ethical deliberation', but only as 'one quite fitting form in which the social critic can clothe his witness'.[11] To some extent this is correct. For Barth made it quite explicit that the political guidelines in 'The Christian Community and the Civil Community' were 'merely intended to illustrate how the Church can make decisions on a Christian basis in the political sphere . . . to illuminate the analogical but extremely concrete relationship between the Christian gospel and certain political decisions and modes of behaviour'.[12] However, there is no evidence that Barth intended his illustrations to be taken with anything less than seriousness. Therefore the elusiveness that characterizes the logic by which many of them are derived from theological premisses is fair game for the criticism that has been levelled at it. Barth was not mistaken in supposing that (some) Christological and ecclesiological tenets have moral or political implications. But he was mistaken in sometimes supposing them to be far more direct and specific than, in fact, they are.

[7] Robert E. Willis, *The Ethics of Karl Barth* (Leiden: E. J. Brill, 1971), 402.
[8] Ibid.   [9] Barth, *Community*, 171–9.
[10] Karl Barth and Johannes Hamel, *How to Serve God in a Marxist Land*, trans. Thomas Wieser (New York: Associated Press, 1959), 58.
[11] Yoder, *Karl Barth and the Problem of War*, 128.
[12] Barth, *Community*, 179.

BIBLIOGRAPHY

I. WORKS BY KARL BARTH

English editions are cited first. Corresponding German editions follow in parentheses.

Against the Stream, ed. Ronald Gregor Smith, trans. E. M. Delacour and Stanley Godman (London: SCM, 1954):

'Blessed are the Meek, for They shall Inherit the Earth' ('Selig sind die Sanftmütigen, denn die werden das Land besitzen', in *Christliche Gemeinde im Wechsel der Staatsordnungen*).

'The Church between East and West' (*Die Kirche zwischen Ost und West* (Zollikon-Zurich: Evangelischer Verlag AG, 1949)).

'The Christian Community in the Midst of Political Change' ('Die christliche Gemeinde im Wechsel der Staatsordnungen', in *Christliche Gemeinde im Wechsel der Staatsordnungen*).

'The Christian Understanding of Revelation' (*Die christliche Verständnis der Offenbarung* (Munich: Christian Kaiser Verlag, 1948)).

'From a Discussion in Budapest on the Morning of April 1, 1948' ('Aus der Diskussion in Budapest am vormittag des 1. April 1948', in *Christliche Gemeinde im Wechsel der Staatsordnungen*).

'Political Decisions in the Unity of Faith' (*Politische Entscheidung in der Einheit des Glaubens*, Theologische Existenz heute, ns 34 (Munich: Christian Kaiser Verlag, 1952)).

'The Real Church' ('Die wirkliche Kirche', in *Christliche Gemeinde im Wechsel der Staatsordnungen*).

Anselm: Fides quaerens intellectum, trans. Ian W. Robertson (London: SCM, 1960) (*Fides quaerens intellectum* (Munich: Christian Kaiser Verlag, 1931)).

The Christian Life, Church Dogmatics, iv/4, Lecture Fragments, trans. G. W. Bromiley, (Edinburgh: T. & T. Clark, 1981) (*Das christliche Leben, Kirchliche Dogmatik*, iv/4, Fragmente aus dem Nachlaß, Vorlesungen 1959–61 (Zurich: Theologischer Verlag, 1976)).

Christliche Gemeinde im Wechsel der Staatsordnungen: Dokumente Einer Ungarnreise, 1948 (Zollikon-Zurich: Evangelischer Verlag AG, 1948).

The Church and the Political Problem of Our Day (London: Hodder & Stoughton, 1939) (*Die Kirche und die politische Frage von heute* (Zollikon: Verlag der Evangelischen Buchhandlung, 1939)).

The Church and the War (New York: Macmillan, 1944):
　'The Churches of Europe in the Face of War' ('Die protestantischen Kirchen in Europa: Ihre Gegenwart und ihre Zukunft', in *Eine schweizer Stimme*).
　'A Letter to American Christians' ('Brief an einen amerikanischen Kirchenmann', in *Eine schweizer Stimme*).
Church Dogmatics, 4 vols., ed. G. W. Bromiley and T. F. Torrance (Edinburgh: T. & T. Clark, 1936–77) (*Kirchliche Dogmatik* (Zollikon-Zurich: Evangelischer Verlag AG, 1942–70)):
　Vol. i: *The Doctrine of the Word of God*, part 1, 1st edn., trans. G. T. Thompson (1936); 2nd edn., trans. G. W. Bromiley (1975) (*Die Lehre vom Wort Gottes*, pt. 1 (1947)).
　Vol. i, pt. 2, trans. G. T. Thompson and Harold Knight (1956) (*Die Lehre vom Wort Gottes*, pt. 2 (1945)).
　Vol. ii: *The Doctrine of God*, pt. 1, trans. T. H. L. Parker, W. B. Johnston, Harold Knight, and J. L. M. Haire (1957) (*Die Lehre von Gott*, pt. 1 (1946)).
　Vol. ii, pt. 2, trans. G. W. Bromiley, J. C. Campbell, Iain Wilson, J. Strathearn McNab, Harold Knight, and R. A. Stewart (1957) (*Die Lehre von Gott*, pt. 2 (1942)).
　Vol. iii: *The Doctrine of Creation*, pt. 1, trans. J. W. Edwards, O. Bussey, and Harold Knight (1958) (*Die Lehre von der Schöpfung*, pt. 1 (1945)).
　Vol. iii, pt. 2, trans. Harold Knight, G. W. Bromiley, J. K. S. Reid, and R. H. Fuller (1960) (*Die Lehre von der Schöpfung*, pt. 2 (1948)).
　Vol. iii, pt. 3, trans. G. W. Bromiley and R. J. Ehrlich (1961) (*Die Lehre von der Schöpfung*, pt. 3 (1950)).
　Vol. iii, pt. 4, trans. A. T. Mackay, T. H. L. Parker, Harold Knight, Henry A. Kennedy, and John Marks (1961) (*Die Lehre von der Schöpfung*, pt. 4 (1951)).
　Vol. iv: *The Doctrine of Reconciliation*, pt. 1, trans. G. W. Bromiley (1956) (*Die Lehre von der Versöhnung*, pt. 1 (1953)).
　Vol. iv, pt. 2, trans. G. W. Bromiley (1958) (*Die Lehre von der Versöhnung*, pt. 2 (1955)).
　Vol. iv, pt. 3. 1, trans. G. W. Bromiley (1961) (*Die Lehre von der Versöhnung*, pt. 3. 1 (1959)).
　Vol. iv, pt. 3. 2, trans. G. W. Bromiley (1962) (*Die Lehre von der Versöhnung*, pt. 3. 2 (1959)).
　Vol. iv, pt. 4 (Fragment), trans. G. W. Bromiley (1969) (*Die Lehre von der Versöhnung*, pt. 4 (1967)).
Community, State and Church: Three Essays, ed. Will Herberg (Gloucester, Mass.: Peter Smith, 1968):
　'The Christian Community and the Civil Community', trans. Stanley

Godman (*Christengemeinde und Bürgergemeinde*, Theologische Studien 20 (Zollikon-Zurich: Evangelischer Verlag AG, 1946)).

'Church and State', trans. G. Ronald Howe (*Rechtfertigung und Recht*, Theologische Studien 1 (Zollikon-Zurich: Evangelischer Verlag AG, 1944)).

Eine schweizer Stimme, 1938–45 (Zollikon-Zurich: Evangelischer Verlag AG, 1945).

Ethics, trans. G. W. Bromiley (New York: Seabury, 1981) (*Ethik i 1928* (Zurich: Theologischer Verlag, 1973); *Ethik ii 1928/29* (Zurich: Theologischer Verlag, 1976)).

God Here and Now, trans. Paul van Buren (London: Routledge & Kegan Paul, 1964):
    'Christian Ethics' (*Christliche Ethik* (Frankfurt-on-Main: Freies deutsches Hochstift, 1946)).

How I Changed My Mind, ed. John Godsey (Edinburgh: St Andrew Press, 1969).

How to Serve God in a Marxist Land, trans. Thomas Wieser (New York: Associated Press, 1959) (together with Johannes Hamel).

The Humanity of God (Richmond, Va.: John Knox Press, 1960):
    'The Gift of Freedom: Foundation of Evangelical Ethics', trans. Thomas Wieser (*Das Geschenk der Freiheit: Grundlegung evangelischer Ethik*, Theologische Studien 39 (Zollikon-Zurich: Evangelischer Verlag AG, 1953)).

'Im Namen Gottes des Allmächtigen!', in *Eine schweizer Stimme*.

Karl Barth's Table Talk, ed. John D. Godsey, Scottish Journal of Theology Occasional Papers No. 10 (Edinburgh: Oliver & Boyd, 1963).

Letters, 1961–68, ed. Jurgen Fangmeier and Heinrich Stoevesendt, trans. G. W. Bromiley (Edinburgh: T. & T. Clark, 1981).

A Letter to Great Britain from Switzerland, trans. E. H. Gordon and George Hills (London: Sheldon Press, 1941):
    'First Letter to French Protestants' ('Ein Brief nach Frankreich', in *Eine schweizer Stimme*).
    'A Letter to Great Britain from Switzerland' ('Ein Brief aus der Schweiz nach Großbritannien', in *Eine schweizer Stimme*).
    'Second Letter to the French Protestants' ('Eine Frage und eine Bitte an die Protestanten in Frankreich', in *Eine schweizer Stimme*).

The Only Way (New York: Philosophical Library, 1947):
    'The Germans and Ourselves' ('Die Deutschen und wir', in *Eine schweizer Stimme*).

Unsere Kirche und die Schweiz in der heutigen Zeit (St Gallen: Verlag der evangelischen Gesellschaft, 1941); also in *Eine schweizer Stimme*.

Verheißung und Verantwortung der christlichen Gemeinde im heutigen

Zeitgeschehen (Zollikon-Zurich: Evangelischer Verlag AG, 1944); also in *Eine schweizer Stimme*.

2. OTHER WORKS

ADAMS, R. M., 'Divine Command Metaethics as Necessary a Posteriori', in Paul Helm (ed.), *Divine Commands and Morality* (Oxford: Oxford University Press, 1981), 109–19.

—— 'A Modified Divine Command Theory of Ethical Wrongness', in Paul Helm (ed.), *Divine Commands and Morality* (Oxford: Oxford University Press, 1981), 83–108.

BALTHASAR, HANS URS VON, *The Theology of Karl Barth*, trans. John Drury (New York: Anchor, 1972).

BARR, JAMES, *The Bible in the Modern World* (New York: Harper & Row, 1973).

BARTON, JOHN, 'The Place of the Bible in Moral Debate', *Theology* (May 1985), 204–9.

BIGGAR, NIGEL, 'A Case for Casuistry in the Church', *Modern Theology*, 6/1 (Oct. 1989), 29–51.

—— (ed.), *Reckoning with Barth: Essays in Commemoration of the Centenary of Karl Barth's Birth* (Oxford: Mowbray, 1988).

BIRCH, BRUCE C., and RASMUSSEN, LARRY L., *Bible and Ethics in the Christian Life* (rev. edn., Minneapolis: Augsburg, 1989).

BONHOEFFER, DIETRICH, *Ethics*, ed. Eberhard Bethge, trans. Neville Horton Smith (New York: Macmillan, 1955).

BRENNAN, J. M., *The Open Texture of Moral Judgements* (London: Macmillan, 1977).

BRUNNER, EMIL, *The Divine Imperative: A Study in Christian Ethics*, trans. Olive Wyon (Philadelphia: Westminster Press, 1937).

—— *Dogmatics*, 2 vols., ii: *The Christian Doctrine of Creation and Redemption*, trans. Olive Wyon (London: Lutterworth Press, 1952).

BUSCH, EBERHARD, *Karl Barth: His Life from Letters and Autobiographical Texts*, trans. John Bowden (Philadelphia: Fortress Press, 1976).

CHILDRESS, JAMES, 'Scripture and Christian Ethics', *Interpretation*, 34/4 (Oct. 1980), 371–80.

CLARK, S. R. L., *Civil Peace and Sacred Order: Limits and Renewals 1* (Oxford: Oxford University Press, 1989).

CULLBERG, JOHN, *Das Problem der Ethik in der dialektischen Theologie* (Uppsala: Appelbergs, 1938).

CURRAN, CHARLES, *Catholic Moral Theology in Dialogue* (Notre Dame, Ind.: University of Notre Dame Press, 1976).

DALFERTH, INGOLF, 'Karl Barth's Eschatological Realism', in S. W. Sykes (ed.), *Karl Barth* (Cambridge: Cambridge University Press, 1989), 14–45.

FORELL, G. W., 'Can We Endorse the Barthian Ethics?', *Dialog*, 3 (Winter 1964), 55–6.

FREI, HANS, 'An Afterword: Eberhard Busch's Biography of Karl Barth', in H. MARTIN RUMSCHEIDT (ed.), *Karl Barth in Review* (Pittsburgh: Pickwick Press, 1981), 95–116.

FRIES, HEINRICH, 'Kirche als Ereignis: Zu Karl Barths Lehre von der Kirche', *Catholica*, 11 (1957), 81–108.

GADAMER, HANS-GEORG, *Truth and Method* (New York: Seabury, 1975).

GESTRICH, CHRISTOF, *Neuzeitlichen Denken und die Spaltung der dialektischen Theologie: Zur Frage der natürlichen Theologie*, Beiträge zur historischen Theologie 52 (Tübingen: Mohr, 1977).

GUSTAFSON, JAMES M., *Can Ethics Be Christian?* (Chicago: University of Chicago Press, 1975).

—— *Christ and the Moral Life* (Chicago: University of Chicago Press, 1968).

—— *Christian Ethics and the Community* (Philadelphia: Pilgrim Press, 1971).

—— *Ethics from a Theocentric Perspective*, 2 vols., ii: *Ethics and Theology* (Chicago: University of Chicago Press, 1984).

—— *Protestant and Roman Catholic Ethics: Prospects for Rapprochement* (Chicago: University of Chicago Press, 1978).

—— *Theology and Christian Ethics* (Philadelphia: Pilgrim Press, 1974).

HAUERWAS, STANLEY, *Character and the Christian Life: A Study in Theological Ethics* (San Antonio: Trinity University Press, 1975; 1985).

—— *A Community of Character* (Notre Dame, Ind.: University of Notre Dame Press, 1981).

—— 'On Honour: By Way of a Comparison of Barth and Trollope', in Nigel Biggar (ed.), *Reckoning with Barth* (Oxford: Mowbray, 1988), 145–69.

—— *The Peaceable Kingdom: A Primer in Christian Ethics* (Notre Dame, Ind.: University of Notre Dame Press, 1983).

—— *Vision and Virtue: Essays in Christian Ethical Reflexion* (Notre Dame, Ind.: Fides Press, 1974).

HELM, PAUL (ed.), *Divine Commands and Morality*, Oxford Readings in Philosophy (Oxford: Oxford University Press, 1981).

HERBERG, WILL, 'The Social Philosophy of Karl Barth', in Karl Barth, *Community, State and Church*, ed. Will Herberg (Gloucester, Mass.: Peter Smith, 1968), 11–67.

HOOD, ROBERT E., *Contemporary Political Orders and Christ: Karl Barth's Christology and Political Praxis* (Pittsburgh: Pickwick Press, 1985).

HUNSINGER, GEORGE (ed. and trans.), *Karl Barth and Radical Politics* (Philadelphia: Westminster Press, 1976).

IDZIAK, JANINE MARIE (ed.), *Divine Command Morality: Historical and*

Contemporary Readings, Texts and Readings in Religion Series (New York: Edwin Mellen Press, 1979).

JEANROND, WERNER, 'Karl Barth's Hermeneutics', in Nigel Biggar (ed.), *Reckoning with Barth* (Oxford: Mowbray, 1988), 80–97.

—— *Text and Interpretation as Categories of Theological Thinking* (Dublin: Gill & Macmillan, 1988).

JÜNGEL, EBERHARD, 'Invocation of God as the Ethical Ground of Christian Action: Introductory Remarks on the Posthumous Fragments of Karl Barth's Ethics of the Doctrine of Reconciliation', in E. Jüngel, *Theological Essays*, trans. J. B. Webster (Edinburgh: T. & T. Clark, 1989), 154–72.

KELSEY, DAVID, *The Uses of Scripture in Recent Theology* (Philadelphia: Fortress Press, 1975).

KIRK, KENNETH E., *Conscience and Its Problems: An Introduction to Casuistry* (London: Longman, Green & Co., 1927).

LEEUWAN, A. T. VAN, 'Oorlog als ultima ratio', *Wendig* (Jan. 1953).

LEHMANN, PAUL, *Ethics in a Christian Context* (New York: Harper & Row, 1963).

LOVIN, ROBIN W., *Christian Faith and Public Choices: The Social Ethics of Barth, Brunner, and Bonhoeffer* (Philadelphia: Fortress Press, 1984).

MACKEN, JOHN, *The Autonomy Theme in the 'Church Dogmatics': Karl Barth and His Critics* (Cambridge: Cambridge University Press, 1990).

MEYNELL, H. A., *Grace versus Nature: Studies in Karl Barth's Church Dogmatics* (London: SCM, 1965).

MITCHELL, BASIL, 'Ideals, Roles and Rules', in Gene Outka and Paul Ramsey (eds.), *Norm and Context in Christian Ethics* (London: SCM, 1968), 351–65.

NELSON, PAUL, *Narrative and Morality: A Theological Inquiry* (University Park, Pa.: Pennsylvania State University Press, 1987).

NEWBIGIN, LESSLIE, *The Household of God* (London: SCM, 1953).

NIEBUHR, REINHOLD, 'The Moral and Political Judgements of Christians', *Christianity and Crisis*, 19 (6 July 1959), 99–103.

—— *The Nature and Destiny of Man*, 2 vols., ii: *Human Destiny* (London: Nisbet, 1943).

—— review of Karl Barth, *Against the Stream*, *Christianity and Society* (1954/4).

—— 'We are Men and Not God', *Christian Century*, 65/43 (27 Oct. 1948), 1138–40.

OGLETREE, THOMAS, *The Use of the Bible in Christian Ethics* (Oxford: Blackwell, 1984).

OUTKA, GENE, 'Character, Conduct and the Love Commandment', in Gene Outka and Paul Ramsey (eds.), *Norm and Context in Christian Ethics*, (London: SCM, 1968), 37–66.

—— and RAMSEY, PAUL (eds.), *Norm and Context in Christian Ethics* (London: SCM, 1968).

PALMER, RUSSELL, W., 'Methodological Weaknesses in Barth's Approach to Ethics', *Journal of Religious Thought*, 26/1 (1969), 70–82.

PESCHKE, K., 'Karl Barth in Confrontation with Natural Non-Christian Ethics', *South-East Asia Journal of Theology*, 11 (Autumn 1969), 20–4.

QUINN, PHILIP, L., 'Divine Command Ethics: A Causal Theory', in Janine Marie Idziak (ed.), *Divine Command Morality* (New York: Edwin Mellen Press, 1979), 305–25.

RAHNER, KARL, *Theological Investigations*, vi (London: Darton, Longman, & Todd, 1969).

RAMSEY, IAN T. (ed.), *Christian Ethics and Contemporary Philosophy* (London: SCM, 1966).

—— 'Moral Judgements and God's Commands', in Ian Ramsey (ed.), *Christian Ethics and Contemporary Philosophy* (London: SCM, 1966), 152–71.

RAMSEY, PAUL, 'The Case of the Curious Exception', in Gene Outka and Paul Ramsey (eds.), *Norm and Context in Christian Ethics* (London: SCM, 1968), 67–135.

—— *Deeds and Rules in Christian Ethics*, Scottish Journal of Theology Occasional Papers No. 11 (Edinburgh: Oliver & Boyd, 1965).

—— (ed.), *Faith and Ethics: The Theology of H. R. Niebuhr* (New York: Harper & Row, 1957).

—— *War and the Christian Conscience: How Shall Modern War be Conducted Justly?* (Durham, NC: Duke University Press, 1961).

RENDTORFF, TRUTZ, *Theorie des Christentums: Historisch-theologisch Studien zu seiner neuzeitlichen Verfassung* (Gütersloh: Mohr, 1972).

RUMSCHEIDT, H. MARTIN (ed.), *Karl Barth in Review: Posthumous Works Reviewed and Assessed* (Pittsburgh: Pickwick Press, 1981).

SØE, N. H., 'The Three "Uses" of the Law', in Gene Outka and Paul Ramsey (eds.), *Norm and Context in Christian Ethics* (London: SCM, 1968), 297–332.

SYKES, S. W., 'Authority and Openness in the Church', in S. W. Sykes (ed.), *Karl Barth* (Cambridge: Cambridge University Press, 1989), 69–86.

—— (ed.), *Karl Barth: Centenary Essays* (Cambridge: Cambridge University Press, 1989).

THIELICKE, HELMUT, *Theological Ethics*, 2 vols., i: *Foundations*, ed. William H. Lazareth (Grand Rapids: Eerdmans, 1979).

THOMPSON, JOHN (ed.), *Theology beyond Christendom: Essays on the Centenary of the Birth of Karl Barth, May 10, 1886* (Pittsburgh: Pickwick Press, 1986).

TORRANCE, T. F., *Karl Barth: Biblical and Evangelical Theologian* (Edinburgh: T. & T. CLARK, 1990).

VERHEY, ALLEN, *The Great Reversal: Ethics and the New Testament* (Grand Rapids: Eerdmans, 1984).

VILLA-VICENCIO, CHARLES (ed.), *On Reading Karl Barth in South Africa* (Grand Rapids: Eerdmans, 1988).

WERPEHOWSKI, WILLIAM, 'Command and History in the Ethics of Karl Barth', *Journal of Religious Ethics*, 9/2 (1981), 298–320.

—— 'Divine Commands, Philosophical Dilemmas: The Case of Karl Barth', *Dialog*, 201/1 (1981), 20–5.

WEST, CHARLES C., *Communism and the Theologians* (Philadelphia: Westminster Press, 1958).

WILLIS, ROBERT E., *The Ethics of Karl Barth* (Leiden: E. J. Brill, 1971).

YODER, JOHN HOWARD, *Karl Barth and the Problem of War* (Nashville: Abingdon, 1970).

INDEX